# THORNTON WILDER:
## HIS WORLD

Other Books by Linda Simon

THE BIOGRAPHY OF ALICE B. TOKLAS
GERTRUDE STEIN: A COMPOSITE PORTRAIT (editor)

# THORNTON WILDER: HIS WORLD

*Linda Simon*

*Doubleday & Company, Inc.*
*Garden City, New York*
*1979*

Grateful acknowledgment is made for permission to include the following copyrighted material:

"Come In" from *The Poetry of Robert Frost*, edited by Edward Connery Lathem. Copyright 1942 by Robert Frost. Copyright © 1969 by Holt, Rinehart and Winston. Copyright © 1970 by Lesley Frost Ballantine. Reprinted by permission of Holt, Rinehart and Winston, Publishers.

Excerpt from *The Flowers of Friendship: Letters Written to Gertrude Stein*, edited by Donald C. Gallup. Copyright 1953 by Donald C. Gallup and reprinted by permission of Alfred A. Knopf, Inc.

"Teacher" from *Guest Book*. Copyright 1935 by Alfred A. Knopf, Inc. Reprinted with permission of the Witter Bynner Foundation for Poetry, Inc.

ISBN: 0-385-12840-1
Library of Congress Catalog Card Number 78-73193
Copyright © 1979 by Linda Simon
ALL RIGHTS RESERVED
PRINTED IN THE UNITED STATES OF AMERICA
FIRST EDITION

*for*
*Kay and Samuel Perlin*
*and*
*Sylvia and Samuel J. Simon*

# PREFACE

When Thornton Wilder became famous in 1928, he was a quiet schoolteacher who had written a slim, quiet book, *The Bridge of San Luis Rey.* During the nearly fifty years of his literary career, as his fame grew, he always retained something of the quiet schoolteacher in his manner. He was emblematic of no decade. His novels and plays, though enormously popular, protested no generation. And the conduct of his life, even at its most exuberant, was thoughtful and dignified. He was a scholar, a deeply reflective man, often a vulnerable and sensitive one. He was generous with advice to younger writers, whether friends or, briefly, strangers. He was a gentleman and a gentle man. He tried to live his life with integrity.

He was rare in his lack of vanity, in his genuine humility, and rare, too, in his abiding faith in humanity, which never wavered even through two major wars, several smaller ones, and numerous domestic "revolutions." Thornton Wilder could always shake his head knowingly and predict that we would survive, if only by the skin of our teeth. That faith underlies all of his works and endears them to generation after generation of readers. *The Bridge of San*

*Luis Rey* endures as a haunting tale; *Our Town* is the "home" of nostalgic wishes.

Like any other writer, Thornton Wilder transformed his life into art, drawing more or less upon his imagination, more or less upon the particulars of his existence, as his work required. To know of his life is to understand his work more deeply, to appreciate its meaning more accurately, to see the world—ours, and his—more clearly.

For Thornton Wilder, Goethe was the writer, above all others, who formed an aesthetic ideal. And so it is well to look to Goethe for an epigraph for this book:

> For it seems to be the main object of biography—to exhibit the man in relation to the features of his time, and to show to what extent they have opposed or favored his progress; what view of mankind and the world he has formed from them, and how far he himself, if an artist, poet, or author, may externally reflect them.

# ACKNOWLEDGMENTS

Working on this book has proved to me, beyond any doubt, that a person *is* reflected by the company he keeps. Thornton Wilder's many friends, students, and colleagues extended to me the same gracious kindnesses Wilder himself had given to so many younger writers. They responded to my questions with warm letters, tapes of anecdotes and reminiscences, and hours of conversations. The only admonition, from a few, was to "do a good job," to write a book worthy of a man they loved and respected. If I have, it is because of their generosity; and so I most sincerely thank:

Frederick B. Artz, Walter Blair, Kay Boyle, Dick Carlotta, Everett R. Clinchy, Louis H. Engel, Jane and John Fitzpatrick, Anna Freud, Emily Hahn, Franklin Heller, Francis S. Hutchins, Harry Levin, the late Luther Mansfield, Dexter Masters, William Miles, Harry Thornton Moore, Elizabeth H. Paepcke, Nikos Psacharopoulos, Marshall Sprague, Robert Stallman, Holly Stevens, Samuel Steward, Donald Sutherland, Flora Symons, Gene Tunney; and Henry Hagenah, for his help in translating correspondence.

Of course, a great deal of material came from libraries and

collections throughout the world. For their assistance with re-
search that was often arduous and time-consuming, my thanks to:
Alice Jeffries, Altoona Area Public Library; Meyer Mathis, The
American National Red Cross; Horace Hewlett, Amherst Col-
lege; Jack Hall and Gerald F. Roberts, Berea College; Douglas
MacDonald and Howard B. Gotlieb, Mugar Memorial Library,
Boston University; James Kraft, The Witter Bynner Founda-
tion; Suzanne Hamel, Goddard Library, Clark University;
Susan Lundal, The College of Wooster; Kenneth A. Lohf, Eliz-
abeth B. Mason, Rose Valenstein, Columbia University; Kath-
erine R. Hall, Cornell University Library; Walter W. Wright,
Baker Memorial Library, Dartmouth College; B. M. McKewen,
Department of the Air Force; Dan O. Clemmer, Jr., James A.
Donovan, Jr., and most especially J. Manuel Espinosa of the
Bureau of Educational and Cultural Affairs, Department of
State; Patricia Prince, The Dramatists Guild; Iain Crawford,
Edinburgh International Festival; Elizabeth McBride, Emory
University; K. R. Eissler, The Sigmund Freud Archives; E. M.
Kandora, Consulate General of the Federal Republic of Ger-
many; Frank K. Lorenz, The Burke Library, Hamilton and Kirk-
land Colleges; Louis A. Rachow, The Walter Hampden–Ed-
win Booth Theatre Collection and Library; Rodney Dennis and
Suzanne N. H. Currier, Houghton Library, Harvard University;
William Ingoldsby, The Huntington Library; Jo August, Hem-
ingway Collection, Kennedy Library; Dean H. Keller, Kent
State University Libraries; Thomas B. Greenslade, Chalmers
Memorial Library, Kenyon College; Jerry J. Donovan and espe-
cially Elizabeth C. Miller for her painstaking, indefatigable,
and always gracious efforts, The John Dixon Library, The
Lawrenceville School; John C. Broderick, Paul T. Heffron,
Wayne D. Shirley, and William Matheson, The Library of
Congress; Linda Hanson, The Lyndon Baines Johnson Li-
brary; Conrad S. Spohnholz, The MacDowell Colony; Shirley
Thayer, Maine State Library; Betty Bruce, Monroe County
Public Library; Mary C. Henderson, Friends of the Theatre and
Music Collection, Museum of the City of New York; Ronald
E. Swerczek for the care and interest he took in helping me to

document Amos Wilder's government career, Diplomatic
Branch, Civil Archives Division, National Archives and Records
Service; Edith G. Selig, Lazrus Library of Intergroup Relations,
National Conference of Christians and Jews; A. Cox, National
Library of Scotland; Charles Cummings, The Newark Public
Library; Katharine B. Wolpe, The Abraham A. Brill Library,
The New York Psychoanalytic Institute; Paul Myers, Theatre
Collection, Library and Museum of the Performing Arts, New
York Public Library; Albert M. Donley, Northeastern University; R. Russell Maylone and Patrick M. Quinn, Northwestern
University Library; Gertrude M. Cordts, Oakland Library;
Mary E. Cowles and W. E. Bigglestone, Oberlin College Library; Marie Catlin Larrabee, Peterborough Historical Society;
Sally Stearns Brown, Peterborough Players; Ann Geisel, Peterborough Town Library; Earle E. Coleman, Robert E. Van Vranken, Jr., and Ann Farr, Princeton University; Missy Daniel,
Eva Moseley, and Elizabeth Shenton, The Schlesinger Library,
Radcliffe College; J. A. Edwards, Reading University Library;
Helen Jacobsen, San Francisco Unified School District; Kenneth W. Duckett, Morris Library, Southern Illinois University;
Leslie Fox, State Historical Society of Colorado; James L. Hansen and Joanne E. Hohler, The State Historical Society of Wisconsin; Alfred G. Brooks, Max Reinhardt Archive, State
University of New York at Binghamton; Nell Ezequelle,
Stockbridge Library; Jean Waggener, Tennessee State Library
and Archives; Denise C. Miller, The Thacher School; Mary W.
Roe, Transcript Printing Company, Peterborough; Ivan
Schwartz, Dag Hammarskjöld Library, United Nations; R. A.
Lee, Universal City Studios; H. Viebrock, Englisches Seminar,
Der Universität Frankfurt; Irene Moran and Alma Compton,
The Bancroft Library, University of California at Berkeley; Jane
Colokathis and Ruth Halloran, The University of Chicago;
Frances Jackson, University of Hawaii at Manoa; Maynard
Brickford, University of Illinois at Urbana-Champaign; Charles
A. Chambers, William K. Wallach, and Karen Klinkinberg,
University of Minnesota; Toni B. Taylor, University of New
Hampshire; Neda M. Westlake, Van Pelt Library, University of
Pennsylvania; Ellen S. Dunlap, Humanities Research Center,

University of Texas; Ann Marie Harkins, Alderman Library, University of Virginia; Eleanor Nicholes and Leslie Perrin Wilson, Wellesley College Library; Lawrence W. Beals, Williams College; Judith A. Schiff, Wesley H. Poling, Gloria P. Locke, and Patricia L. Bodak, Yale University.

There are moments in the writing of any book when a word of encouragement might inspire a whole chapter—or at least a good night's sleep. A special thank-you each, then, to Rhoda Weyr and Lisa Drew.

And then there are three who make everything possible: Laurence and Freddie and Aaron—thank you.

# THORNTON WILDER:
## HIS WORLD

# I

*Man is not born to solve the problems of the universe, but to find out where the problem begins, and then to restrain himself within the limits of the comprehensible.*

GOETHE

# ONE

———◆———

O F course we need to know the origins of the man, where he
came from and how he grew; which moments shaped him,
which sounds echoed for him, which visions haunted him. We
want to find something in the early years that marked his spirit,
somehow, and set him apart. He remembered something for us—a
phrase often repeated by one of his teachers to quiet the class:
"Be still a moment," he told them, "and you can hear the world
falling through space!" The class would almost hold their breath
to listen, but what they heard was only the soft whistle of far-off
trains, and then silence. Perhaps Thornton Wilder listened
longer.

The Wilders came from Shiplake, England, in the mid-1600s
and settled in Hingham, Massachusetts. Some two hundred years
later, one of their descendants, Amos Lincoln Wilder, was born in
Calais, Maine. He left briefly to study dentistry in Baltimore and
returned as Dr. Wilder to practice in Augusta and start his own
family. His wife, Charlotte Topliffe Porter, six years his junior,
was the daughter of a prominent lumber merchant, shipowner,

and railroad president. They had three children: two sons, Amos Parker and Julian, and a daughter, Charlotte.

At forty-five, Dr. Wilder made a sudden shift to a very different enterprise. He founded an oilcloth manufacturing company on Rear Water Street in Hallowell, which he managed into a thriving $150,000-a-year business. Soon Amos Wilder became as much known for his successful firm as he had been for his unconcealed intemperance.[1]

His son Amos was a bright and active child, educated in Augusta's public schools and, more often, in Augusta's shops and streets. After school, he was rarely at home. "I was 'all over the place,'" he remembered, ". . . peddled things, carried water for elephants, worked in a grocery, and especially in a bookstore at odd hours. . . ." The local newspaper publisher took a liking to him and taught him telegraphing; the clerks in a neighborhood shop would perch him on the counter each evening before closing and request "'a few remarks,' at one time . . . taking the form of a farewell to the Senate."[2]

After graduating from Augusta High School, with a year spent at the Highland Military Academy in Worcester, Massachusetts, Amos entered Yale. There the bold, self-confident child became, in a new and larger world, an anxious young man. "I was in terror at times of being 'dropped,'" he admitted, "and in my relations to my mates I felt ever 'beating beneath what I was the man I might be.'" Other students seemed to him "choice men"— choicer, at least, than he felt himself to be. Nevertheless, he was successful both academically and socially. He was a member of Kappa Sigma Epsilon, Psi Upsilon, Skull and Bones; he sang in the class and university glee clubs, edited the *Courant* in his senior year, and acted as one of the class historians. His greatest disappointment—an embarrassment he was never to forget—came during his freshman year. He was selected for the staff of the *Record*, but was quickly dismissed for incompetency. "This was the severest humiliation I have ever known," he wrote later. In his small room on High Street he felt deeply dejected; but, characteristically, he summoned his strengths and rallied.

Though his memories of Yale were mixed, he always believed his undergraduate years afforded him "a rich legacy. . . . While I was too immature and undisciplined to know what was going on in the class-room, yet having associated with as good men as the nation was producing at that time, and noting that in some ways I held my own, I emerged with a feeling that I had parts to an extent and need not be inferior unless I so elected."

He had no plans to return to his family in Maine. For the first year after he graduated in 1884, he taught at Bartlett's School in nearby Old Lyme, Connecticut. The next year he moved west to Faribault, Minnesota, and taught at the Shattuck School there. In 1886, however, he was able to take a position more to his liking. Once again he moved, this time to Philadelphia, where he served as a reporter on the *Press* until 1888. He then returned to New Haven, enrolled for his doctorate at Yale, and took over as editor of the New Haven *Palladium* for the next four years. As editor, he freely dispensed his strong opinions. "I have never dared to consult the files of that period," he admitted later. ". . . What miles of nonsense my pen must have reeled off—but there was no one to edit my copy and I could at least be myself. I had a directorate of business men to deal with, and they were a kindly lot. This quick transition from a sense of abysmal failure to Quinnipac fame confirmed my theory that one should never be permanently discouraged." Editing was his new career, and only by catching classes at odd intervals during the day and studying at midnight did he manage to earn his Ph.D. in the Department of Social Sciences by 1892. His thesis was entitled "The Municipal Problem" and dealt with the difficulties of governing American cities and possible ways to overcome those difficulties.

He might have stayed on at the *Palladium,* but his editorial on "The Big Four" caused so much controversy that he was forced at last to leave. Not having an immediate opportunity in sight, he pondered his choices and headed for New York. There he worked on the *Mail and Express* and *Commercial Advertiser* until, two years later, he took a trip that changed his life.

"The year 1894 was an eventful one for me. I took a western trip in the spring, seeking an opportunity to invest in some modest daily newspaper, convinced that salaried journalism was not a secure call for such as I. Madison, Wis., was on my itinerary. Here I tried to sell some literary articles to the chief owner and editor

of the *State Journal,* at the same time suggesting he sell me an interest in his paper mainly on credit. He declined both propositions and I left for Milwaukee. A telegram, however, called me
back and he later told me my persistence had made an impression." With his savings of $5,000 and loans from some friends,
Amos Wilder found himself in possession of a one-quarter interest
in one of Madison's foremost papers. He was thirty-two years old.

That winter he also began lecturing for the University of Wisconsin, traveling to six cities in the northern part of the state to
speak on municipal government. He also took time from his newspaper work to marry, on December 3, 1894, Isabel Thornton
Niven, twenty-one, of Dobbs Ferry, New York, the daughter of a
Presbyterian minister. The couple settled in Madison, where, nine
months later, their first child was born, a son they named Amos
Niven.

By 1901 Amos had gained full controlling interest in the *State
Journal* and was an important figure in Wisconsin politics. He
reveled in his independence and knew that his personality required it. In New Haven he had often come under attack for his
ideas. What he needed, he once wrote to a friend, was a place
where he could do things completely in his own way and show
himself as he was.[3] In his own unpredictable way, then, he first
supported Senator Robert M. La Follette and suddenly, in 1903,
switched to the opposition. He also alienated a number of political leaders by his strong stand on liquor. No doubt drawing on
childhood memories, Amos's opinions on temperance were iron-
bound. He would not be swayed, and throughout his career repeatedly found himself in difficulties because of that one issue.

At home, as at his newspaper, Amos dominated. Isabel was
unlike her husband in temperament. While Amos was outgoing,
forceful, a fiery speaker, his wife was quiet and reserved. Though
she had not been highly educated, she was artistic and refined. At
Sunday school in her father's church, the teacher had found her
"brilliant and highly cultivated." She had had aspirations of attending college or becoming a teacher, but her father, the Reverend Thornton MacNess Niven, had definite restrictions for the
education of his daughter. An old-school Presbyterian, taciturn
and stern, Niven had come to the South Presbyterian Church in

Dobbs Ferry from Halifax County, Virginia. In 1867 he became pastor, causing some consternation among his parishioners because he had previously served as a chaplain in the Confederate Army. Nevertheless, he quickly won their respect and esteem. Like the Reverend Niven, Amos, too, showed a skepticism of Isabel's artistic inclinations. He was ever the patriarch and, for his wife and some of his children, a formidable force to confront.

In the first years of their marriage, money was scarce, since Amos had to repay loans for his interest in the newspaper. He settled his family in a small apartment at 140 Langdon Street. It was there that his second son was born. On April 17, 1897, Isabel was delivered of twin boys, one stillborn, the other to be christened Thornton Niven, after her father. The next year, on August 28, 1898, Charlotte Elizabeth was born. With a growing family, new quarters were needed. In 1899 Amos found an apartment at 211 West Gilman Street, where another daughter, Isabel, was born on January 13, 1900.

Even with a young family to demand her time and attention, Isabel found moments to devote to aesthetic pursuits. Neighbors would often see her taking her children on afternoon outings: her oldest son, Amos, was barely walking, steadying himself by holding on to the baby carriage with the three younger children inside, and Isabel herself would be pushing the carriage as she read a book of poetry.[4]

Although city life was pleasant, Amos decided that his children should have the experience of a more rustic existence. In 1901 he found a cottage at Maple Bluffs on the shores of Lake Mendota and named it, imaginatively, "Wilderness." There his family spent the months from early spring to late fall in a small home lined with knotty pine and surrounded by trees. The children would ride his old horse, Billy Bones, swim in the lake, eat biscuits and butter on the shore or bowls of bread and milk on their shady porch. Their physical growth was measured by notches beside a door, indicating how tall "Thorntie" was the year they had the measles, or how tall Charlotte had been the time their mother took a trip to Europe. Their intellectual growth was overseen by both parents, with each contributing something in accordance with his or her personality. Amos preferred Scott, Dickens, and

Shakespeare; Isabel, Yeats and Maeterlinck. Amos was concerned with imparting moral lessons; Isabel, a sense of beauty.

Thornton would always remember the months at the lake, the mist rising in the morning and the cobwebs shining with dew. At the water's edge he found stones covered with seaweed moss. Beside the piers he discovered crayfish holes. Those particular memories would be among the happiest of his boyhood.[5]

Back in Madison, Amos insisted that the children attend church with him each Sunday. A "devout layman," as Thornton later described him, Amos sat among his four children in one pew of the Congregational church and, to keep them still, would stretch out his arms to allow them to draw pictures on the cuffs of his shirts. The image seems disparate with Amos's usual demeanor, but Wilder family legend persists.

Afterward Thornton would accompany his father to his offices on East Washington Avenue, where the smell of ink and paper left an indelible memory. "Dad was quite a paternalistic editor in those days," he knew. "One time he sent a reporter out to do some kind of a country survey, and then promptly decided he wanted the reporter back again. He didn't know how to reach him, but he did know he'd be reading the paper.

"So all he did was put a big, black notice on the front page—'Walker, come home'—and Walker came in a hurry!"

As Thornton knew, his father expected the same obedience from his children as he did from his employees.

The quiet life in Madison and at Lake Mendota continued for several years until Amos decided to enlarge his world and seek a diplomatic post.[6] In 1905 he applied for appointment as United States Minister to Uruguay-Paraguay. Despite earnest recommendations, his appointment was not approved. Undaunted, on January 6, 1906, he applied to be considered for a post as Consul General at Hong Kong. At five feet ten and one hundred ninety pounds, he described himself as being in perfect health. His sponsors included Charles Hopkins Clark, Bishop J. W. Bashford, and Anson Phelps Stokes. Their letters to Theodore Roosevelt point to Amos's distinction as a Yale man and his loyalty as a conservative Republican. The lawyer Charles Sherrill of New York provided significant details:

It has come to the attention of his many friends in New York City, that Mr. Amos Parker Wilder of Madison, Wisconsin is an aspirant for a diplomatic post under our Government. Mr. Wilder was, for some years, a resident of this city, being at that time a member of the editorial staff of the "Mail and Express." During that time he became very largely known and popular in this city as he then showed the quiet but forceful character which had brought him his later successes. He has always been willing to assist our party in any and every proper way. Last year I succeeded in persuading him to come on from his home in Wisconsin to New York City to speak at the annual dinner of the Twenty-ninth Assembly District Club here as it was felt that we needed a strong and enthusiastic speaker who was heartily in accord with the government's policy. He so thoroughly fulfilled the purposes desired, that last fall, with the same purpose, we again persuaded him to come on to New York City and speak at the very splendid meeting held by the Business Mens Association at Carnegie Hall, at which, also, Secretary Taft spoke. I cite these as but a couple of examples of his willingness to assist us in the political problems that we find them [sic] in New York. The western vigor and enthusiasm which he brought into the campaign in this city last fall was particularly satisfactory to the Lawyers Roosevelt and Fairbanks Club, which organization I had the honor to represent in the Business Mens Association. Therefore, I beg, Sir, very respectfully to submit that if you should deem it wise to regard his present aspiration with favor, it would be heartily approved by our organization in this city, as we would feel that you would have selected a man not only of ability, but also of staunch patriotism, much tact and fully worthy to represent our Country in any post to which he might be appoint[ed].

His political views seemed in line with Roosevelt's. His State Department rating was 8.4 out of a possible 10. This time, on March 7, 1906, his appointment was confirmed, and on May 7 he and his family landed in Hong Kong.

Nineteen hundred six was not an auspicious year to be in China. The country had not fully recovered from the Boxer Rebellion six years before, which had aimed to remove all foreigners from Chinese soil. After it failed, armies of the "great powers" that sought economic control of China marched to the capital, slaughtering, raping, looting, and otherwise humiliating the inhabitants. In June 1905 there had been a general boycott by China of American goods to protest the treatment of the Chinese in the United States and the strictures on Chinese immigration. Yet trade, in general, had been increasing between China and the United States. And it would be Wilder's duty to see to it that the trade continued at an upward rate.

Partly because of the unstable and potentially volatile political atmosphere and partly to provide a sound education for her youngsters, Isabel took it upon herself to remove the children from Hong Kong. After barely half a year with her husband, she and her family left China and sailed for California. Undoubtedly with Amos's approval, she set up a home in Berkeley and remained there for the next few years.

Thornton attended the Emerson Grammar School in Berkeley and on Sundays, this time without his father's admonitions, sang in the choir at St. Mark's Episcopal Church. His exemplary attendance record and behavior earned him a small gold harp, which the family treasured. However confusing the trans-Pacific crossings might have been for the children, life with Mother was more congenial than it had been with their father. Thornton benefited especially.

There seemed to be a special affinity between Mrs. Wilder and Thornton. "Our mother had the same kind of excited, enthusiastic curiosity about not only being alive and what the world held, but especially music and art, for all that could be learned and seen in Europe and for languages and especially poetry," Isabel remembered later.[7] Even as a young child, Thornton was busily writing plays for his brother and sisters, and their mother provided yards of cheesecloth for draped costumes.

Thornton had other talents to be encouraged, too. In 1906 he began violin lessons with a certain Miss Brightman. A few years later, when Charlotte began studying piano, he taught himself to play. The University of California sponsored a series of concerts and Isabel, though she couldn't afford to buy tickets for the whole family, managed to find friends willing to take a child or two along. Also, Thornton sometimes served as his mother's escort for nights at the theater, where stock companies performed raunchy, rollicking musicals.

Amos's visits were rare, though he kept in close contact with his family by letters. He was especially concerned with the children's education, and when he did arrive in California, his presence was not as welcome as all might have hoped. He frequently dispensed assignments to the children—the memorization of some passage or other, for example—and expected that their schoolwork and marks be uniformly excellent.

When in Hong Kong, Amos diligently performed his consular duties. Sometimes, however, his staff was totally confused by his odd office practices. He would write important messages on any scrap of paper, stuff them into an envelope, and send them out. ". . . We had the dickens of a time trying to figure out what he meant," one of his workers recalled. And it seemed that Amos had as much trouble deciphering many of the reports he received. One day he could stand it no longer and became enraged. "Assume no intelligence at this end," he ordered in his next memo.[8]

Amos's work took him to southern China, where he visited some remote areas. He also traveled to the Philippines and then, in 1909, to Japan. While there, he received word that he was being promoted and transferred from Hong Kong to Shanghai. Before returning to China, however, he paid a short visit to his family. By June 1, 1909, he had taken up his new post. He made only one more visit to California, in the fall of 1909, and this time he left with the plan that Isabel and the children would again join him in China.

Though his work in Hong Kong seemed to have proceeded smoothly, his position in Shanghai had an inauspicious beginning. On December 29, 1909, he received a letter from a New York importing firm to which he could make only one response. The firm desired "to increase the sale . . . of Caroni Bitters" and asked for the names "of the leading wholesale drug and liquor dealers in Shanghai."

Because of his strong personal convictions, Amos felt that he could not co-operate. He wrote to the Secretary of State in February, asking for "instructions," and received an explicit reply.

The consular service exists for the promotion and protection in foreign countries of the legitimate interests of all American citizens, and it is especially necessary that consular officers exert their best efforts to aid in the development of American export trade. It is not for this Department, or for any officer serving under it, to deny the support of the consular service to any individual or firm engaged in a class of business not prohibited by law or public policy. . . . Inasmuch as all legitimate American interests are entitled to its impartial support it must insist that consular officers shall render such assistance as may be in their power and consistent with their other duties to further the interests of every manufacturer and exporter. It cannot admit the principle of permitting a consular officer to regulate his official conduct by his own personal views of propriety or morality where that course would result in the withdrawal of his support from Americans engaged in a trade the legitimacy of which has been recognized from time immemorial.

Of course, Amos was not satisfied. Beyond his personal aversion to liquor, he believed it immoral to foist alcohol on the Chinese. "The studied effort to force alcoholic drink on the Chinese people," he wrote to the State Department, ". . . is a task in which I must decline to share even the most casual participation." Though he would not sabotage the government's official policy, he felt he must be "true to the light I have on this question [rather] than that I should fall in with the conventions of government. The conventions of government," he added, "always lag behind the convictions of the few; and if the few who think they have new light accepted as unchanging the policies of the day, civilization would have no advances to report." On June 14, 1910, he offered to resign.

But the problem proved less momentous than it seemed. He did not resign, and when his family arrived later in 1910 he managed to settle them comfortably in their new country. Now there were five children: Janet Frances had been born on June 3, 1910, in Berkeley. The elder children were sent to schools, and Isabel was occupied with her infant daughter. It was Amos who bore alone the burdens of his chosen post.

Thornton later recalled that spending part of his childhood in China made him "no stranger to the unfathomable misery in the

world." In 1911 the misery was graphic when China experienced
one of her recurrent famines. Again Amos found himself opposing
official government policy. In April the U. S. Army transport *Bu-
ford* arrived with supplies from the United States. At a cost of
$50,000, the ship had carried across the Pacific large quantities of
American flour and various canned goods. But the flour, Amos informed the State Department, was not palatable to the Chinese
unless it was mixed with equally large amounts of bean cake. To
purchase the bean cake, the canned goods were sold, and Amos
would have liked to sell the flour, too, to be able to devote the
money toward the purchase of kaoliang, an indigenous grain, and
rice. Here he was strongly opposed. The representatives of the
*Christian Herald*, donors of half the flour, and flour agents in
Shanghai wanted the Chinese to receive the twelve hundred tons
in the form it was sent. Furthermore, the flour agents in Shanghai
believed that an auction would impair their business in China.
Tactfully, Amos suggested an alternative. "I heartily approve of
this magnificent giving," he wrote, "for when a man is dying on
one's doorstep is not time for academic wisdom or carping criticism . . . , [but] I am of the opinion that in the future the phi-
lanthropy of American [*sic*] could best be expressed by gifts of
cash."

Speaking before the Central China Famine Relief Committee,
he urged that generous funds be raised. Here the conservative Republican spoke as a Christian and humanitarian. "It is futile to
say that the way to force the [Chinese] Government to correct
conditions is to let the people perish—futile, if not a saying without mercy," he told his audience. "The Chinese have been perish-
ing for centuries, and the canals are silted up, and the dykes fallen
down. The issue of what Government does for the people is one
for Chinese Government and Chinese people, and the present
state of the Empire indicates that the logic of conditions is not
lost on the people; but for the on-looker the one fact is of Need,
Suffering, Starvation, Death. . . . The man who loves his fellowman, whose heart goes out to helpless, innocent children, cries, 'I
give what I can,' and he conditions only that it be applied to the
best of human wisdom."[9]

As Amos knew, the "logic of conditions" was indeed not lost, and the famine was not the only crisis through which he worked in 1911. A revolution was brewing against the Manchu regime and the Westerners who held so much power in the huge country. By February 1912 the six-year-old Manchu Emperor, P'u-yi, had abdicated, and China was technically a republic. By March 14 Amos had arrived in San Francisco and reported to the Secretary of State that he would not return to China until, at the earliest, September.

Besides the emotional strain of the past year, Amos was suffering from sprue, a severe digestive disorder, which had caused considerable loss of weight and general weakness. On his doctor's advice, he had returned to the States and a San Francisco sanitarium for observation. He had been told in Shanghai that he must avoid the Chinese summer, and planned, therefore, to remain in California until the fall.

Then, restored somewhat, Amos sailed back to Shanghai and resumed his post—again without his family. This time he was confronted with considerable controversy over whether or not he should be retained as Consul General. The Secretary of State received numerous letters in his support, and many that spoke against him. Those who urged his retention cited his "personal integrity and high moral standards." "He is a high-minded, princely man," one writer offered. "It is a scandal when the United States will send out a gambling, whiskey drinking, blaspheming, licentious man to represent us."

Yet others were not so kind. "Old Dr. Wilder is no good and does no harm," another wrote. "Take him home, send out a 'live' man." One of the sorest disagreements in which Amos had become involved was, as might be expected, over the serving of liquor at official functions. Friction had occurred, it seemed, when the American Association planned to serve champagne at its Fourth of July celebration. Amos not only refused to attend, but planned a reception on the same day, a few hours later, at which no champagne would be served. The American Association saw this conflicting party as a deliberate affront and complained to the Secretary of State that at a Washington's Birthday Ball, at which Amos was Chairman of the Executive Committee and one of the hosts, he not only attended the reception but tried "to dominate it." The conflict, according to the representative of the American Association, was not merely one of a difference of opinion but "resolves itself into the question as to whether the American community are going to be run by Dr. Wilder, or whether they will conduct their own affairs. . . . I feel sure that I echo the sentiments of a great many of the prominent business men here when I say that there is a fairly general hope that the good of the service will demand that Dr. Wilder be transferred from this post, and some one sent here who will enter to a greater degree into the life of the community; and, incidentally, who would improve the general manner in which the Consulate is conducted."

A few months later, Amos again found himself the subject of letters to the State Department, this time being accused of "talking too much." The contretemps occurred at a meeting of the "Saturday Club," an informal group of Chinese and foreigners organized to better relations between the two communities. On September 20, 1913, a luncheon was held, which was reported in the Shanghai *Times*. An editorial accused Amos of having participated "and with every manifestation of approval in the proceedings, in a regular political demonstration of a character virulently hostile to the Central Government of China. . . ." Wilder later admitted that he "had talked too much . . . ," the paper went on, and a certain Mr. Tucker—the same man, coincidentally, who had launched the Fourth of July attack—once more wrote bitterly to the Secretary of State. He enclosed clippings from the Shanghai *Times*, *The China Press*, and *The China Republican* that were highly critical of Amos. "Dr. Wilder's attitude," Tucker wrote, "during the present disturbances in China has been of a character calculated to give overt sympathy to the rebels against the constituted Government. . . . China is in a very difficult position. The Peking Government is making every effort to establish stable conditions throughout the country, and deserves the sympathy and aid of all foreigners, especially those who live here. It would seem that, temperamentally, Dr. Wilder is unable to preserve the nice balance which his official position would dictate, and, while I express it only as a personal opinion, I feel safe in saying that it would be echoed by the great majority of responsible Americans here, that he be changed to another field of activities, and some one be sent here who would more perfectly represent what I believe to be the sentiments of your Department and the American Government."

To Tucker's accusations Amos responded with dignified strength. The club, he explained, was a forum he himself had organized to present speakers of expertise on a wide range of topics. "Apart from the September 20th session," he added, "there has been hardly a ripple of censure;—only congratulations that such a force for international goodwill was in existence in Shanghai." He thought the article in the Shanghai *Times* only another evidence of the "emaciated condition" of the newspaper and the "whimsical" editorial policies of its editor, John O'Shea. Attacks against the Saturday Club, Amos felt, resulted from the disapproval of one of the *Times*'s supporters, who had himself begun an "International Institute" with similar aims. Moreover, he believed that the attack was really against two speakers rather than against his own presence at the luncheon and his refusal to withdraw from the session after having heard the content of the speeches. Instead of admitting that he "talked too much," he implied that his silence was taken as tacit approval of the speeches.

One speaker was T. H. Lee, a Yale graduate and vice-president of the YMCA, whose political analysis of the recent rebellion did not heap praise upon the existing government. Some people, Amos thought, might be "annoyed by his failure to confine . . . all blame to those Chinese who report disappointment with the Administration at any point," but for Amos, Mr. Lee's ideas were "constructive in the best sense,—not seditious but finely patriotic."

The other speaker, and the one on whom the controversy centered, according to Amos, was Dr. W. E. Macklin. Macklin had been invited to discuss conditions at Nanking during the rebellion. A long-time resident and "staunch friend" of China, Macklin nevertheless spoke scornfully of the troops of Chang Hsun, the invading horde who had sacked the city and massacred its inhabitants. He contrasted their brutality with the order and bravery of the defending soldiers and wondered whether Chang Hsun's troops "were loyal to Peking or preparing violence as an independent contingent. . . ." As temperate as his remarks seemed to many of his listeners, Macklin's words stirred up some reporters who publicized the meeting and Amos's apparent support of the speeches.

Though Amos seemed confident as he defended himself, the new controversy evidently did little good for his health. Apparently, too, he realized that his effectiveness in Shanghai was at an end. On September 27, 1913, just five days after Tucker wrote his damning letter, Wilder unconditionally resigned.

I have the honor to inform the Department that my physician is of conclusive opinion that I should not longer live in China. When I returned from the United States a year ago, I was not wholly recovered from my trouble, but I hoped it would disappear. Increased loss of weight, combined with lack of energy are factors that cannot longer be disregarded with safety. Medical counsel is to the effect that permanent transfer to another climate should restore me to health and former vigour, my malady (the beginning of sprue) being confined to the Orient; but that I must not work longer in the Orient. It is with great regret that after 7½ years in China, during which time I have become interested in the activities and forward movements of the Nation and people, I must withdraw.

He requested transfer to Canada or Britain, but instead retired permanently from diplomatic service and returned to Berkeley, California, and his family. At the time of his retirement he had been earning $8,000 a year, and despite his difficulties with the Shanghai community, his "Standing in District" was rated as "Excellent." As far as his consular administration, however, he was rated "Very poor," which may give some indication of why he was not transferred to another post.

Amos left the consular service with a clear conscience and fond memories. He felt he had given his best and learned a great deal. For the children, however, the impressions of China would be deep and everlasting and somewhat more romantic.

# TWO

———◆———

THORNTON first attended the Kaiser Wilhelm School for a short time and then transferred to the China Inland Mission Boys' School at Chefoo, on the Yellow Sea. Many of his classmates' parents were missionaries, and he was shocked at first when he discovered that "(perhaps covertly) they regarded the Chinese as a primitive people."[1] He was convinced otherwise. Nevertheless, he wrote later, he had brief desires of becoming a missionary "to a really primitive tribe."

Schooling at Chefoo did not encourage Thornton's artistic nature. Diversions took the form of cricket and soccer or, perhaps more appealing, cross-country runs through fields of enormous graves. "There had been a great deal of corporal punishment," he remembered, "from the teachers on the students, and from the students on one another." Those who were the last three to finish a quiz received three strikes on the hand with a ruler "and could watch for hours the rising blue welts." Greek and Latin were part of the curriculum in the early grades, placing other students ahead of the Berkeley-educated youngster. Even in the dormitories, the boys' slang was mixed with Latin.

Worse than the weekly visits with Amos to the Congregational church in Madison were the three services required of the boys at the mission school. ". . . We were all falling in and out of religious conversions a good deal of the time," Thornton recalled.[2] There was no instruction, however, in the culture of the Orient, and whatever Thornton gleaned from his stay there was based on intuition. He thought, for example, that the Chinese "believe that hatred, in itself, kills. . . ."[3]

More than the physical impressions that Thornton retained of the vast land were the aesthetic sensibilities that the culture evoked. He first confronted a sense of timelessness, of antiquity, which would forever influence him. And he sensed a profound linking of all things of nature, which he expressed many years later. There were only seven Chinese words he could remember, he said: "one, two, three, four, chicken—egg—cake." The metaphorical translation was, he decided, "All nature is one."[4]

Far different, but rigorous in its own way, was Thornton's next environment, the Thacher School in Ojai, California.[5] Located in the lush Ojai Valley, some four hundred miles south of the family's residence in Berkeley, the surrounding towns were said to offer "pleasant, cultivated society, with churches, schools, and the moral and intellectual atmosphere of a New England community." The school itself was nestled amid mountains rising to heights of six thousand feet and boasted the healthful benefits of its situation. Outdoor life was an integral part of education at Thacher, and hearty, sports-loving boys were encouraged. Less robust young men—Thornton was one—were accepted, however, if it was thought they might improve under the school's regime. Housed in simple, unheated rooms, the boys participated in baseball, basketball, tennis, golf, riding, calisthenics, trail-making, mountain climbing, "and a little hunting of small game and trapping of coyotes, wild-cats and foxes. . . ." In a nearby canyon, beside a small stream, some groups of boys had built rustic "shacks" and retreated there on weekends, chaperoned by a faculty member, to learn "the use of tools, some wood craft, and a little of the art of cooking . . . along with the enjoyment of most wholesome pleasures out of doors." In the fall and spring, camping excursions to the Sespe Valley were made on horseback, a ride of about three hours. The privilege of this trip, however, was granted only once a month—provided, of course, schoolwork and conduct were acceptable.

For all its emphasis on a rugged physical program, Thacher's curriculum was meant to provide a sound basis for college admission and included Latin, Greek, French, and German; English grammar and literature; algebra, geometry, and trigonometry; physics and chemistry; Greek, Roman, English, and American history; and debates. Examinations were held every six weeks, followed by reports to parents. Intellectual life was further extended by evening readings of Scott, Dickens, Austen, James, Kipling, or Howells, with a lengthy reading from the Bible on Sunday. At eight o'clock each morning, the headmaster opened the school day with an appropriate comment "on morals and manners . . . followed . . . by the reading of some valuable poems, with so much comment and description as may insure appreciation. The idea was suggested by Goethe's assertion that no day should go by without the reading of a good poem."

Thornton, at fifteen, was a member of the Middle School, required to rise promptly at 6:30, and go to bed at 9:15—twenty minutes later on Saturday but ten minutes earlier on Sunday. One of his subjects was algebra, in which he had some difficulty. In class, he dreamily covered the flyleaves of his text with imagined titles of future works. Young authors, he wrote later, spend a great deal of time making up interesting titles and composing elaborate tables of contents. But their ability is far below their dreams. They are better at writing lofty prefaces, unearthing Latin and French quotations, and setting down moving dedications than at realizing the works which they planned.[6] Daydreaming, which would have provided enough of an obstacle to the learning of algebra, was compounded by what he thought was an inborn inability to remember numbers. But his teacher, a kindly old man who was nearly deaf, patiently spent time after class helping him.

Nor was Thornton more adept at the rigors of grammar and spelling. His English teacher, Talcott Williamson, concerned at Thornton's lack of interest on these points, once sent for him. "Now, Thornton," he told the young student, "you've got to learn how to capitalize and spell and punctuate and have some idea of the connection between paragraphs. . . ." Thornton, he recalled, "was very pleasant and smiled and said, 'Well, I don't know. I'll always have a stenographer.' "[7]

Though Thornton later recalled the "friendly masters," "sunny days," and "congenial fellow-students" at Thacher, it is likely that the "impressive stars above the Sespe" were more inspiring than the gymnastics and games. Besides competing with the other students, he also had to try to live up to his brother's reputation. Amos, a year ahead, was an excellent student and a better athlete than Thornton, especially in tennis, for which he won praise and prizes. Bookish and withdrawn, Thornton was not a typical Thacher boy, and after a year at the school he returned to Berkeley.

Berkeley High School, which Thornton attended with his sister Charlotte, saved the Wilder family the tuition of Thacher and offered Thornton a chance to display his talents—which lay more in acting and playwrighting than in sports. In the first month he was at the school, his skit *The Advertisers* was performed in the fall Vaudeville Show, to the delight of the audience. His "original conception" won praise, as did his acting the part of Mr. Lydia Pinkham. In the spring Vaudeville Show, he again produced a sketch, this one "full of action and variety." What's more, he acted the part of Le Beau in *As You Like It*, a performance, the yearbook reported, that "will never be forgotten."

His creative life continued beyond the walls of the high school. A walk in the country might inspire an idea, a plot, and of course an enticing title, for a major work. But when he returned home to try to write, his enthusiasm waned. Being an adolescent author was discouraging, he found. He had high hopes but could never realize his plans. He felt a fellowship with great authors, but his own notebooks were a great disappointment. Much of what he wrote sounded like poor imitations, with convoluted sentences, purple prose, and a mass of half-remembered styles.[8] Nevertheless, he did write some short plays in the spring of 1915 from which he rescued two, *Brother Fire* and *Proserpina and the Devil*, for inclusion in a volume published thirteen years later.

Each play intimates his later work in the theater. *Proserpina and the Devil* is a play for marionettes, set in the Venice of 1640. Four puppets are worked by two puppeteers who, in turn, are overseen by a manager. The atmosphere is one of chaos and disillusion. The puppeteers argue behind the scenes. When the manager suddenly leaves for a drink, the arguments worsen. Here the creators of theatrical illusion fail in their roles.

*Brother Fire* is more conventional in style, but the theme will be echoed in Wilder's more mature work. Set again in Italy, which the young Thornton had not yet seen, the characters are Annunziata, a peasant woman who thinks fire is wicked; Isala, her eight-year-old daughter, who likes to play with fire; and St. Francis, who claims fire is "our brother, and one of the best things in the world."[9] Among Francis' other lines is one that will reappear in other forms in later novels and plays: "Bring me not logic, sister," he tells Annunziata. "She is the least of the handmaids of Love. I am often troubled when she speaks."[10]

In the fall of 1915 Thornton Wilder became a freshman at Oberlin, where his brother was already enrolled. The rest of the Wilder family had moved to New Haven after Amos took a position as executive secretary and treasurer of the Yale-in-China program. Perhaps to spare his sons the shock he had felt on entering Yale as a freshman, Amos chose for them a small and less socially lofty school. A self-supporting student at Oberlin was more respected than one coming from a wealthy family, and there was something appealing to Amos, too, in the unwavering principles on which the school was run. "Oberlin cared nothing for money and nothing for fame," a contemporary alumnus later remembered. "By the same token it did not object to being ridiculous on principle. In perspective the silly regulations of my time endear Oberlin to me not for what they were but for what they represented. They represented a spirit so independent that all Oberlin's conventions were unconventional. The answer to all objections to those conventions was simple, complete, and characteristic. If we didn't like it we knew what we could do. . . . Once a professor's son I knew was detected in the act of smoking with Mr. Braithwaite, the genial engineer at the water works. He was summarily expelled, and the community agreed that the only thing for that boy to do was to join the navy."[11] The president of the college himself admitted shame whenever he caught a cold. And most im-

portant, rigorous intellectual work was required. ". . . Without
the intellectual virtues," it was believed at Oberlin, "the moral
sense rests on habit and precept alone."[12]

The atmosphere at Oberlin would not stifle Thornton's spirits.
He was brought up to believe that men came into the world to
work, and years later told a friend that "the older he grew the
more he found himself moving away from people who weren't in
some way clear about that."[13] Besides the classes, there were exciting activities on campus that sparked his interest. In the fall of his
freshman year, the students were rehearsing Bernard Shaw's *Can-
dida*. On Sunday afternoons, informal gatherings were held at the
home of one much-admired faculty member and his gracious and
cosmopolitan wife, Professor and Mrs. Martin. There Thornton
soon showed himself to be "a leading light" with his talk of literature and the theater. He quickly became a member of the Oberlin
Dramatic Association, and even found a forum for his own plays
—the parlor of the Men's Building.

That spring, four students who called themselves "The
Strollers" performed two short plays by Thornton: *The Last
Word About Burglars* or *A Fantasy*, in which the playwright
played the Burglar; and *A Fable for Those Who Plague*, in which
Thornton played Frederick Bennett, the fiancé of Doris Elston.
One classmate remembered another about an artist viewing an exhibition of his own paintings. Here Thornton played every role:
the artist and each visitor, including a pretentious critic who made
"the most hilariously moronic remarks."

Thornton stood out among his classmates. One young man,
who later became chairman of Oberlin's History Department, recalled him vividly.

What a fantastic freshman he was. He spoke in an excited and exotic manner, highly punctuated with epigrams. Everything about
him—appearance, dress, speech, and manner,—was precise, even precious. One might have imagined him a porcelain figurine of a witty
French abbé of the Enlightenment come to life. There was something of the 'gamin,' the mischievous boy, about him, too. And no
one could have guessed his age, for if he was not old in appearance,
certainly neither was he exactly youthful looking. . . . I am re-

minded of Wilde's comment on Max Beerbohm, "Max was born
with the gift of eternal old age!"[14]

The unconventional freshman was becoming known as an ur-
bane yet unpretentious young man, worldly yet somehow "small-
town" and comfortable, a combination of qualities that would always attract others to him. One such friend was Robert Maynard
Hutchins, whose father, William, was Professor of Homiletics in
the Theology School. Robert, a handsome and personable young
man, easily won the presidency of his freshman class. He and
Thornton were classmates in German, sharing an enthusiasm for
Goethe which began during that first year. Though the friendship
between the two students was casual, Robert's mother showed a
genuine fondness for Thornton, and he frequently visited the
Hutchins home.

Robert's memories of Oberlin included an affectionate chiding
of its many requirements and rules. "I can remember sitting every
day in this room on the most uncomfortable of all chapel seats
trying hard not to hear what the speaker was saying. I can remember the dancing rule, the rules confining ladies to their rooms
at earlier and earlier hours in inverse proportion to the time they
had spent in college, and the smoking rule, which I abhorred but
was not robust enough to violate."[15]

Thornton's most outstanding memory of the time he spent
there, however, was a singular professor: Charles A. Wager, who
taught courses on Burke, Victorian Prose, Early Nineteenth Century Prose, and Old and Middle English. An erudite scholar, Wager's enormous success with his students came not so much from
his learning but from "his charm and, above all . . . , his style in
writing and speaking." For Wilder, Wager was a lifelong inspiration. Wherever he would teach, whatever material he used, he
said he was giving his Wager imitation. He was not alone in his
evaluation of the man. Many others agreed that "Wager was the
greatest teacher I ever had."[16]

Hardly an issue of the *Oberlin Literary Magazine* was published
without a contribution by Thornton Niven Wilder '19. The first,
appearing in December 1915, was a short play, *St. Francis Lake: A
Comedy in Cages.* In the single scene, we see a brief meeting be-

tween Julia and Jane, two elderly sisters whose life is spent running a glove shop in a small city. Once a year they take turns at
one-week vacations in a neighboring village, St. Francis Lake. Jane
is now returning home, but Julia tries unsuccessfully to convince
her to go back to the lake. Both know they must face reality, however, and the scene ends with Julia hurrying to board the train
and Jane tearfully returning to her job.

*St. Francis Lake* described two women caught in psychological
cages. Thornton's next offering, *Flamingo Red: A Comedy in
Danger*, was a vignette set in a certain tearoom in one Hotel
Cour de Lion. The playlet, which appeared in the January 1916
issue, featured Madame Flamingo, a woman with "a mystic temperament," who presided over her "medievally furnished room."
In the scene, she serves Charles and Dora, a young married couple
who seem not to be compatible. Though Charles is all patience,
Dora is perversely intent on starting a quarrel. Finally Madame
Flamingo, distressed at their bickering, convinces them that it is
the "red Spirit" in the room which is causing them to quarrel and
admonishes them to be constantly alert to it. They agree and, preoccupied, they stop arguing.

Thornton's next appearance in the magazine was a celebration
of his literary prowess. He had written the Prize Essay in the
school's Shakespearean Contest, and his winning words were published in March 1916. His thoughts on drama give definite indication of his own later work.

In his essay, Thornton focused on the language that Shakespeare used to convey emotion, contrasting it with the poverty of
modern speech. In a recent play, he tells us, the heroine could do
no better than exclaim, "How awful! How awful!" upon hearing
the news of the death by violence of her husband. "We have lost
a living, expressive speech," Thornton concluded, "our emotions
must be suppressed; we live in the great Anglican calm; we must
meet the crisis of our lives with a few awkward monosyllables."
He was not, on the other hand, advocating the use of inflated dialogue. "Great plays," he said, "need great, but natural language."
Playwrights must use living, vibrant speech—like swearing. "One
might almost say that Shakespeare's plays are great because everyone swore in his day."

With brilliant use of language, Thornton believed, the actor had no need of constant prodding toward interpretation. "These plays," he wrote, "do not need the close stage direction of the moderns who are so perpetually anxious to impress on the reader and performer that the scant text conceals deepest distress." Of the modern writers who succeeded in their own use of language, Thornton cited Synge and Ibsen.

Besides his usual entries of plays, Thornton published three prose pieces in the magazine. One, in April 1916, was a short short story, "Sealing Wax," the merest breath of a ghost story. In it a man chides his wife for using sealing wax, malodorous and old-fashioned, just a few moments before she dies. Thereafter, he is haunted by visions of her always accompanied by the distinctive odor of sealing wax. Finally, when he is lying on his deathbed, he requests that sealing wax be burned; he sees her once again until, at last, "she became—real. . . ."

The other two prose pieces are much closer in style and theme to what is later to be found in *The Bridge of San Luis Rey* or *The Woman of Andros*. "Two Miracles of Doma y Venuzias," published in the fall of Thornton's sophomore year, relates two tales about Doma, the saint of a small Spanish village. More mystical than the motherly Madame Flamingo, Doma is a dark, ethereal woman whose miracles include preparing the Infanta for her imminent death and taking upon herself the wantonness of two prodigal sons returning to their aged, loving mother. The language is close to that of *The Bridge*; the tales have a timeless, biblical quality characteristic of much of Wilder's later work.

Perhaps the most striking of his publications is "The Marriage of Zabett," which appeared in June 1917. Here we have the story of Zabett der Derken, a woman who hates the caresses of men and is repulsed by the idea of her coming marriage. She seeks deliverance from the event that all consider inevitable, and is advised to postpone the ceremony and await some sign. When no sign comes, she is desperate and miserable, and she allows the plans to proceed. Shortly before the rites, however, she finally receives her instructions and runs away to found a convent.

St. Zabett, as she later became known, is uncharacteristically sensual. Her burning revulsion to the affections of her betrothed is an emotion rarely found in Wilder's works. Clearly she is the heroine not only for her adoption of the spiritual life, but also for her success in overcoming an acquiescence to the sexual stereotype to which she might have been condemned. ". . . Me and many another she spared from that exile of a woman's soul from Heaven, the marriage of the body," the author concludes. "She is our intervention; without her we should be dead, slain by the caresses of our husbands."

The two years at Oberlin had given Thornton the confidence that Amos had hoped would ensure his future success. In 1917 Amos called him back to New Haven and enrolled him in his alma mater, Yale. Thornton said later that he had by then grown "completely devoted" to Oberlin and "deeply resented" his father's transferring him to another school. But if he presented any opposition to Amos's plans, he was overruled. Thornton was not to be Oberlin '19 after all, but Yale, class of 1920.

Amos had already made plans for his son's summer, too. He had contacted the Reverend William Goodell Frost, the president of Berea College, to arrange for his son to enroll at the school for the summer. On June 15, 1917, Thornton arrived in Kentucky ready—if not eager—for the unusual program Berea offered its students.

Berea was founded after the Civil War to serve black and white students in Appalachia. In fact, it was not until 1915 that non-mountain students were admitted—and even then, it was by quota. Besides being proudly interracial—a difficult feat under early Kentucky state law—Berea required its students to enroll in a work program. One of its aims still remains "to demonstrate through the Labor Program that work, manual and mental, has dignity."

Thornton was to take some regular courses—one was typing—and was assigned to work in the garden. As he told one friend later, he and the other gardeners spent a great deal of time praying for rain.[17] Another of his chores was to tend the cows, during which he would "declaim . . . the judge's speech from Barrie's 'The Legend of Leonora.'" He was, at the time, shifting his literary admirations from such writers as Barrie and George Moore to Sophocles, Dante, and Cervantes, choices influenced by Charles

Wager. And always he kept in mind Wager's warning: "Beware of what you admire when you're young; because admiration is the only school for the will."[18]

Amos's close direction of Thornton's life was caused not only by his own domineering personality, but also by his deep conviction that his son was headed for failure. "Poor Thornton, poor Thornton . . . he'll be a burden all his life," Amos would often say. Thornton wrote, but had no desire to follow his father as a journalist. "To me it smacked too much of the manipulation of public opinion, however sincerely prompted,"[19] he decided. His ambitions were as diverse as archaeologist and actor, but included nothing that Amos considered fitting and potentially remunerative. Thornton himself admitted that his personality could be exasperating to others. He was, at times, childlike. He knew he was neither aggressive nor competitive. He could be happy with simple amusements. "I often appeared to be vacant or 'absent.' This irritated some; even valued friends, both men and women (perhaps including my father), broke with me charging me with 'not being serious' or calling me a 'simpleton.' "[20]

When Thornton entered Yale in the fall of 1917, he was twenty years old. He had never before disobeyed—and would not then disobey—his father's wishes. Years later, he would compare a man's devotion to country with his role in a family, pointing to the difference between "nations that speak of their unity in the feminine: mother country, *la patria, la patrie*; and in the masculine, like V*aterland.* A mother you protect," he said, "a father you obey, and no man over twenty-one should obey his father."[21]

But however definite Thornton felt about a patriarch in later years, his relationship with Amos was one of submissive son to omnipotent father. It had been so at ten, it was so at twenty, and it would continue to be so for almost two decades longer.

# THREE

---

"THORNTON showed extraordinary versatility. He wrote plays, poems, short stories, essays, played the piano and composed music, acted in college dramatics, was a member of the Pundits and of the Elizabethan Club and thought Lola Fisher, the actress, was so beautiful that she ought not to be at large. His conversation was better than that of most good men at forty. . . . I believe he is a man of genius."[1]

The opinion of William Lyon Phelps, a professor of English, was not unique among the Yale community, although Phelps had long been an admirer of members of the Wilder family. As a freshman, he had known Amos at Yale when Amos was a senior and "one of the ablest and wittiest men in college, a shining light in public speaking." When he was twenty-three, he had taught Sunday school in a certain Presbyterian church in Dobbs Ferry, where he had encountered the extraordinary fifteen-year-old Isabel. Now he found Thornton to be "a star of the first magnitude . . . unusually versatile, original, and clever."

Yale's literary circle was quick to respond to the talented junior. Among Thornton's friends were Philip Barry, later to achieve

fame as a playwright, and Stephen Vincent Benét, the poet. Even
Thornton admitted his own popularity. "Stephen Vincent Benét,
Harry Luce and I were considered the outstanding poets of the
class of '20 at Yale," he told an interviewer.[2] Of the three, it was
Thornton who composed the college's Ivy Ode.

As one classmate remembered, Thornton was not interested in
joining the various societies and associations that proliferated on
campus.

> He was independent and even somewhat scornful of these tradi-
> tions. The artistic life of the college centered around the Eliza-
> bethan Club, where undergraduates, graduates and professors gath-
> ered . . . of an afternoon or evening to smoke and talk.

> Here one would find most of the English faculty. Thomas Beer was
> an occasional visitor. Wayland Wells Williams, writing his novels,
> and residing in New Haven, contributed his biting comments on
> the college world. Archibald MacLeish would pay a quick visit from
> Cambridge, where he was then studying law. It was a volatile and
> eager gathering and in this crowd Wilder was a somewhat retiring
> but decidedly definite figure. I can remember that he was always
> willing to talk, but that he preferred a small group to a large one.
> His wit was sudden and devastating, and while it made him close
> friends, it frightened away the dullards.[3]

Besides joining the Elizabethan Club, a small number of aspiring writers formed a group they called the S-4N, which published
—sporadically—a pamphlet-size magazine. The group included
Thornton, Stephen Benét, and Ramon Guthrie, among others,
guided by Norman Fitts. Thornton's nonliterary friendships included his roommate, Barets Oscar Benjamin, a native of Denver
and long-time resident of New York City.

As at Oberlin, Thornton again became associated with the college's literary magazine, this time as an editor as well as contrib-
utor. His plays and reviews began appearing in the fall of 1917
with *The Angel on the Ship*, a brief piece set on the stranded
*Nancy Bray*. The crew are reduced to prayer, but the object of
their devotion is a carved figurehead whom they call Lily. When
they finally see the approach of *Maria Theresa Third* and know

their prayers have been answered, they fear they will be called pagans for "bowin' down to wood and stone."

Besides publishing his own creations, Thornton reviewed Yeats's *Per Amica Silentia Lunae* and Rupert Brooke's *Death and Burial*. He had always been a wide and voracious reader, and his own work was being influenced by the authors he was discovering during his college years. Literature, he thought, comes from "two curiosities": one about human beings, which bordered precariously on love; and the other, an absorbing curiosity for those rare few masterpieces of literature.[4] He read Newman and Swift, and borrowed the theme from Ben Jonson's *The Alchemist* for what he later termed "a callow play," *The Trumpet Shall Sound*. The play was published in four issues of the *Yale Literary Magazine* from October 1919 through January 1920, and Thornton described it succinctly: "Master departs on a journey of indefinite length, leaving his house in charge of faithful servants; servants gradually assume the mentality of masters; liberty leads to license; Master returns unannounced and puts an end to their riotous existence. Lively writer, Ben Jonson," he added.[5]

Of all the plays, *Childe Roland to the Dark Tower Came* is the most poetical and mysterious. Set in a kind of Flemish half-light, the play presents a wounded knight, Childe Roland, approaching the Tower of Death. The knight "blows his horn; the landscape collects itself to listen." Within the tower he finds two women, one a gentle red-haired girl who would give him red wine and delight in his verse; the other, a dark-haired girl who understands his longing for death and finally alleviates his suffering by putting a chalice of poison to his lips. Though he would have wished death to come more quickly, she explains the delay and urges him to be courageous: "How slow you have been to believe well of us," she tells him. "You gave such little thought while living that we have made this little delay at your death." Wilder may have borrowed his title from Browning's poem or from an allusion in *King Lear*, but the theme is his own. Those who give "such little thought" to life will reappear as characters throughout his future work.

By the time Thornton entered Yale in 1917, the war had changed the lives of many of its students. Thornton's brother,

Amos, had enlisted in the Ambulance Corps and was serving in France. His friend Robert Hutchins, who, like Thornton, had planned to transfer to Yale from Oberlin, also was overseas. But Thornton's eyesight prevented him from experiencing the war firsthand. Instead, he joined the Army and was sent to a division of the Coast Artillery at Fort Adams in Newport, Rhode Island. Though he would spend his time in the service unimpressively "having defended, unopposed . . . Narragansett Bay," his time away from Yale, and away from home, was not wasted. There were free hours in which he took long walks past the boarded-up cottages of the wealthy, and came to know the multi-levels of Newport society, from its summer visitors to its modest natives. By the time his brief career as a soldier had ended—he served only from September 14 to December 31, 1918—he felt a great affection for Newport, its bay, its ambiance, even "the night sky."[6]

It was in the Army that he first met some types of people vastly different from those with whom he usually associated. An impassioned listener and watcher, he was especially impressed by soldiers who had come from rural areas, who had never been away from a rustic home, a tightly knit family, and a small society. For such young men, Fort Adams was a world apart, and they would often weep from homesickness. To Thornton the plight of these men was just another example of the depth of suffering inherent in being human. Thornton longed, not for the first time, to be able to know people of all backgrounds and not just the able, well-mannered, well-educated men and women among whom he had been raised.

Thornton returned to Yale in January 1919, to his literary work and to a renewed friendship with Robert Hutchins. The bond between the two was stronger than it had been at Oberlin; both found they had in common a similar upbringing that fostered a similar outlook. "Having fun," Robert once said, "—that was a wholly impertinent question for me. Coming from a structured family with its roots in the ministry, I wasn't supposed to have fun, and I've never overcome the notion that having fun is a form of indolence.

"I feel an obligation to work although I'm allergic to it. I was not brought up to look out the window, and the fact that it may be pleasant to look out the window would be a very poor reason for doing it. Life is supposed to be rigorous—no question about that."[7]

His father, like Amos Wilder, had brought him up "along ascetic lines, which included getting up at 5:30 A.M. . . ." Working at his studies during the day and in an ice cream factory at night, Robert managed to graduate with honors and became elected to Phi Beta Kappa—but like Thornton, he had no specific plans for his future. After Yale, he took a teaching job at the Lake Placid School in New York. Amos, however, had plans for his son.

As Thornton put it, in 1920 he "was sent abroad to study archaeology" at the American Academy in Rome. A visiting student, he spent the year among artists and classical scholars, learning Italian, brushing up on Latin, and hungrily absorbing Roman history. Becoming an archaeologist, he admitted, had once been an ambition, inspired by Schliemann's discovery of Troy and his uncovering of the strata of cities that were buried at the site. But it was not to indulge a fancy that Amos sent Thornton to Rome; rather, it was an extra year to mature, to gain an added urbanity, to obtain some useful knowledge.

Thornton immediately felt the impact of a foreign landscape. As his train approached the city, he knew he was at last in "Virgil's country and there was a wind that seemed to rise from the fields and descend upon us in a long Virgilian sigh. . . ."[8] If Amos thought the wind would clear his son's head of some "simple-minded" notions, he was wrong. Thornton would be inspired, instead, to write. In Rome he would begin his first novel.

He lived in quiet elegance at the Villiero Belleacci, one of the Academy's residences, and his studies included work on excavations under a visiting professor, McDavid. Often the students would be taken out on digs, unearthing the past with their own hands. They found a road that was two thousand years old, with ruts still identifiable though long buried. Millions of people had passed over it "laughing . . . worrying . . . planning . . . grieving." For Thornton, the dig was a revelation. "It freed me from the oppression of vast numbers and vast distances and big philosophical questions beyond my grasp."[9] Suddenly everything in his own world seemed distant, as if it were being looked at through the wrong end of a telescope. "You look at Times Square as a place about which you imagine some day scholars saying 'There appears to have been some kind of public center here.' "[10]

In Rome, Thornton uncovered not only past worlds, but a new, attractive and vibrant world of the present. He frequently visited the home of Adolfo de Bosis, a poet and translator of Shelley. His wife was a daughter of a Methodist minister, born in New England, but raised in Rome and displaying none of the Puritan qualities to which Thornton was accustomed. Particularly intriguing was their son Lauro, a nineteen-year-old chemistry student at the University of Rome. Lauro was a complex and idealistic young man. His parents had instilled in him a love for poetry and literature; he himself was inclined toward philosophy, and he was fascinated with the implications of coming advances in science. Moreover, he was politically liberal, disturbed by the ardent nationalism that had arisen in Italy after World War I and fearful of its consequences. Thornton was much attracted to Lauro de Bosis and to the aristocratic, esoteric world in which he lived. It was this world which Thornton recorded in notebook after notebook, and which eventually would inspire a novel, *The Cabala*.

As the year came to an end, Thornton's career was again a major question to which Amos, as usual, found an answer. He sent a telegram to his son informing him of his future. "HAVE JOB FOR YOU TEACHING NEXT YEAR LAWRENCEVILLE, LEARN FRENCH," his father cabled;[11] and Thornton dutifully set off for Paris.

The Lawrenceville School, a boys' preparatory school in Lawrenceville, New Jersey, was then headed by Mather Abbott, formerly a professor of Latin at Yale and a close friend of William Lyon Phelps. Abbott, a descendant of Cotton Mather, brought to the school a proud Puritan morality. Thornton's study of French had ended in his second year at college, but his facility at languages enabled him to learn whatever else he needed for success as a teacher. Besides his classroom duties, he was made assistant master of Davis House, working with Edwin Clyde Foresman in overseeing some twenty-five adolescent boys.

The house system, he thought, did encourage warm relationships between faculty and students. The academic standards were high. The students were, for the most part, responsive.

Though Thornton described Abbott's personality as "bracing," he found Mrs. Abbott more congenial, and he settled into the Lawrenceville community as well as he could.

He was especially fond of Foresman, known as Clyde, who had been teaching at the school since 1913 and had been master of Davis House since 1920. Clyde had the reputation among his boys as being "the squarest man on the faculty," an understanding adviser and an enthusiastic football coach. Another of Thornton's close friends was C. Leslie Glenn, a teacher of mathematics who later became an Episcopalian minister. Thornton felt a good deal of sympathy with Glenn's ideas on religion, and once, during a conversation, suddenly turned to him and said, "'What we believers forget is that no one is happy without God, no one!'"[12] The friendship that began at Lawrenceville was to last for fifty years, with Glenn closely following his friend's writings, especially where he saw an expression of Thornton's religious feelings.

Thornton was interested in those boys who were the nonconformists of the class—not the athletes but those who spent their energies on literature, music, and art. The second year he was at the school, he founded the Almanack Club, which consisted of six or seven members whose sole purpose was "the consideration of good writing and good music. . . ."[13] Together, he and the students would walk across the golf links and through the school woods munching on popcorn and exchanging ideas. The group, which met informally, existed for three years, after which its members graduated, not to be replaced.

At Lawrenceville, Thornton found what he considered to be his true vocation—teaching. His study was usually crowded with chattering, questioning students. He was fascinated by each—by their backgrounds, their interests, their ambitions. "Teaching," he said later, "is a natural expression of mine."[14] Decades after, when he was a world-renowned and much-lauded author, the space on his passport for "occupation" would read "educator,"[15] and teaching would always seem to him the most authentic of his roles.

Only at night, after his boys had gone to bed, would he turn to writing. On the floor below, the drowsy students often heard his pacing; they knew his evening's work had begun. The manuscript he was assembling and revising was drawn from the notebooks he had kept in Rome. It was to be called *Memoirs of a Roman Student*, but it contained little that was autobiographical. Instead, it dealt with an exotic group of aristocrats who lived in their own special world. They were called the Cabala, explained by one character as "a pocket of archaic time in the middle of a world that has progressed beyond it." They found, as Virgil had written, that "This world where Time is, troubles me," and so created for themselves a community apart from the political and social realities of Italy in the 1920s.

As his first major effort at writing, *Memoirs of a Roman Student*, finally titled *The Cabala*, was different from the plays and short pieces Thornton had published as an undergraduate. Where he usually read his work to his mother, depending on her comments and encouragement, he now welcomed another opinion. Fortunately, he had access to a willing ear.

During his return trip from Rome, he had met on shipboard the drama critic for *The New Republic* and *Theatre Arts Monthly*, Stark Young. Impressed with Thornton, Young had given him the address of Edith Isaacs, the editor of *Theatre Arts*, advising him to contact her and bring her some of his work.

Isaacs, like Young, immediately recognized a new talent. "Although he was still very young," she thought, "he had seen more of the world than many men ever see." Her colleague described Thornton as someone "full of talent and human quality. . . ." Her feelings were in complete agreement. "Although very shy," she remembered, "he was unusually friendly; although he was surprisingly learned, he was never pedantic; he was as deliberate in his thinking as he was explosive in his speech, letting the words roll off his tongue one on top of the other but every one the right word aimed exactly at expressing the right idea. He was both temperate and enthusiastic, bold and unafraid but very modest, and above all he was one of the most amusing young men I had ever met. . . . If there were twenty people who could talk as well and listen as well as Thornton Wilder could, they might easily revolutionize American social life."[16]

She asked him to read from the notebook he had brought, and he perched beside her on the couch to read—at first "shyly," she said—from his *Memoirs of a Roman Student*. As he went on, he read with more feeling, almost acting out the individual characters and dramatizing the work. Isaacs thought his dialogue was written with "theatrical precision" and believed that Thornton had an "innate sense of theatre speech."

Edith Isaacs was not alone as Thornton's audience that afternoon. From her favorite spot beneath the family's grand piano, Hermine, Edith's small daughter, listened enchanted. There was something appealing to the child in the "eager" young man; and she knew her mother was delighted by him.

When Thornton finished his reading, Edith suggested that he type up part of the manuscript for magazine publication. " 'Don't you think,' " he asked her, " 'it might be just as well not to hurry? I am glad you think it is good enough but I have always believed that a little Greek temperance would be helpful in such matters.' " Still, he was so buoyed by her enthusiasm that when he left, instead of taking the elevator, he happily ran down fourteen flights of stairs.[17]

# FOUR

HOWEVER satisfactory Wilder found teaching, he knew he wanted to devote more time to writing. With the support of Edith Isaacs, he applied for residence at the MacDowell Colony in the summer of 1924 and was accepted. In June the group of "MacColonists" already in residence met their new guest. He was "a rather slight, dark-haired man of medium height with gray eyes half hidden behind horn-rimmed spectacles, and a sensitive mouth beneath a closely cropped moustache. He never kept still for any length of time and talked very fast, gesticulating constantly."[1]

The residents that summer included the poet Leonora Speyer, composer Mabel Daniels, dramatist Esther Bates, Padraic and Mary Colum, writer Nancy Byrd Turner, Elinor Wylie and William Benét, the newly divorced Tennessee (Mrs. Sherwood) Anderson, and Edwin Arlington Robinson. Anagrams with Nancy Turner filled many an evening. Elinor Wylie talked of her new novel, *The Venetian Glass Nephew*, and made Thornton promise to send her some historical information about Venice. He also promised Bill Benét, the brother of his Yale friend, that he would

send on some of his short plays for his opinion. But the most congenial spirit was that of E. A. Robinson, the heavy-drinking, pool-
playing poet who resided at MacDowell for several months each
year. "Outside of discussing literature or music and holding his
liquor, pool was . . . E.A.'s only fully developed, conventional social exercise," one guest remembered, "though even so, he never
initiated a game but would merely stand at the table, looking
silently receptive, till someone else proposed it."[2] He drank his gin
straight, untainted by such additions as orange juice, tumbler after
tumbler, yet never became an alcoholic, or even a loose talker.
He always maintained a certain reticence, and clearly skirted
topics in which he had no interest. "E.A. was responsive and explicit where a particular person was concerned, or a particular experience or particular expression in literature. But he had little time for generalizations of a cosmic or social order. As he frequently proclaimed without shame, he had no rational philosophy
or sense of 'society' as a living reality."[3] Once, when he and
Thornton were discussing Shakespeare, Robinson asked if he had
ever read *Macbeth*. "Of course," Thornton replied; but the poet
was not satisfied. "No . . . , I mean have you ever *really* read
*Macbeth*?" he asked, leaving Thornton to wonder if, indeed, he
had.[4]

Robinson succeeded in convincing Thornton that a writer must
never mix politics with art.[5] The poet himself did not join groups
of publishers and authors, would not take part in literary arguments. For him, life as a writer was sacred and had to be pro-
tected from distractions.

During the day, each resident was obliged to concentrate on
work in an assigned studio. But at dinner and in the evenings, camaraderie was encouraged. Tennessee Anderson quickly took a liking to Thornton and tried to capture his interest. One evening she
managed to sit him beside her on the floor, throwing her arm
around his shoulders to keep him immobile. Thornton, thoroughly engrossed in a conversation with two other writers, went
on talking as if oblivious of his ensnarement. He talked "steadily
and with stammering and supersonic speed, waggling his finger at
all, sundry, and nobody in particular, and two or three times

breaking away from Tennessee only to be snatched back, still orating, not skipping a syllable."[6]

The summer seemed too brief for all the work Thornton had hoped to accomplish. He was trying to finish two full-length plays and work on his Roman novel. But he managed to procrastinate as much as he could, and he complained to a friend that his fountain pen sometimes seemed inordinately heavy. Suddenly it was September, and one dawn he was awakened to the sound of pebbles being thrown at his window. He hurriedly dressed to be driven to the train and, a few hours later, was back in New Haven.

His mother listened, receptive as always, as he read his summer's work. After a short visit with his family, Thornton went on to New York to see some plays, a respite before the school year began once more. Then he returned to Lawrenceville, to the routine of teaching—admonishing students, seeing that they all went to bed on time, correcting French grammar, and attending faculty meetings.[7] But his life was widening more and more to include his writing and his love for the theater.

He spent the holiday season of 1924–25 attending plays in New York for a round-up review in *Theatre Arts Monthly*. Though the task should have been pleasurable, the season's offerings, Thornton found, were generally disappointing. Productions of imported works seemed especially thin, coming from "the second shelf" of such authors as Galsworthy, Molnár, Hermann Bahr, and J. M. Barrie. Molnár's *Carnival*, for example, had been awaited with high expectations and was produced with great care. The sets and costumes were brilliant; the leading lady, Elsie Ferguson, "beautiful" and "persuasive," if unfortunately cast. But the dialogue itself—perhaps because of an inept translation—made viewing the play a tedious experience.

Bahr's *The Mongrel*, as adapted by Elmer Rice, also bored Wilder, who thought that mourning a dead dog was an insufficient theme for a play. Even the settings did not capture his interest. These, he said, had that look of shiny newness more appropriate to a store display. At least Galsworthy's *Old English* had two exciting acts—first and last—to compensate for a dull second act in which all color and flavor seemed to be lost from an evocation of the business world of old London. Even the weakness of

the play, however, could not detract from a masterful performance by George Arliss, whose "bold and simplified" style Wilder
much admired. And Barrie's offering, too, was weak, lacking
meaning and ending nowhere, though bearing, Thornton said, the
unmistakable sign of an expert playwright.

He was much more satisfied with the work of his contemporaries: Philip Barry's *The Youngest* and Mary Kennedy and
Ruth Hawthorne's *Mrs. Partridge Presents*. Barry's was the
stronger play, but one performer in *Mrs. Partridge Presents* struck
Thornton as memorable. "Ruth Gordon," he wrote, "did more
than her share in compensation in her much discussed performance of a minor role. One imagines her observing scores of silly,
meaningless rich girls and finally from the notebooks of her memory offering us the fine extract of her malice, an arrangement in
pauses and lines not notable in themselves, delivered in a William
Gillette pianissimo that forces a house to breathless attention. It
is the only performance," he added, "one remembers long."

The highlight of the season for Thornton showed his personal
inclination toward farce and fun that would someday emerge in
*The Skin of Our Teeth*. John Howard Lawson's *Processional*, "A
Jazz Symphony of American Life," was produced by the Theatre
Guild. "What could be more attractive," Thornton asked, "than
a play that intermingles strips of vaudeville patter, exciting drama
and burlesque, a Ku Klux Klan ballet and a negro song-and-dance;
in which a man in a silk hat steps to the footlights and announces
tenderly that it is Mother's Day; in which the stage is framed by
famous American advertisements and yet contains a pathetic love
story and a fine sober climax?" The author fell short of the play's
promise, though, by offering "shallow" and "unexhilarating" dialogue. Yet something in the play caught Thornton's imagination:
"American civilization has been proved crazy," he wrote, "and the
only solace in despair is the ever-present jazz-band." At the end
the cast formed "a jigging parade," and invited the audience to
join them and go "God knows where. . . ." Thornton was
delighted.

Also apart from his duties at Lawrenceville was his work on his
novel. In the spring of 1925 he submitted a portion of the manuscript to the publishing firm of A. & C. Boni, where Lewis Baer, a

former classmate at Yale, was on the staff. Baer was receptive to
his talent and encouraged him to complete the book. Nights were
spent writing; evenings were often spent at the nearby Princeton
library—pleasant hours, Thornton recalled, in the basement of the
venerable building.

The proximity of Princeton was a lure for Thornton. The university offered the wider world of scholarship together with the se-
curity of once again being a student. The daily chores at Lawrenceville, after four years, were beginning to seem unstimulating.
Moreover, he was being urged by his father to enter a graduate
program, "to go on and get a higher degree and . . . progress in
your teaching."[8] Thornton applied for, and was accepted into, a
master's program at Princeton and arranged for a two-year leave of
absence from his job. His major was to be French language and
literature, a choice he sometimes regretted. But he found life as a
graduate student a refreshing change.

Though his classes did not always excite him, one professor provided as much inspiration as had Charles Wager. Louis Cons was a
Frenchman who had been an assistant professor at Princeton
since 1919. A graduate of the University of Paris, he had been a
tutor to the royal family of Prussia before World War I and a
teacher at the University of Berlin. Sprightly and witty, Cons was
an expert on French drama and on Villon, Baudelaire, and Ver-
laine, frequent subjects of his lectures.

Out of class, however, Thornton found his most sympathetic
company. "Kierkegaard evenings" were spent at the home of
Walter Lowrie, theologian and scholar. Dr. Lowrie, an alumnus of
Lawrenceville and one of the first fellows—in Christian architecture—at the School of Classical Studies in Rome, had in common
with Thornton a respect for hard intellectual work. Toward the
end of his life, he commented that his output had hardly been
startling—"barely 12 items a year, one a month, in the course of a
long and misspent life."

At the time, Thornton was concerned about his own output. In
the spring of 1926 his first full-length volume was published.
Though it sold only a few thousand copies, *The Cabala* was
widely reviewed and engendered interest in its twenty-nine-year-
old author. The *Times* called him "a mystic" and "a fine stylist;

he clothes mysticism in his style and lightens it with jewels of charming observations and felicitous expression. . . ." But there were reservations, too, when the reviewer remarked that the work "contains no substance, as yet, which will appeal to the rank and file of the world."[9] Yet the book was thought to be distinctly original, a "sophisticated extravaganza," another reviewer decided, which "uneven as it is in its total effect, often makes thoroughly good reading." Disorganized structure and writing that seemed to the *Saturday Review*'s reader "more perfectly Carl Van Vechten than the best of 'Peter Whiffle'" were minor criticisms. ". . . The fascinating characters in the course of the novel . . . do frequently galvanize the whole affair into a brilliant, if intermittent, life. . . . Altogether, if you care for unlikely people doing improbable things in an irresponsible manner against supernaturally picturesque backgrounds," he concluded, "you will like the antics of Mr. Wilder's *Cabala*."[10]

The "antics" in Thornton's first novel concerned a small group of bored aristocrats living well in contemporary Rome. Into this group stumbles the amiable American, eventually nicknamed Samuele by a Cabalist, whose innocence, intelligence, sensitivity, and Puritan morality suggest the author himself. Samuele is a Wilder prototype, a character who will be transformed in several other novels, but whose function remains the same: he stands as an example of rationality and stability in environments that lack or pervert these qualities; he is capable of benign intervention into the lives of others while remaining intact and emotionally independent; he is staunchly American, with the same spiritedness and newness of the most wide-eyed Henry James character.

Samuele is introduced to the group by one James Blair, a Harvard graduate and classical scholar, who has come to Rome from Sicily, where he was archaeological adviser on a film "bent on transferring the body of Greek mythology to the screen." Blair is a darker personality than Samuele, but still a facet of Thornton's prism. He seems to be what Thornton wants to avoid in his own character—a young man once "frightened by life" who turns to books for solace. He pursues learning almost maniacally. He is afraid to confront the world as if such a confrontation would reveal a fearful sight: "the world, dissolving in ruin." Yet his scholarly pursuits lead nowhere. He does not really enjoy the research; he publishes nothing. His work "was not so much the will to do something as it was the will to escape something else. One man's release lies in dreams," the author tells us, "another's in facts."

The Cabala immediately become fond of Samuele and involve him in three episodes which together form the structure of the book. The first centers around a handsome young man, the sixteen-year-old Marcantonio, whose very name conjures up a romantic image. Marcantonio is about to marry, but his fiancée's family is aghast at his licentious behavior and wants him to settle down for a while before the wedding takes place. Samuele is called in to reason with the boy, though clearly he is at a loss to understand the impetuous, restless spirit that motivates him. One evening, in fact, Samuele watches in disbelief at what appears to be an allusion to incest between Marcantonio and his half sister, Donna Julia. That morning he is awakened at about three by Marcantonio, fully dressed and nearly incoherent. Distinguishable only is the phrase "You were right." Then Marcantonio flees from the room. His body is discovered later in the morning.

Marcantonio's suicide does not impede the novel's progress. In the next episode, the lovely Alix becomes hopelessly infatuated with James Blair, is spurned, and finds comfort only in Samuele's company. It is she who gives him his nickname, after her dog, a delightful setter who could spend his days doing nothing more than watching people "with a look of most intense excitement." Alix is charming and endearing, but deeply vulnerable. She wants to protect Blair, to watch over him. He wants only his independence. Samuele, of course, is ineffectual. He cannot substitute for his friend. He can hardly console the distraught Alix; yet his presence alone brings her a certain calmness. After a tempestuous period of trying to cope with her despair, Alix returns to the Cabala, where she is enveloped and sustained.

The final "antic" deals with Astrée-Luce, a woman who gilds herself with religion. She is constantly occupied with pious thoughts and the possible doing of good works; "but she had no brains." Astrée-Luce is a fervent admirer of the Cardinal Vaini, a cynical prelate whose early service in China seems to have colored his views of the Cabala and the world. His true nature is lost on

Astrée-Luce, however, and she, a royalist, has designed a plan to induce him to write for her cause. She explains her plan to Samuele: together, they would "prop up the Cardinal so that the Cardinal could prop up Europe."

Samuele refuses to help but does go to see the Cardinal on his own. The ageing curate mocks Astrée-Luce's childlike beliefs, not only in Samuele's presence, but before Astrée-Luce herself. She becomes so confused and disturbed at his attitude that she attempts to kill him—but fortunately misses. For the Cardinal, the crisis he provoked shows "that belief had long since become for him a delectable game." He books passage to China, but dies on shipboard before reaching his destination.

For Samuele—and for the reader—the Cabala is a mystery. Toward the end of the book, one character offers Samuele an explanation, but clearly he is unsatisfied. The ancient gods, she tells him, at first did not die with the advent of Christianity, but they did lose worshipers. And when they lost believers, their divine attributes began to wane. Suddenly they were forced to confront death. When a god died, however, his "godhead" passed to someone else, an unsuspecting mortal who knew he had been blessed when he discovered "that to wish for a thing is to command it." These new gods were, of course, attracted to Rome: hence, the Cabala.

But Samuele runs from that ancient land back to "the rich new country that will grow more and more splendid. . . ." He takes the advice of the shade of Virgil, which appears to him on shipboard: "The secret is to make a city, not to rest in it." He knows he is called upon to found "some city that is young." He rejects Europe and embraces America.

Samuele was running in the opposite direction from that of many young, intellectual, artistically inclined Americans. And Wilder was praising New York when fellow writers were buying one-way tickets to Paris. Nineteen twenty-six saw the publication of another young novelist's work: Hemingway's *The Sun Also Rises*; and the contrast between the two authors is immediately evident. Wilder's background, firmly ingrained in his personality, would never allow him to become an expatriate—often an emotional, rather than geographical, state. He was not trying to break from his past but rather to find a way to use that past as a fertile ground for his creations.

Hemingway's epigraph from Ecclesiastes might well have been taken by Wilder, but Gertrude Stein's remark about the "lost generation" would have been rejected. For Wilder, the cyclical progression of humanity was a fitting theme for a novel; but the celebration of rootlessness and hopelessness was not. "This Hemingway of the middle twenties . . . ," Edmund Wilson saw, "expressed the romantic disillusion and set the favorite pose for the period. It was the moment of gallantry in heartbreak, grim and nonchalant banter, and heroic dissipation. The great watchword was 'Have a drink'. . . ."[11]

However sophisticated Wilder's style and allusions were in *The Cabala*, he thought of his audience as including the small-town reader, the middle-class American, who would accept his premises and applaud them. The most telling line in the novel comes during a conversation between Samuele and Cardinal Vaini over the fate of Marcantonio. The Cardinal, well aware of the youth's amorous entanglements, is against any intervention. The boy should be left alone, he thinks, and be allowed to follow his caprices. Suddenly Samuele understands what the Cardinal is really saying. "How clear it makes all Italy, all Europe," he realizes. "*Never try to do anything against the bent of human nature*. I came from a colony guided by exactly the opposite principle." Thornton was not one to rail against the fates; he was still, after all, his father's son.

# FIVE

⬥

THORNTON was awarded a master of arts degree in June 1926, spent part of the summer at MacDowell, and then worked at Lake Sunapee Camp, a tutoring school, in New Hampshire. He still had one year's leave of absence from Lawrenceville, which he wanted to devote to his writing. In the fall of 1926 he sailed for Europe in charge of a young man to whom he was to show the sights of the great cities. Living in a grand style, touring through castles, viewing operas and plays, visiting museums, Thornton was unhappy. His charge, Andy Townson, was bored and restless. The boy wanted nothing more than to spend his days in his hotel room, and even then preferred to rush from city to city rather than to visit leisurely. The two traveled to Rome, Naples, Florence, Paris, London, Oxford, and several cities in Germany. Thornton was dismayed at his lethargic companion and looked forward to the day when the boy would return to America. At least then, Thornton wrote to Lewis Baer at Boni, he could continue work on his second novel.[1]

Thornton had definite ideas for his next book, and more came to him as he walked through Europe with his uncongenial com-

panion. He thought Germany would provide an especially felicitous atmosphere for writing and was sure that, as soon as he found
himself alone, he would be able to complete the manuscript
quickly. In any case, he asked Baer to hold off from typesetting
the first sections he had already submitted. All was to be changed,
he now planned. The weeks of frustration when he could not write
forced him to compose the book in his mind and in hastily jotted
notes. He now had a full sense of *The Bridge of San Luis Rey*,
and full confidence in its merits.

But *The Bridge* was not to be written in Germany. After Andy
left, Thornton traveled to the South of France and on Christmas
Day was in a village midway between Cannes and Nice. There he
came upon a group of Rhodes scholars and suddenly he felt so
homesick—at his advanced age, he ashamedly admitted—that he
shortened his vacation and returned home in little more than a
month. He arrived in New York in time to see a performance of a
play about which he had some misgivings—his own college effort
*The Trumpet Shall Sound.*[2]

Thornton had submitted the play to Richard Boleslavsky, a
friend of Edith Isaacs and the director of the American Laboratory Theatre. The production had opened on December 10, 1926;
Thornton saw the twentieth performance and was aware of the
mixed reviews. His reworking of Jonson's *Alchemist* was set in a
Washington Square mansion of the 1870s. The servants of the
mansion, spurred on by a young maid, let out rooms while their
master is away and face the consequences of his return. The mot-
ley assortment of tenants includes a woman of the streets, a sea
captain who preaches his new-found religion, a wealthy Swedish
woman who pretends poverty, and a pyromaniac.

The New York *Times'* reviewer experienced "a rather murky
evening." The play, he wrote, "assumes the customary kindly, benevolent and tolerant attitude to erring humanity, showing on its
canvas a whole panorama of petty human frailties contrasted
against a background of the sympathy and understanding of the
faintly haloed central figure."[3] Most critics were less than enthusiastic about the play; and even Thornton himself admitted that it
might have needed more work.

At that moment, however, his foremost interest was his new

book, and he worked on it through the summer, completing it at MacDowell. In September, with the manuscript on its way to publication, he returned to Lawrenceville to resume his duties as teacher of French and master of Davis House. But he was not content in a world bounded by school buildings and academic responsibilities. Though he still considered himself an educator, he saw a larger way of transmitting his ideas—through writing. As he explained to a writer friend a few years later, the worth of the world's great books was, not in their recording of history, not in their celebration of art for art's sake, but in their instruction of humanity—gently, almost indiscernibly, but powerfully.[4]

His hopes were in his future as a writer. He had applied for a Guggenheim fellowship which would free him financially to write. Although his support included a strong recommendation from Edith Isaacs, he had been rejected. His reputation rested solely on *The Cabala* and one professional production of a play. He knew his second book would point the direction of his career. *The Bridge of San Luis Rey*, however, seemed an unlikely candidate for fame.

"I write first as if I were writing about people we know," Thornton once said. "Then I do my research after I write—not before."[5] The basis for *The Bridge* was not so much in historical research as it was in the literary enthusiasms and personal obsessions that occupied Thornton at the time. But of course there was a kernel of historical fact in his tale. There had been a bridge, described as being "two hundred paces" long, made of cables handtwisted from the fibers of the maguey plant. In heavy wind, it swung frighteningly over a dark abyss, above threatening waves that thundered against the rocks. It had been built across the Apurímac River in Peru in about 1350 and had lasted for hundreds of years, supported on either side by stone pillars. It was a much used thoroughfare, and every two years the cables were renewed and the wood planking replaced. But when the wheel came into common use among the Indian population, the bridge was allowed slowly to decay. It collapsed, and the few travelers upon it were plunged to their death.

Like many before him, Thornton asked, "Why? Why were those particular travelers chosen to die? Or were they chosen at all?" But his questions came from another source as well, a passage from the Bible that continually rang in his mind:

> Or those eighteen, upon whom the tower in Siloam fell, and slew them, think ye that they were sinners above all men that dwelt in Jerusalem?[6]

The passage set the theme; the characters were drawn from many sources.

The book is divided into five parts, with the central three describing the lives of the victims: the Marquesa de Montemayor and her servant Pepita, Esteban, Uncle Pio, and a young boy, Don Jaime. It is the self-imposed task of a Franciscan monk, Brother Juniper, to investigate their deaths and determine if "we live by accident and die by accident, or we live by plan and die by plan." For Brother Juniper there is no doubt: the accident must have been an act of God, and therefore the life and death of each person involved must have some meaning.

He tells us first about Doña María, the Marquesa de Montemayor, known through legend and her letters to her daughter. Doña María was inspired by Thornton's fascination for Madame de Sévigné, an enthusiasm he could not fully explain. ". . . She is not devastatingly witty nor wise," he admitted once. "She is simply at one with French syntax."[7] So, too, the Marquesa frequently blunders in her dealings with others, but her letters are full of unleashed passion and "flamboyant" language. Doña María, like Thornton's early St. Zabett, rebels against marriage. But she is forced into a mismatched union by her mother and eventually has a daughter, the haughty Doña Clara. Doña María suffers unrequited love for her daughter, and her suffering gives her insight into the isolation of other humans. "She saw that the people of this world moved about in an armour of egotism, drunk with self-gazing, athirst for compliments, hearing little of what was said to them, unmoved by accidents that befell their closest friends, in dread of all appeals that might interrupt their long communion with their own desires." Yet she, too, becomes blind to love and fails to appreciate the singular spirit of her young maid, Pepita, who despite her unhappiness serves her mistress in good faith.

Contrasted with the Marquesa is an Abbess, Madre María del Pilar, loosely modeled on Thornton's aunt Charlotte, his father's sister, then chairman of the International Committee of the YWCA and a woman Thornton admired and respected. The Abbess is an ardent feminist who wants only "to attach a little dignity to women." She realizes, of course, the futility of her goal in eighteenth-century Peru. Yet like a swallow who tried to build a mountain by adding a single pebble to a pile every thousand years, the Abbess perseveres. She sends her protégé, Pepita, to the Marquesa because she knows that not even the suffocating existence of that life will damp the girl's spirit.

Indeed, it is Pepita who ultimately shows Doña María that her life spent in pursuit of her daughter's affections has been wasted; Doña María realizes that she was a coward in both living and loving and resolves to start anew. " 'Let me live now,' she whispered. 'Let me begin again.' " But two days later, she and Pepita die crossing the bridge.

The characters in the next section are closer to Wilder's own life. Esteban and Manuel are orphaned twins, raised by the Abbess, who, despite her generalized hatred of men, grew fond of the two boys. The duality of personalities is treated more emotionally here than it was in *The Cabala*, where Samuele and James Blair are contrasted. For Thornton, the idea of being a twin, of living with a double, was almost an obsession. His dead brother often haunted him; he carried within him the image of an identical likeness.

Esteban and Manuel are so close in spirit that "love is inadequate to describe their profound identity with one another. . . ." They invent their own language and find that telepathy often occurs between them. No matter what they do or where they go, they are certain of one thing: "All the world was remote and strange and hostile except one's brother."

But their bond is broken when Manuel becomes infatuated with a beautiful actress, known as the Perichole. His brother feels estranged and once threatens to leave. There is a crisis, however: Manuel cuts his knee and is badly wounded. Esteban nurses him, but the infection worsens and his brother becomes delirious. Suddenly he begins to curse Esteban for coming between him and the actress. For several nights Esteban suffers under his brother's raving; on the third night, Manuel dies.

Esteban's grief causes near-madness. At first he pretends to be Manuel, and no one is the wiser. But he meets a sagacious sea captain, Alvarado, to whom he tells the truth, and his confession seems to relieve him somewhat. Alvarado invites him to join his crew. Esteban agrees, provided he can take on the hardest work. He knows suicide is proscribed, he tells Alvarado, but clearly he is seeking death in life.

Just before sailing, however, Esteban changes his mind, vacillates, and tries to kill himself. He cannot bear to leave Peru. He cannot bear to live alone. Alvarado tries to comfort him, but he knows how meaningless his words must sound to the young man. "We do what we can," he tells him. "We push on, Esteban, as best we can. It isn't for long, you know. Time keeps going by. You'll be surprised at the way time passes." Esteban, calmed, leaves with the captain and is killed when the bridge collapses.

The Perichole and her benefactor, Uncle Pio, are met again in the fourth section. Uncle Pio is a sympathetic character, a lonely man who discovered the actress when she was the waif Micaela Villegas and transformed her into an idolized figure. Uncle Pio decides early in his life that he will try to fulfill three aims: independence—keeping emotionally detached from people while able to act as "an agent" in their lives; proximity to beautiful women who would depend on him when they were in trouble, though they would not, he thought, love him; involvement with those who loved Spanish literature and its masterpieces, especially in the theater. His life with the Perichole seems on the surface to fill all three, but gradually it becomes evident that Uncle Pio is hardly detached from the young woman. He realizes that the world may be divided into two groups, "those who had loved and those who had not." His devotion to the actress places him among the former.

Though Uncle Pio's attachment to the Perichole transcends a mentor-student or father-daughter relationship, it never implies sexuality. Instead, Uncle Pio understands the rare communion between the two, and does not want to lose it. When the Perichole retires from the stage and finds a position in Peruvian high society, he urges her to return with him to Madrid and to the theater. But she refuses, mocking his dreams, and turns him away. Uncle Pio does not give up, however. Even when the Perichole contracts smallpox, he tries to see her, and one day comes upon her accidentally unveiled, her scars revealed as she tries to cover them with make-up. Enraged, she throws him out of her house. Still he persists. Finally he implores her to allow him to take her young son and raise him for a year. He will educate the boy as he did her; and the child will be his new companion. She relents and sends her beloved Jaime to Uncle Pio. The next day the two leave for Lima—and cross the bridge.

Despite Brother Juniper's dogged efforts, the author is not convinced that the collapse of the bridge was a deliberate and meaningful act of God. Surely there are lessons to be learned from the close examination of any life, but what these lessons teach are ambiguous. Each in a different way, the victims sought love; each was the victim of love. The dead live in the memory of the living until they, too, die and are forgotten. "But the love will have been enough; all those impulses of love return to the love that made them. Even memory is not necessary for love. There is a land of the living and a land of the dead and the bridge is love, the only survival, the only meaning."

Hardly anyone—least of all Thornton—was prepared for the accolades bestowed upon *The Bridge of San Luis Rey* when it appeared in late fall. "A new talent, and a very distinguished one, has appeared in American letters," Lee Wilson Dodd declared in the *Saturday Review*. While *The Cabala* had hinted at promise, Thornton's full talent was not yet evident. "It grows clear with his second book . . . ," Dodd saw,

> that Mr. Thornton Wilder is not just another literate and sophisticated young man. 'The Cabala,' his first book, had distinction, passages of genuine insight and beauty; yet there was about it an air of the tentative, the experimental. One felt that Mr. Wilder had wings, that they would prove to be good wings—and even enchanted wings; but one felt, also, that he was merely trying them out a little before they were fully fledged. There was a general atmosphere of flutter eddying round the whole charming performance.

But *The Bridge*, Dodd thought, was ". . . a tale which I am grievously tempted to call a masterpiece. . . . This book is a poem, if you will, a romantic poem—for its true matter is human love."[8]

Thornton was heralded also in *The New Republic*, where Malcolm Cowley found that the book "without pretense to greatness is perfect in itself. . . . In 'The Bridge of San Luis Rey,' the texture is completely unified; nothing falls short of its mark; nothing exceeds it; and the book as a whole is like some faultless temple erected to a minor deity. . . ."[9]

By the end of the year, praise for the book had appeared in most newspapers and magazines across the country. And in February an important review appeared in London's *Evening Standard*. Arnold Bennett wrote that he had been "dazzled" by the unsurpassed writing in the novel. "The author does not search for the right word. He calls, it comes."[10] Like his fictional Cabalists, Thornton had found that "to wish is to command." Yet he read each review in hope of some instruction, some advice. He wanted to be evaluated, and though he was more than pleased by the praise he was receiving, he was thankful, too, for less favorable assessments.[11] One of these came in March, 1928.

"And Then The (Bridge) Failed" was John Herrmann's review in *transition*, the Paris-based literary journal.

> Now that it is definitely established that *The Bridge of San Luis Rey* by Thornton Wilder is a classic (Burton Rascoe), a work of genius (William Lyon Phelps), a little masterpiece and of course a contribution to literature (Isabel Patterson), unsurpassed (Arnold Bennett), a great success for the discriminating (Henry Seidel Canby), and able to refresh such a jaded reviewer as Harry Hansen (Harry Hansen), I will horn in with two fingers and point out that the old bunkum is still the cat's eyebrows.

Herrmann thought the plot was "founded on a trick, a chain of feeble attempts at character sketching. . . ." The theme was inconsequential, he went on, and the descriptions "beatific." It would be a best seller only "because there is nothing new about it and readers have gotten used to it." But Herrmann scored the critics for heaping undeserved praise on what was, in his view, a failure.

Fortunately, Herrmann's view was in the minority, and the winter of 1927–28 was a time of celebration. In December, Thornton rushed from the year's final meeting at Lawrenceville and headed for Florida, where he hoped to relax in the sun and take long naps.

His former professor and stalwart supporter William Lyon Phelps was vacationing in Miami, as was a man Thornton was unexpectedly invited to meet—the boxer Gene Tunney. Tunney, too, had come from a recent triumph—the defeat of Jack Dempsey in Chicago on September 22. But his interests went beyond the boxing ring to include literature, music, and art. "On the day he fought Dempsey in Chicago," Phelps learned, "he had a good dinner at three o'clock, then read Somerset Maugham's novel *Of Human Bondage* for an hour and a half, and actually forgot he was to fight that evening!"[12] Phelps was as impressed with Tunney as Wilder was, and after talking with him for a while about Shakespeare, invited him to address his English class at Yale. The date they set was Shakespeare's birthday, April 23, and the subject would be Tunney's favorite play—*Troilus and Cressida*.

Thornton returned north in high spirits and to his duties at Lawrenceville with renewed exuberance. He managed to slip out several evenings—once to attend a festival of Max Reinhardt's plays in New York; another time to visit F. Scott Fitzgerald's home, Ellerslie, a gracious mansion in Edgemoor, Delaware. Fitzgerald was an admirer of Wilder, thinking *The Cabala* "the very best thing that had come out . . . since Hemingway. . . ."[13] At Ellerslie, Thornton first met the critic and novelist Edmund Wilson, who had not yet read either of his books. Wilson had, however, been reading Proust in the original, a diversion he had in common with Thornton. "I had had the impression," Wilson remembered, "that his [Wilder's] novels were rather on the fragile and precious side, and was surprised to find him a person of such positive and even peppery opinions. He had his doubts about *Le Temps Retrouvé*; he declared that too many of the characters turned out to be homosexual."[14] Besides literary conversation with Wilson, Thornton, at dinner, talked with Esther Strachey about

Colette, commenting about the merits of some of her Claudine books. The rest of the company was engaged in casual banter, interrupted only by playwright Zoë Akins' recitation of Shakespeare. All were inspired by the luxurious surroundings and the fine wine. But, Wilson noticed, though Thornton imbibed as much as anyone, he was "extremely responsive [and] remained sharply and firmly non-soluble."[15]

One of Thornton's few digressions from his father's dictates was his liking of liquor. His father had made him take a solemn pledge of temperance at an early age, and admonished him frequently to shun the evils of alcohol. " 'Now dear boy,' he would say, twirling his amethyst watch fob, 'even if you are at a bishop's table and you are served wine, I want you inconspicuously to turn down the glass.' " As Thornton added with a smile, "He meant 'conspicuously.' "[16] At home, grape juice replaced red wine and mineral water substituted for white. Imported ginger beer was always a favorite.[17] Nevertheless Thornton drank—often much more than his friends—with great pleasure and no unsightly effects.

In a euphoria of fame, recognition, congratulatory letters, parties, and celebrations, Thornton began to think of his next book, a novel based on the first half of Terence's *Andria*; plan a trip to Europe—this time with his sister Isabel; and give up, at least for the present, his teaching position at Lawrenceville. His correspondence reveals a content and confident writer, modest about his achievements, but hopeful about his professional future. And he had every reason for happiness: on May 7, 1928, he won his first Pulitzer Prize.

# II

*It is obvious that the effects of the best
poets and aesthetic writers of all nations
have now for some time been directed towards
what is universal in humanity.*

GOETHE TO CARLYLE, 1827

# SIX

———◆———

A former classmate from Yale, John Farrar, visited Thornton at Lawrenceville and found him hardly changed from his college days. "Slim, dark, wiry, eager, his appearance is characterized by quickly moving hands, flashing eyes. His speech is remarkably quick. His words rush over one another so rapidly that it is almost impossible to follow what he is saying when he is excited." Nor had his personality changed. "Do you think many people are going to read it?" he asked ingenuously about his latest work.

He seemed thoroughly at home and comfortable at Davis House, a graceful white building surrounded by trees, somewhat distant from the classrooms of the school. At the time of the visit, his rooms were filled with students waiting for Thornton—"Sir," to them—to sign checks. "If they're not very quiet, you must excuse them," Thornton explained. It was prom time, and excitement was pervading the school. Nevertheless, the boys stayed to be introduced and talk for a while. When they left, Thornton told Farrar a little about each one. "They are so simple, honest, and fresh in their reactions to life," he added. "Do you wonder that I do not want to give it up?"

He had arranged for one year's leave of absence, but intended to return. "I think it likely," he told Farrar, "that I will go on teaching. I should miss it very much. I should be afraid to leave it, because I believe I need that sort of quiet, academic atmosphere and the stimulation of study to do my best work."

The publicity over his prize winner had provided another kind of stimulation, exciting, but distracting. First he began to receive many books from publishers seeking his comments. Then his mail had become voluminous and he felt it would be rude not to answer every letter. Farrar told him not to answer anything unless it was a business letter or one he really wanted to answer, but the advice was hard for Thornton to follow. He was invited to publicity gatherings; interviews were scheduled for him. He began to meet some of his fellow writers. Throughout all, however, he managed to maintain an innocent enthusiasm and modest self-assurance.

Once, at a New York party arranged by his publishers, the "lion hunters" were amazed to find him so gregarious and unassuming.

At that party it was difficult to find Mr. Wilder because he dashed from one group to another. As soon as a crowd collected about him, he vanished. He kept taking one newspaperman aside and talking to him again and again. "It's the first time I've ever been interviewed," he said, "and I like it." The interviewer repeated the remark . . . as a joke. It was no joke. The interviewer was talking to Wilder and asking him questions. He found it much more palatable than the murmured flatteries of the assembled multitude.[1]

One afternoon he traveled up from Lawrenceville to attend a going-away party for the novelist and poet Glenway Wescott, who was sailing—permanently, he thought—for Europe. Though Thornton did not yet know Wescott, he knew he had been born in Wisconsin, so there was a common, if tenuous, bond between them. Wescott, along with Hemingway and Fitzgerald, was among the contemporary writers Thornton admired, thinking that they "seem . . . to be sincerely trying to express something that they see in life, something that they feel keenly."[2] He had dinner with Edna Ferber, to whom he suggested that a school of Wisconsin writers be formed, and with Louis Bromfield, to whom he proposed a great many well-meaning toasts.[3] He renewed his friendship with Gene Tunney, planning a hiking tour in Europe for the fall of 1928.

Tunney, who was training for a bout with Tom Heeney on July 26, planned to be married in early October. He would sail for Ireland in mid-August; Thornton planned to leave in July. "We shall spend about a month and a half," Thornton told an interviewer, "in a leisurely ramble through the small towns of France and Germany." More details of the trip would be worked out when Thornton visited his friend at Speculator, a training camp in the Adirondacks, where Tunney was working out.[4]

On June 28, Thornton was at the camp, and he and Tunney decided to take a canoe trip on the Kunjamuck River. The waters were decidedly chilly, as the two found out when their canoe overturned and both had to swim to shore. The boat was recovered, however, and even Thornton's pipe, which had sunk to the bottom, was found.[5] The plans for the trip withstood the minor mishap and were made definite by the time Thornton left.

In early July, Thornton sailed for Europe accompanied by three Lawrenceville students. He was to meet his mother and his sisters Isabel and Janet at a house he had rented in Surrey, England, after he spent several weeks in London. The three young men from Lawrenceville enjoyed being in the company of a literary lion. "It seemed that almost all the passengers and crew of the S.S. *Adriatic* wished to meet T.W. The fans included a librarian from Dartmouth College, a Vice-President of the Corn Exchange Bank, a doctor from the Mayo Clinic, and a pretty girl from Emma Willard," recalled Clark Andrews, one of the students. They discovered that Thornton had some odd practices they had not noticed at school. He rose at dawn and read for three hours before breakfast, for example. And he walked around the deck, absorbed in thoughts about writing, for some five miles each day. "He'd invent characters, devise plots, plan lectures and, for a breather, recite Shakespeare," Andrews noted. "It was understandable that passengers in their deck chairs were startled when a man hurried by their luxurious indolence gesturing to the ocean air and saying, 'Welcome, dear Rosencrantz and Guildenstern. . . .'" As gregarious as he was, though, he refused to attend the masquerade dance held toward the end of the voyage, preferring, he said, to watch the revelers through a porthole.

Thornton's volubility was at its most bubbling in London. "T.W. kept up an incessant chatter," Andrews remembered. "'Boys, look at the country! There's history in every speck of dirt. The Romans were right here—centuries ago. Think of that! Come now, don't go to sleep. Take deep breaths. You've got only seventy years. Keep turning your head in all directions—don't blink. Everybody buy a notebook and write down your impressions—write your mothers.'"

They stayed at the Metropole Hotel and visited every guidebook recommendation, took every tour. They sat in pubs, especially the Fitzroy Tavern, sipping ale and observing real London life. After an exhausting few weeks, they went on to Surrey, where the Wilder women were installed in a gray stone house. "The house was large, with many rooms, corridors, alcoves, nooks, and crannies, chock-full of a combination of Edwardian and French furniture," Andrews described. "The most vivid memory I carry of the house was its capricious electrical system. The slightest thunderstorm would knock it out. But no one seemed to mind. T.W.'s mother and two of his sisters had put candles everywhere."

Mrs. Wilder, Andrews saw, was a reserved, well-bred woman who expected complete deference from her son. ". . . A request for a glass of water, for Thornton to have the lawn mowed, or for him to drive to the village for some special kind of cake" would all be complied with immediately. "And she was always after him to buy a new suit," Andrews said. "'Something else besides gray, please,'" she would add.

To the Wilder children, Mrs. Wilder was the parent who instilled their aesthetic sensibilities and nurtured their refinement. For Thornton, especially, her support and approval were vital. She followed his career and his writings with the attention and interest that Amos could not show. Thornton's friendships with Edith Isaacs, Sibyl Colefax, Gertrude Stein, Alice Toklas were patterned on his devotion to his mother. These other women, too, offered him solicitous attention and maternal protectiveness that he would not have found among many women his own age.

Only his sister Isabel equaled her mother's devotion to Thornton. "She followed him around like a puppy dog," Andrews saw, "catering to his every wish." In later years, she would share his home, manage the smooth running of the house, help with his correspondence, act as his representative in literary matters, protect him from publicity-seekers, accompany him on social engagements.

Janet, Andrews decided, was very unlike Isabel and Thornton. "She was young and shy and told me she felt a little out of things with her literary family. At tea, mandatory every afternoon at five, she said little, although she listened intently with a frown of concentration."[6]

In August the family attended a tea given by Lady Sibyl Colefax, at which Thornton met the French writer André Maurois and his English admirer Arnold Bennett. Bennett thought Wilder a likable young man.

As Thornton told André Maurois when he visited with the writer on August 18, "I'm thirty . . . like all writers of twenty-six." He always felt older than others of his generation and knew he was separated by other qualities, too. "My weakness is that I am too bookish," he told Maurois. "I know little of life. I made the characters of *The Bridge* out of the heroes of books. . . . The method has served me well, but I don't want to use it again. I shall not write again before I have actually observed men better."[7]

It hardly mattered what subject a writer chose. "By the time of Euripides," he said, "they had all been dealt with already, and all one can do is to pick them up again." Shakespeare took his characters from history or traditional stories; the Romans copied from the Greeks, "Molière from the Romans, Corneille from the Spaniards, Racine from Corneille and the Bible. . . . No," he added, "there is nothing new that a writer can hope to bring except a certain way of looking at life."[8] For Thornton, an important theme was the unhappiness inherent in being human, caused in large part by the conflict between human desires and the inability to satisfy them in a civilization. Freud, he thought, had helped greatly in bringing to light an understanding of those desires. "Sexual life is so important," he concluded.

Thornton's own sexual life was kept private and discreet. Friends believed his homosexuality was a great burden to him throughout his life. "He was perhaps the most closeted one of his day," a friend of his wrote. "Despite all his advice and lecturing to me about the great homosexuals of the past, he would not have dared admit he was one of them; and all his life was spent in a series of elaborate charades to explain away his bachelorhood."[9] A writer's life was so absorbing, he would claim; a creative life had no place for marriage.

Indeed, many of those who knew Thornton did not know he was homosexual and believed that he was asexual, with preference for neither men nor women, and that sex played little part in his life. A reading of his works tends to reinforce that view. Sexual encounters occur offstage, are in no way erotic or graphic, and are clearly not integral to the understanding of his characters. All encounters are heterosexual, but most are unbelievable. Many readers thought Thornton's own puritanical feelings toward sex led to his inability to deal with the subject in his books; rather, his inexperience with heterosexual relationships caused his descriptions to be contrived and stilted.

Thornton's comment to Maurois was a general statement not intended to reflect his own personality. His sexual life would not have been a subject for discussion with a casual acquaintance.

Maurois remembered a pleasant afternoon in which the talk turned to music and theater. Realizing the erudition his visitor brought to his work, he questioned the friendship with Gene Tunney. "A strange companion," Maurois commented. "Don't think that," Thornton replied. "I'm very fond of him."[10]

Tunney's earnestness about art and literature endeared him to Thornton. They met on August 26 and by September were back in Paris ready to begin their trip along the Rhone and into Italy. Whenever Thornton would mention the title of a book he thought exceptional, Tunney would want to buy a copy, and he scoured English-language bookshops in the cities through which they passed.

Thornton had visited Paris last in 1926 with his bored young companion. Though he could now be considered a literary lion, he still did not seek out the notable salons—Gertrude Stein's or Natalie Barney's, for example—of the time. The closest he came to Stein was a visit to Sylvia Beach's bookstore, Shakespeare and Company, a few blocks away. Beach found Thornton refreshingly modest. "His manners were the best of any of my friends'," she remembered; "he was rather shy and a little like a young curate; his background seemed quite different from that of others of his generation in Paris."[11] Thornton did take Tunney to meet a fellow writer, however, remarking enthusiastically, "This man is going to be great!" The writer, Tunney recalled, was Ernest Hemingway.[12]

In England, the two visited Bernard Shaw. Tunney thought the two writers would have a great deal in common, but, as it turned out, Shaw, who had boxed in his youth, acted in a rather superior way to both men. It was only Mrs. Shaw, an admirer of Thornton's books, who softened the atmosphere of the meeting.

As the hike progressed, Tunney found his companion to be an able mountain climber and a tireless walker, sometimes averaging twelve to fourteen miles a day. Also, Tunney recalled, Thornton could outeat him, a feat not easily matched.

Tunney and Thornton traveled to Chamonix, Arles, Nîmes, Marseille, Nice, Genoa, and finally to Rome, where Tunney was to be married to Mary J. Lauder on October 3. Wilder was asked to be the best man, but he declined the honor, although he did serve as moral support for the nervous groom. Tunney's anxiety was over the publicity he knew his marriage would engender, and which he wanted to spare his fiancée. Thornton was surprised to see the usually calm man betraying inner turmoil; he himself, he realized then, always seemed excited and nervous, but was actually quite tranquil.[13] With the Tunneys safely off to their honeymoon on the island of Brioni, Thornton returned to France.

At the end of October he was settled at the Pension Saramartel in Juan-les-Pins, where he renewed his friendship with Glenway Wescott. Wescott was flattered by Thornton's attentions and thoroughly enjoyed their walks and conversations. "For two or three hours on successive days," he remembered,

we strolled here and there in and around Villefranche, looking
down upon its famous harbor scooped out by Hercules on his way
from one of his more famous labors to another, with anchorage
deep enough for ocean liners and battleships, including our battleships; visiting the cemetery where some nineteenth-century U.S.
Navy personnel lie eternally sleeping; descending into the Rue Obscure which is a sort of elongated open-ended cellar under the tenement houses on the quay, coming back up into the Riviera sunshine, gladly exhaling the sour old crypt-like atmosphere, and
inhaling the fragrance of the commercial flower beds, carnations
and stock, distributed upon the shelving foothills, and strolling
along elsewhere, I have forgotten where. Perhaps I ought not to say
strolling: we went so vigorously, and at intervals stopped and stood
face to face, in a rapture of articulateness, with gestures.[14]

As he had admitted to Maurois, Thornton told Wescott that
his two novels had been based on people he had read about,
rather than on those he had actually observed. "For each and
every sophisticated up-to-date Roman," Thornton said, speaking
of *The Cabala*, he "had in mind some hero or heroine of bygone
fiction or drama, or haunting figure out of someone's correspondence or memoirs." He seemed almost ashamed at first to
admit it, and intent on widening his experiences as sources for his
future work.

Wescott maintained a fond image of Wilder in his days of
early fame. Though Thornton conceded the need for publicity, he
warned Wescott not to take seriously most of the reviews he received. Though outwardly sophisticated, Thornton seemed, still,
to have a charming naïveté. "At times," Wescott wrote, "he made
me think of a boy climbing a tree, carefully placing his feet on
limb above limb, finally peering into a bird's nest containing eggs
or little birds, and holding his breath, in order not to sully anything with his human odor, not to disillusion or disincline the parent birds when they got back."[15] His laughter showed "a general
joy of living rather than a sense of fun at the time and in the circumstances." His eyes flashed, and when he spoke he punctuated
his sentences with his hands and fingers "somewhat in the manner of clergymen of a past generation or of old-time political cam-
paigners."[16]

Besides his leisurely afternoons with Wescott, Thornton used the time to work on his next book and on a play. He was also preparing some lectures, in anticipation of a speaking tour when he returned; and though he sometimes felt homesick, he realized that he could work best away from the distractions that threatened the solitude of a well-known writer.

In November he left the Riviera and went north, where Isabel met him in Germany. Together the two would spend a month viewing plays in Munich and Vienna for a major article in *Theatre Arts*. On his third night at the theater, Thornton discovered his favorite auditorium. Munich's Kammerspiele, he wrote, "isn't beautiful nor historic nor impressive in crimson and crystal, but a beehive of industry, ambition and intelligent stage-lore." The theater held about four hundred, and the stage was small and close to the audience. The theater was clearly more impressive than the play.

A few nights after, Thornton again became excited by a technique rather than by the content of the play. At the Residenz-Theater in Munich he found the "use of a revolving stage as an integral part of an otherwise realistically set play. . . . To give continuity and heighten the mood of danger and suspense, the stage turns and without lowering the curtain, the new scene appears and instantly the dialogue begins." And again, in December, after the exhausting viewing of scores of performances, Thornton took special note of the setting at Vienna's Deutsches Volkstheater. "Steps and ramps and backcloths on which whole towns and landscapes were painted in flat colors with mathematical contortions" seemed to him striking.

Christmas was spent in Grindelwald, where his aunt Charlotte joined him and Isabel as spectators at the two-week festival of winter sports. And by the end of January, the tired travelers were on board the S.S. *Cedric* heading for home.

During the month of "Playgoing Nights," a collection of Thornton's short plays was quietly published in America. *The Angel That Troubled the Waters* was originally to have been called *Three-Minute Plays for Three Persons* and contained some of his early Oberlin works together with some more recent additions. Short plays, Thornton wrote in his introduction, "satisfied my passion for compression." Besides, he added, since many were written at Davis House, in the short time he had between marking papers and getting his own rest, three minutes seemed the perfect length.

The plays were not meant to be staged. In fact, Thornton thought of them more as poetry than as drama.[17] He was especially concerned with explaining the plays' theme, which was, he said, "religious, but religious in that dilute fashion that is a believer's concession to a contemporary standard of good manners." As a schoolteacher, he well knew that he could not impart his moral beliefs by coercion; "beauty is the only persuasion." In a sense, he was trying to revive the spirit of Christianity in a time when ordinary language made it difficult to speak of pity, charity, humility, hope, and faith without seeming outmoded and trite. But he saw a hidden meaning in the challenge. ". . . It at least reminds us that Our Lord asked us in His work to be not only as gentle as doves, but as wise as serpents."

Thornton's theme did not surprise his readers, who already— from The Cabala and The Bridge—accepted and appreciated his morality and humanism. But The Angel That Troubled the Waters was not destined for the success of his previous books. Though there was grace and wit in the plays, one reviewer noted, they were "very seldom moving, 'everywhere not deep.'" Thornton's would-be evangelism did not strike the reader as powerfully as he might have intended. "Not even the most orthodox Christian could object to such sugaring of the pill. . . ." In short, the collection seemed immature, slight, too slim to be considered a major literary contribution. ". . . It is a pity that this notebook for what must be a more solidly considered achievement should have been ripped untimely from him," was this reviewer's conclusion.[18]

The book took its title from a passage in the Gospel of St. John, the story of the Pool of Bethesda where physical disabilities are cured through supernatural intervention. "For an angel went down at a certain season into the pool, and troubled the water: whosoever then first after the troubling of the water stepped in was made whole of whatsoever disease he had." For Wilder, the implications of troubled waters and metaphysical cures had a wider range. In the short play of the same name, one character wishes to be healed, but is told by the Angel, "In Love's service only the wounded soldiers can serve." Suffering, transformed by art, brings beauty and enlightenment. The theme is more directly dealt with in *Nascuntur Poetae*, perhaps the most beautiful of the plays in the collection.

Here we find an innocent boy addressed by an ethereal woman who tells him that some, before they are born, are chosen to carry on in the spirit of past artists. ". . . When on the winds toward birth the souls of those about to live are borne past them, they choose the brighter spirits that cry along that wind. And you were chosen." The boy is excited by the revelation and cannot wait to "astonish" life. But first, he is told, he must meet the woman in deep red, another creature, who will bestow upon him a special gift. The boy is afraid of this woman and draws back from her gift, a golden chain. But the chain is necessary, she tells him. It will bring tears that will enable his eyes to perceive truth. It will inspire a certain madness that will stir him to create. It will bring loneliness and misery, too, for he will forever yearn for "a lost meaning and a more meaningful love." In the end, the boy is no longer as eager as he was. But his fate is set, and he is led to life.

*Nascuntur Poetae* is Thornton's most moving statement of his conviction that an artist is set apart from the rest of humanity, those who lack the gift, and yet, at the same time, must celebrate life for them and define its meaning. On the surface, the play had little to do with the theme of Christianity that he proposed in his introduction; yet it is written with the deepest emotion. Contrasted with *Nascuntur Poetae* we find such humorous creations as *The Flight Into Egypt*, where Hephzibah, an argumentative donkey, finds itself carrying Our Lady and the Lord. After a contrary conversation about theology with Our Lady, the donkey is finally reminded of its precious burden. But it is not abashed. Laconically, it remarks, "Well, well, it's a queer world when the survival of the Lord is dependent upon donkeys. . . ."

# SEVEN

---

IN Europe, as he was preparing for his speaking tour, Thornton wished he could somehow break his contract with agent Lee Keedick to deliver one hundred lectures. "Speaking is so natural and so happy with you," he wrote to William Lyon Phelps, "that you can scarcely imagine my dread of it; but it's very real."[1] He would much rather have been working on his novel, which he explained to Phelps was "a picture of life on an Aegean island, the pagan world shot through with intimations of Christianity." Nevertheless, he unpacked his bags from his European jaunt and repacked them for his tour of colleges and lecture halls. His subject would be his own writing, and he had a chance to explain *The Bridge* to any readers who may have been puzzled.

"I meant to show it was just like yesterday's or today's motor car accident in Kansas City," he told an audience. "Some might say God meant those particular motorists to die or be injured. Others will say 'accident' and shrug their shoulders."[2] There were few questions he could not field, although he admitted some difficulty when a reporter in Toronto asked him to name his ten favorite Canadian authors.[3]

A pleasant side trip took him to Berea, where Robert Hutchins' father, William, had taken over the presidency. There he read to a group of faculty members and spoke to the college students;[4] he also discovered one street in Covington, Kentucky, which seemed to come from another age when men wore beaver hats and women full-skirted crinolines. It was more like a stage set than reality, he decided.[5]

Thornton's friendship with Robert Hutchins had become warmer as the two matured. "Thornton . . . used to say that he and I were brought up in the 'late foam-rubber period of American Protestantism,'" Robert remembered. "And the worst of that, he said, was that we didn't have the courage to think what he called 'window-breaking thoughts.'" Such ideas, he told Robert, would awaken the rich and the idle from their lives of complacency. "'The enemy was philistinism, parochialism, narrow specialization. The object of education—indeed of the whole of life— was the expansion of imagination.'"[6]

Robert's views were similar, and it was those views which caused him to be considered for an extraordinary position: in September 1929 he was to become president of the University of Chicago, the fifth administrator of the thirty-seven-year-old school and the youngest college president in the country. As "perpendicular, independent and somewhat stubborn" as he described his ancestors,[7] Hutchins had definite and unconventional notions about the running of a college. He wanted to bring to the university a wide range of talented minds, and one of his immediate choices was Thornton.

As late as June 1929 Thornton had not made a public announcement of his decision to leave Lawrenceville. He had intended to return to teaching—but now a more enticing and important opportunity had arisen. Hutchins' plans for the school were undeniably exciting: there would be a new administrative structure; the Schools and College of Arts, Literature, and Science would be reorganized; the Great Books Program would be instituted. Eventually, credits and course examinations would be abolished, along with compulsory class attendance and arbitrary residence requirements. Instead, there would be a general examination of competency, to be taken by each student when he or she felt ready. The object of the university would be "to give a general education and to eliminate, wherever possible, courses with a professional aim."[8] Robert's enthusiasm was contagious, and Thornton accepted his offer. In April 1930 he would join the English faculty of one of the most prestigious colleges in the country.

Thornton returned to MacDowell in July to rest and to work. And in mid-August he took his mother to Europe again, partly as a vacation and partly to take her away from the pressures involved in the building of her home in Hamden, Connecticut. With the royalties from his most successful novel, the book he had dedicated to his mother, he was now building for her the house she had always wanted. It was, he said, "the house *The Bridge* built." Isabel was to oversee the building, sending detailed letters to Mrs. Wilder. By September the two had arrived in Europe, traveling to Bruges, Ghent, Antwerp, Amsterdam. By the end of the month they were in England, visiting Oxford, and by late fall had returned home.

Thornton then took a brief rest before traveling again—this time on another lecture tour to fulfill his contract. At the time he signed the agreement with Keedick, one hundred lectures seemed a reasonable number. After all, he thought, he spent more hours teaching. But as his lecturing progressed, the prospect of more talks seemed almost ominous. Thornton had now widened his topics to include "The Future of American Literature" and "The American Novel."

On January 7 he was at Clark University in Worcester, Massachusetts, the concluding speaker in a series of fine-arts lectures. Usually, when he arrived in a new place, he headed straight for his hotel and then spent a few hours rambling through the town. But in Worcester he was to be the house guest of one of the English department faculty, Loring Holmes Dodd.

Dodd was delighted with his effusive visitor. Thornton tried to be as unobtrusive as possible and freely shared theater gossip and stories of his family. On the lecture platform, however, his personality was changed.

"His stage voice is poor, his manner formal, the friendliness gone," Dodd saw. "He walks up and down like a professor before his class. After an affirmation he reaffirms with a 'Yes' as if to gain time to think or to step to the reading desk to glance at his notes. He rubs his hand in an eye much as a child would. He squeezes his hands together in the manner of a tortured concert singer."[9] But despite his nervousness, he managed to keep his audience attentive with his talk on the "Relation Between Literature and Life."

In early February he was at the University of Minnesota, and his remarks helped to prepare his readers for the book that was to be published within days. "American literature," he said,

> now shows a gulf between highbrows and lowbrows. —I, for one, use "lowbrows" without condescension; perhaps the lowbrows were astonished and relieved to find a book that had all the appearance of a highbrow clique-product, but which nevertheless neither scolded the average mind, nor implied that a belief in the attachments of the family is naïve and immature.
>
> The last twenty years in America has [sic] been the awkward age. Now it may be ready for novels of the inner life, for the springs of action which have always been the true subject matter of literature. Thus, for such books, all the external adventure and obscenity in the world is no sure preparation. One must know his phase of life intimately, not just have a smattering of generalities. . . .
>
> I should like to think that my own work is French in force, from memoirs, non-fiction, letters; German in emotion, from German music, such as Bach, Beethoven and Mozart; and American in eagerness.[10]

*The Woman of Andros*, published in 1930, does not seem, at first, to be aimed at a mass audience. It is set in pre-Christian Greece, on the island of Brynos, and the characters are at least as exotic as those in *The Cabala* and *The Bridge of San Luis Rey*. Yet the plot is timeless; and the theme, as one character expresses it, is simple: "How does one live? . . . What does one do first?"

Chrysis is the central character, a woman whose sensibilities place her outside of her society and ahead of her time. Her home is a gathering place for such troubled and questioning young men as Pamphilus, who are trying "to see what life is about." Pamphilus' future has been partly arranged—he is to marry Philumena, a young woman for whom he has no special feelings. It is understandable, then, when he falls in love with Chrysis' younger sister, Glycerium, a lonely, gentle girl. Glycerium becomes pregnant, and Pamphilus' predicament enlarges. This time, however, he cannot depend on Chrysis for advice; she is dying, and her words seem vague to the young man, and unrelated to his problem. She tells him of some mystery she foresees, some change that the world is about to undergo. She tells him that he may marry Glycerium or someone else; it does not matter. "It is the life in the mind that is important." And in her last moments, when loneliness overtakes her, she asks only to be remembered kindly "as one who loved all things and accepted from the gods all things, the bright and the dark."

It is the dark that befalls Pamphilus and Glycerium. She is sold into prostitution, but is saved at the last moment by Pamphilus' father, a sensitive if somewhat bewildered man. Yet when she is brought back to his home, she is so weakened that she dies, with her infant, during childbirth. Pamphilus, distraught and confused, remembers Chrysis' last words and takes comfort in them. And the last image is meant to comfort the reader: ". . . in the East the stars shone tranquilly down upon the land that was soon to be called Holy and that even then was preparing its precious burden."

Just as Wilder had intended *The Bridge* to parallel any accident in Kansas City, he meant society in Brynos as a metaphor for his own world. It was a world in which "the living too are dead," in which human beings are fully alive only in rare moments "when our hearts are conscious of our treasure; for our hearts are not strong enough to love every moment." It was a world in which, in each mind and in each heart, there lay a fear of not being vitally needed by someone, of impending separation. "The loneliest associations are those that pretend to intimacy," Thornton knew. It was a world in which the "highest point toward which any existence could aspire was to be a member of an island family, living and dying on one farm, respected, cautious, and secretly wealthy. . . ." And yet two characters, Pamphilus and Chrysis, saw beyond that world. To Pamphilus it seemed that the world consisted not of physical, tangible, palpable objects, but of spirits burning "with the perpetual flames of love,—a sad love that was half hope, often rebuked and waiting to be reassured of its truth." Chrysis put it more succinctly: it was a world evolving. " 'Lift every roof,' " she would sometimes say, " 'and you will find seven puzzled hearts.' "

Thornton's novel of "the inner life" did not receive unqualified praise. Edmund Wilson, though he admired Wilder's "accomplished technical skill," sensed "a broken-hearted Proustian sob which had welled up, all too unmistakable, from the peculiar sentimentality of our own time and not from any state of mind that one can associate with the Greeks. . . ." The book, according to Wilson, "strikes me as being a kind of thing that there is no longer much point in doing." He thought that Wilder was becoming imitative, adding that "just because he is evidently a first-rate man, one would like to see him more at home."[11]

Henry Hazlitt, in *The Nation*, agreed. Thornton was approaching a stage in his writing where he was beginning "to betray his limitations: his manner, his fictitious world gradually harden into a fixed mold; the reader can draw a definite circle around him." Of course there were merits to Thornton's writing: as always, he took "scrupulous care" in his language and style. Some passages were undeniably beautiful, and there were "flashes of real insight and wisdom. . . ." Many of the characters were appealing. But on the whole, Hazlitt was disappointed. ". . . Somehow the novel leaves me cold," he wrote. "The situations seem to me patently arranged, the plot shopworn, and at no time . . . was I able to lose sight of Mr. Wilder in the act of being a fine stylist. The whole thing, in fact, seems to me primarily an exercise in style. . . ." The book, he concluded, was "a trifle anemic."[12]

Thornton did find his supporters, however. Among them was Henry Seidel Canby, writing in the *Saturday Review*. For Canby, *The Woman of Andros* was no less than a masterpiece, just as he considered *The Bridge of San Luis Rey*. "It is not . . . the theme which calls for praise, however much it may fix attention; nor the characters of this simple, poignant narrative of love irradiating, burning through, transcending the petty life of an island where only the tradition of the home is lovely. . . . It is the ideas and situations that burn. . . ."

He admitted that Wilder would never be thought great for his innovations in fiction. But his craftsmanship was outstanding, "not as preciosity or display, for there is not one self-conscious word or superfluous phrase in the book, but because with skill and a patience and an understanding of the lofty ideas in a beautiful setting with which he deals, Wilder has been willing to carry his writing over those leagues beyond impressionism which our journalist-novelists have never tried to follow, the pain of labor, or the haste of composition, being too great." For Canby, the two writers of note in the coming generation were Thornton Wilder and Ernest Hemingway, each bringing his own talent to the writing of fiction. *The Woman of Andros* was a clear example of Wilder's special touch. The book, Canby thought, was "the quiet, perfectly finished meditation of a scholar in literature, bookish, philosophic, slight in narrative, and yet touched with a fire of beauty, and raised by a fine imagination into an understanding that is more than esthetic and intellectual."[13]

# EIGHT

"**B**OB is as happy as a king in your identification with the University," William Hutchins wrote to Thornton. "Your comradeship will mean much to him."[1] In his early days at Chicago, Robert Hutchins did, indeed, value the support of those he recruited. Both his presidency and his innovations were met with skepticism by many of the tenured professors. Heralded as a "boy wonder" and near-genius, Hutchins was under no illusions about the importance of his appointment. "I was chosen . . . because of a prevailing euphoria and the lack of general discrimination. If you can't recapture the spirit of that era, you can't understand how it happened. The feeling was 'we got to have a president, and it doesn't matter how old he is.' I couldn't have been elected two years earlier or a year later. I took office on the first of July, 1929, and the market broke in October."[2]

He had come to Chicago from Yale, where, at twenty-eight, he had been appointed dean of the law school. According to his later recounting, his early career was a series of happy accidents. While he was a law student, a professor "died or got appendicitis" and Robert was asked to take over his course. Then another professor quit, and he was assigned another course. And as long as he was on the staff, he was asked to serve as acting dean when the position became vacant. That position in the academic community made it possible for him to be interviewed for the presidency at Chicago. And the times, he thought, allowed him to be chosen.

"Our idea there was to start a big argument about higher education and keep it alive," he said once. And a lively controversy did ensue over the Chicago Plan. The program combined the last two years of high school and the first two years of college; emphasis was placed on a core course of Great Books, which Hutchins developed with Mortimer Adler, who had seen a similar program work effectively at Columbia. Above all, Hutchins wanted to redirect the course of higher education from its tendency toward "vocational" courses to a truly liberal curriculum. "My contention is that the tricks of the trade cannot be learned in a university," he said. "All that can be learned in a university is the general principles, the fundamental propositions, the theory of any discipline. If education is rightly understood, it will be understood as the cultivation of the intellect."

One of Hutchins' favorite cartoons reflected his educational ideas. It was a drawing by James Thurber "of a man sitting by himself at a party with his head on his fist, like Rodin's *Thinker*. One guest pointing to the solitary brooder says to another, 'He doesn't know anything except facts!' . . ." When Hutchins asked to buy the original from Thurber, the cartoonist responded that he would present it to him as a gift. "Dr. Hutchins used to say," a friend recalled, "that he was more pleased with Thurber's drawing than with the millions from a foundation that arrived that same day. . . ."[3]

Shortly before Thornton was to begin teaching, he placed a notice in the university's student newspaper. "I shall be offering two courses," he wrote, "and they will not be snap courses." One class was to be in creative writing, open only to a selected fifteen; the other was to include classics in translation—open to all as a lecture course. His warning in the newspaper drove no one away, and as his reputation quickly spread across the campus, the lecture hall overflowed. It became the only literature course that attracted even football heroes and campus playboys.[4] ". . . I once visited his packed classroom of undergraduate students," one young man observed, "while he paced the floor with Dante's *Inferno* in one hand, while with the index finger of the other hand he put into italics every point he uttered. He staged a most dramatic perform- ance, impassioned even when he voiced his insights in whispered innuendo."[5]

"He was a marvelous teacher," a student remembered, "—in my opinion and in that of everyone I knew who had him—responsive and accessible, to be sure. . . . But those are fairly passive virtues and Wilder's real attractions and abilities as a teacher grew from the sense of excitement with which he surrounded everything and everyone he talked about—together with the excitement of his talk itself, delivered often enough on half-runs punctuated with sudden stops and sharp turns. What kept these performances from being put-ons, as they might sound to a non-witness, was the absoluteness of Wilder's involvement with what he was saying. He knew what he was talking about, he was talking about things you either wanted to hear or were made to want to hear, and he obviously loved talking about them, and so you loved to listen. I don't really know whether my understanding of Dante, say, is bet- ter than it would have been without Wilder . . . but it seemed to me to work at the time, and his students talked not only about Wilder but Dante."[6]

As students filed into the lecture hall in the Social Science building, they usually saw Thornton pacing slowly up and down, thoughtful, waiting for the class to assemble. Then, as the bell rang, he would suddenly stop, turn, and face the class. At one class, especially vivid in the mind of a student, he leaned forward and, as if imparting a secret, informed the audience that he would speak about the physical aspects of theater in the fifth century B.C. At first the topic seemed academic and dull, but quickly the class was transported.

Mr. Wilder has begun to speak with special intensity. Under the stress of his imaginative words, the Social Science Assembly room becomes an Athenian amphitheatre. We pay our 12¢ for the enter- tainment (in a few years the state will take over the expense), pull out the crimson cushions for the chairs, and sit tense and ready for the festival of Dionysius to begin. . . . We are astonished by its [Greece's] color, the polychrome statues and architecture. Even the occasional white has the character of a color: it is an accent. Nor does life seem any longer pale, serene, poised. 'Great ages have no time for poise.' We understand that now. Here it is erratic, iridescent, nervous. The excitement of the competition has penetrated the whole spirit of that vast crowd, thousands of people all seated according to tribes. They are speculating about the new plays. . . .

So, day after day, we went into that astonishing theatre of the imagination. Again and again we returned to celebrate the sunny festival of Dionysius and to watch through Mr. Wilder's words the whole procession of ancient masterpieces. . . . When we came to this class it was not merely to submit our minds to more mature comment, it was to receive the infusion of a tremendous new vitality into our recognition of these masterpieces. . . . They became a part of our lives.[7]

Not all of his students were so completely responsive. Thornton was apparently discouraged once when some seemed not to see the value of studying the material. ". . . In desperation he asked the class in the third lecture if they believed in hell. To his amazement he got a chorus of noes. . . . With the students holding this position, Wilder decided he could not possibly interest them in the *Purgatorio* and the *Inferno*." He brought up the problem a few nights later when he was dining at Hull House with Jane Addams and Ellen Gates Starr. Did they know any damned souls, he asked? "They burst out with stories of dope pushers and pimps, and other instances of contemporary perdition. Fortified with examples . . . , Wilder went back to his students and described hell in Chicago, Illinois. From that time on," a friend of his learned, "they became completely absorbed in Dante's descriptions of hell in eternity."[8]

While many students could benefit from Wilder's lecture performances, only a few could enroll in his writing course. Soon entrance to the class became a coveted prize. "When it was announced that he would teach a course in creative writing to a class limited in number to fifteen," one of the chosen few recalled, "Chicago became the scene of a struggle for survival unrivaled since the earlier years of the Capone gangland massacre. Students fought among themselves. North Shore hostesses fought for entrance not only to the class but to the University. No trustee's arm was left untwisted. No eminent faculty member was left unassaulted for recommendation. Intellectual mayhem, character assassination, well-placed rumors of fakery and plagiarism . . . became the weapons of the moment." Yet despite the cutthroat atmosphere outside the class, within room 102 in Wieboldt Hall there was a friendly camaraderie. ". . . At the first meeting of the class Thornton Wilder . . . looked about at us through his horn-rimmed glasses, rubbed his mustache and laid a question before us. 'There's something I need to know,' he said. 'We're going to discuss creative writing. But I'd like a show of hands. What *form* of writing appeals to you most? If you're granted the conditions that make for final success, what is it you'd like most to write? Novels?'

"One hand went up. . . . Wilder seemed unastonished and surveyed the hands in our laps. The short story? No hands. Poetry? No hands. The play?

"Fourteen hands went up. Wilder snorted. Then the someday author of *Our Town, The Skin of Our Teeth* and *The Matchmaker* lifted his hand too."[9]

Thornton did have definite advice to impart to his students. First he tried to impress them with the need to let their style take form and become established as a personal expression.[10] Then he did not want them to concern themselves with "modernity" in theme. As Charles Wager had told him, "Every great work was written this morning."[11] Thomas Mann had rewritten the book of Genesis. Goethe resurrected Helen of Troy. As long as the writing was sincere and the theme important, the resulting work would be modern in the best sense. He advised against a preoccupation with setting. "The danger to one using local subject matter . . . would seem to be that of becoming absorbed in the local color to the neglect of adequate characterization and construction," he thought.[12]

He did not minimize the work involved in writing—and rewriting—though he admitted that his own writing habits were poor. "I began writing relatively late in life," he apologized, "and never acquired the discipline of regular hours of creative work. I write irregularly, and perhaps in that I get more subconscious development of the theme. I find stimulation in solitary walks. An episode in the novel develops, and I come home with much of it perhaps already composed, memorized, and can sit down and write it."[13] Still, a writer had to be prepared to discard much of what was written, to think of his wastebasket as indispensable. "I forget which of the great sonneteers said: 'One line in the fourteen comes from the ceiling; the others have to be adjusted around it.' Well, likewise, there are passages in every novel whose first writing is pretty much the last. But it's the joint and cement between those spontaneous passages, that take a great deal of rewriting."[14]

For the aspiring playwrights in the class—who at the time included the teacher—Wilder shared his feelings about theater, which he considered "the greatest of all art forms, the most immediate way in which a human being can share with another the sense of what it is to be a human being." Theater allowed an immediacy that the novel did not. It enabled the writer to present characters as he saw them, unencumbered by commentary and analysis. A sensitive dramatist would be able to present "*what is*" without seeming to be didactic or pedantic. "We live in *what is*," Wilder knew, "but we find a thousand ways not to face it. Great theater strengthens our faculty to face it."[15]

Thornton's help with his students' writing was not limited to his classroom hours. One student, Fanny Butcher, who later became literary editor of the Chicago *Tribune*, remembered meeting twice monthly at the houses of one or another of the students. Thornton would be there; his role, he told them, "was as another writer, not a teacher, but his comments were the ones we all craved. Sometimes I came home from a session feeling the way I do after some great symphony concert—as if Thornton, substituting for Saint Peter, had taken me on a guided tour of the condominium awaiting me in the heavenly high-rise."[16]

"The trouble here is that you didn't think hard enough," Thornton would often tell his writing students. The difference between good writing and bad writing was the difference between precise and sloppy thought. They must take care to think through their ideas, he reminded them.[17] He was always there, it seemed, when they wanted to talk, and though he enjoyed a bit of campus gossip now and then, he was just as willing to engage in literary discussions and to unravel personal problems. He resided on campus, in Hitchcock Hall, and usually took his meals in the dormitory's dining room.

It was fun, one student remembered, just to walk across the campus with him, go back to his rooms, and talk for a few hours. And it was even more fun to be invited to accompany Thornton to one of the speakeasies he knew, all of which were "far out of the average college boy's experience." An especially elegant dinner, complete with "Al Capone's best liquor" could be had at a certain restaurant on Thirty-ninth Street and Prairie. It was there that Thornton shared with one young companion a certain limerick that intrigued him because of its intricate rhyme scheme:

> There was a young girl from Rangoda
> Who lived in a golden pagoda
> And festooned the walls
> Of her halls with the balls
> Of the tools of the fools who bestrode 'er.[18]

More than many other faculty members, Thornton seemed to enjoy the companionship of the bright young men and women who attended the University of Chicago in the early thirties. As one student remembered, the atmosphere at the school, especially in the English Department, was exciting and stimulating. Chicago had rigorous academic requirements and a faculty of well-known scholars: W. A. Craigie, Ronald Crane, G. E. Bentley, Robert Morss Lovett among them. Hutchins' presence had, as was intended, brought new life to the university, though not without certain problems.

For Thornton, the problems could be difficult. Without a Ph.D., without solid "academic" credentials, he was subject to the scorn of some of the older faculty members. Furthermore, it was well known that he was a "Hutchins man" and those with any complaints about the new president generalized their feelings to include visiting lecturer Wilder. Thornton, however, retreated

from any involvement in campus political disputes, being consti-
tutionally unable to take one side against the other.

One who supported and was fond of him was Edith Foster
Flint, a pillar of respectability in the English Department. Thornton enjoyed her company and was equally fond of her, but he
could not resist spreading a bit of gossip. He was walking beside
her one day, he told friends, when he noticed that her bloomers
had begun to sag. An extremely large woman, Flint was not the
essence of femininity even without drooping bloomers. But she
handled the problem with equanimity. "These bloomers," she
simply commented as they fell lower; and when they reached her
ankles she merely stepped out of them and continued on her way.
Thornton was amused, too, by her curiosity about the socialites,
actresses, and artists he was rumored to know. At the time, Thornton had the reputation of being a man about town, and Flint was
never at a loss for questions. "There's nothing in the world like a
good woman's curiosity about bad women," he commented.[19]

His most satisfactory social relationships were with his students
and with the cultivated Chicago circle that surrounded the Hutchins family. Robert and his wife, the sculptor Maude Phelps
Hutchins, attracted a young, bright, wealthy group of friends from
among the elite of Chicago's North Shore. Since Thornton was so
frequently invited to dinners and parties, he quickly became one
of their circle, treated with respect for his literary achievements
and with great affection for his warmth and humor. He was often
a guest at the homes of such hostesses as Kate Swift and Bobsie
Goodspeed.

He was teaching at what he repeatedly boasted was "a great
university," and was living in what was, so far in his life, the best
of all worlds. But there would soon be one intrusion—and he was
to be both stunned and hurt.

# NINE

ON October 22, 1930, *The New Republic* published an article by Michael Gold, "Wilder: Prophet of the Genteel Christ." Gold was the author of the autobiographical *Jews Without Money*, well received as a "simple," "stark" tale of life for a Romanian Jew in an East Side tenement. ". . . It is poised and yet aflame," a reviewer noted, "it is tender, and it is merciless."[1] For Gold, Wilder represented irrelevant writing aimed at the wealthy minority of American readers—readers who deliberately, or through ignorance, cut themselves off from the realities of contemporary life. "It is a museum, it is not a world. . . . It is an historical junkshop over which our author presides," he wrote of Wilder's works. For Gold, the past should be drawn upon to evoke "a battle cry"; instead, Wilder had become "the poet of the genteel bourgeoisie."

"Wilder has concocted a synthesis of all the chambermaid literature, Sunday-school tracts and boulevard piety there ever were," Gold went on. "He has added a dash of the prep-school teacher's erudition, then embalmed all this in the speciously glamorous style of the late Anatole France. . . . He is a very conscious craftsman. But his is the most irritating and pretentious style pattern I have read in years. It has the slick, smug finality of the lesser Latins; that shallow clarity and tight little good taste that remind one of nothing so much as the conversation and practice of a veteran cocotte." Gold saw Thornton as a product of the middle class: well mannered, well bred, well educated. He could identify with "aristocratic emotions" and feel comfortable in polite, patrician surroundings.

He was, Gold concluded, an "Emily Post of culture. . . . And nobody works in a Ford plant, and nobody starves looking for work, and there is nothing but Love in God's ancient Peru, Italy, Greece, if not in God's capitalist America 1930!"

From November 5 through December 17, *The New Republic* printed some of the scores of letters it received in support of Gold or Wilder. Finally the editors announced that the debate was ended. "The Gold-Wilder controversy is hereby called on account of darkness," they wrote. "No further letters on this subject will be published." Meanwhile, however, many writers had had their say.

Edmund Wilson, in an unsigned article that appeared on November 26 tried to penetrate the confusion that was felt in many minds over Gold's attack on Wilder. While conceding that Gold was a respected Marxist critic and "important writer," Wilson thought that economic and social realities did not always apply to a work of art. ". . . There are groups which cut through the social classes," he wrote, "and these tend to have an independent existence. The writers make a group of their own; the painters make a group of their own; the scientists make a group. And each of these groups has its own tradition, its own craft and body of doctrine which has been brought down to the present by practitioners that have come from a variety of classes through a variety of different societies." Wilder's craft, then, could not be overlooked.[2]

Still, Wilson had to agree that a certain aspect of Wilder's writing did have the genteel finish that Gold deplored. His drawing upon Proust colored his work with a "rich, luxurious, intoxicating sentimentality" that could not help but appeal to comfortable Americans. "For Proust is surely the writer who, more even than any of the romantics, has made heartbreak a protracted pleasure:

the romantics' hearts broke against desolate backgrounds but Proust's heart breaks at the Ritz. Now, Wilder in *The Cabala*," Wilson went on, "is also at the Ritz and he sticks, in his subsequent books, to a decorative Parisian antiquity that amounts to the same thing." Perhaps Michael Gold was correct, he suggested, in thinking that Wilder's pathos was "a sedative for sick Americans."[3]

Other critics, as respected as Wilson, were not disposed to support Gold. Henry Hazlitt, taking the controversy to the pages of *The Nation*, called Gold's article a "malicious caricature . . . ," and thought its author irresponsible and narrow. "His devotion to the Cause has made him blind to all other values, to any sense of proportion."

Perhaps Wilder's greatest support came in December of 1930, when Sinclair Lewis, the first American to win the Nobel Prize for Literature, gave his acceptance speech and praised ". . . Thornton Wilder, who in an age of realism dreams the old and lovely dreams of the eternal romantic. . . ."

While other writers might have leaped to their own defense, Thornton maintained a dignified silence. He would not involve himself in the arguments, though he was extremely sensitive to the criticism. No later work would be immune from Gold's influence. He weighed his ideas, now, against the possible reaction they might bring from critics preoccupied with economics, politics, or the problems of society. Only several years later did he speak of the controversy in public. His statement is consistent with what he always had said, and always would say, about his own work.

"These radical critics are, in my opinion, wrong in their claim that man is solely the product of the economic order under which he lives . . . ," he said. "If my characters are not starved, if they have a little something for their stomachs, then they will be much the same in any environment. The fundamental emotions, love, hate, fear, anger, surprise are common to all mankind, in any milieu, in any age. My people in the 'Bridge' are not so very far away. What are two or three hundred years? Only a small period in the life of mankind.

"That's one of the troubles with the left-wingers. They think all literature, all life, commenced somewhere around 1900, when they began.

"And they haven't met the first big test, I think. They have produced no samples, no samples of the literature their viewpoint would count as good literature."[4]

For Thornton, his life's work was the production of "good literature." He had committed himself to teach only in the spring semester—and an occasional summer—at Chicago each year. His free months were spent at work on his books. In 1930 he was finishing a collection of plays that were more "American" and timely in setting than his previous works. *The Long Christmas Dinner* included six plays, longer than those in his 1928 collection, but still not the full-length works that would win him acclaim. *The Long Christmas Dinner*, which gives its title to the book, uses few props, no curtain—only a long dinner table set with a turkey. The left portal of the set is trimmed with garlands of fruits and flowers, representing birth; the right portal is hung with black velvet: death. The technique, Thornton admitted, was taken from Chinese drama. At the Christmas dinner of several generations of the Bayard household, we see a repetition of personalities and concerns that have little to do with the particular age in which the family lives. In essence, the house and its inhabitants remain the same for ninety years, though dress, language, "props" may change.

*Queens of France*, the play that follows, is a lighter piece, a farce about a charlatan lawyer who convinces women that they are descended from French royalty. He collects fees from these would-be queens of France, on the pretext of inaugurating a search for verifying documents. Set in New Orleans, the play is a comical period piece, a blithe cartoon.

*Pullman Car Hiawatha* has a more serious intent. Again, there is no scenery but a background balcony. The actors enter carrying chairs. There is a stage manager who interrupts the action from time to time to comment. These are techniques to be seen again in Thornton's work, to greater effect. Even the predicament of a major character will one day be reworked in *Our Town*. Here we see Harriet die, but not willing, at first, to give up the world.

There are two minor plays: *Love and How to Cure It*, dealing with the problem of unrequited love, and *Such Things Only Happen in Books*, presenting a writer who, despite the tumultuous world he lives in, cannot find anything to write about. And then Thornton presents his favorite play, in fact the play that remained his favorite even after others had achieved fame, *The Happy Journey to Trenton and Camden*.

*The Happy Journey* evokes a feeling of nostalgia for the family of American dreams: the strong but loving mother, the innocent children on the brink of adulthood, the bourgeois determination that, one is sure, will get them through any crisis. "I live in the best street in the world because my husband and children live there," Ma Kirby tells the audience. And no one can doubt her.

The characters consist of the five members of the Kirby family and a stage manager who moves the few props and takes the lines of minor roles. The family—Ma Kirby; her husband, Elmer; their children Arthur and Caroline—are taking a trip from Newark to Camden, New Jersey, to visit the elder daughter, Beulah, who has just lost a child and had nearly died during the difficult delivery. The geography was familiar to Thornton, who has the family pass through Lawrenceville on their way south.

Ma Kirby is the central character. She is a pious woman, though her religion is woven through with superstition. She refuses to allow her son to utter a word against God. God, she explains, has done too much for her and she won't abide blasphemy. She frequently spouts homey platitudes. "There's nothing like a good sunset," she remarks once. And when her daughter comments on the multitude living in the entire country, Ma rejoins that every one of them likes "to drive out in the evening with their children beside'm." She thinks New Jersey is the finest state, and George Washington a great man because of his undoubted truthfulness. She wants her daughter to be good and her son honest. Her husband, who works in a laundry, is an upright man, a good provider, and the best driver in the world. To her daughter's despondency over the loss of her baby she offers: "We don't understand why. We just go on, honey, doin' our business." She doesn't want fame or beauty or riches. There is only one thing that can make her happy: being appreciated by her family.

Strangely, *The Happy Journey*, for all its platitudes, never strikes the reader as a satirical work. There is an honesty and trust-worthiness in the Kirby family that seems enviable and desirable. The family is an indissoluble unit, and it is, here, eternal. Ma Kirby is the archetypal mother; she awaits a lost child to enfold in her arms—and for a moment, at least, the reader would like to be that lost child. The play is appealing, and its appeal will later be repeated—and amplified—in *Our Town*.

The theater was occupying more of Thornton's creative time, and the world outside of the university was filling more of his life. One of the most satisfying friendships at the time was with Alexander Woollcott, ten years his senior, the acerbic Round Table wit and *New Yorker* columnist. Thornton, who enjoyed private gossip as long as it was harmless and kept within the boundaries of good manners, seems an unlikely companion for the outspoken Woollcott. After he invented the brandy alexander, Helen Hayes commented, "And well named it was—being both lethal and oversweet, the two extremes he most enjoyed." George S. Kaufman, satirizing Woollcott in *The Man Who Came to Dinner*, called him "the self-centered prima donna riding roughshod over ordinary people's feelings. . . ." To those he did not admire and trust, Woollcott could be willful and moody. But to the few he genuinely liked, he was open and warm—and he did like the ebullient Thornton.

Thornton often visited Woollcott at his Fifty-second Street apartment in Manhattan, the place Dorothy Parker called "Wit's End," and at Neshobe, an island in Lake Bomoseen, Vermont, that Woollcott bought in 1923. "He ran the island as a benevolent monarchy," a friend remembered, "and he summoned both club members and other friends to appear at all seasons of the year; he turned the island into a crowded vacation ground where reservations must be made weeks in advance. . . . Breakfast went on all morning, with Woollcott presiding at the table in a dressing gown." Croquet was his favorite game, played with heavy English mallets on a choppy terrain. "It was nothing for one game of croquet to last three hours. Passions ran high, including Woollcott's, even when the game was played for nothing."[5]

At breakfast once, Thornton found himself seated with Ethel

Barrymore and Paul Bonners. Guests might include Ruth Gordon, writer Alice Duer Miller, Eleanora Mendelsohn, Helen Hayes, Bea and George Kaufman, Harpo Marx, illustrator Neysa McMein, and a favorite of Wilder—a shy, witty, and sad lady, Dorothy Parker.[6] It was no wonder, then, that Thornton found the atmosphere too distracting for any work, though Woollcott, respectful of a writer's craft, would try to ensure privacy and quiet.

To Woollcott, Thornton was a mixture of "'poet, prophet, hummingbird, and gadfly.' . . ." As a gadfly, Thornton tried to inspire Woollcott to write, once suggesting that he at least put together an anthology of his *New Yorker* pieces for publication. "'He came up to Bomoseen and sat on my fat neck until I gave in,'" Woollcott said later. A friend and biographer, Samuel Adams, could not help but notice the disparate personalities of the two friends. Thornton, he saw, was "the gentlest and most charitable of men. Aleck's violence and injustices made him wince. But though he never openly protested, such was his influence that, so their friends noticed, the Woollcott outbreaks were noticeably tempered in his presence. Though neither man was technically religious by bent, their companionship had, I think, more of a spiritual basis than any other association of Woollcott's later years."[7]

For Thornton, Woollcott was someone he could count on to be always interested in theater gossip and amusing stories. Their correspondence reflects their mutual affection and trust. Thornton especially liked to share his latest enthusiasms with Woollcott, from students he thought would someday change the literary world to undiscovered actors or actresses whose potential, he thought, was enormous.

One such actor was described in detail. The young man, Thornton wrote to Woollcott, had gone to Dublin in 1931, when he was sixteen. He spent six months there, visiting friends and touring the countryside with a donkey and cart, stopping now and then to paint a landscape. His friends in Dublin were then helping on the settings for a production of *Jew Suss* at the Gate Theatre, and he stayed to lend a hand. While he was there, he learned that the role of the Duke had not yet been filled, and in an effort to get

the part, pretended to be a veteran actor from the New York
Theatre Guild. His talent impressed Micheál MacLiammóir, who
hired him. He made his debut on October 13, 1931, and the reviews were so astounding that he was kept on to play Othello and
Hamlet.

But acting seemed to him too easy, and he returned to the
States intent on becoming, instead, a writer. Two years later, however, he met Thornton, who, knowing of his performance in Dublin, persuaded him to return to acting and introduced him to
Katharine Cornell. She immediately hired him for her troupe.
The young man, Thornton told Woollcott, had a round face with
a lock of hair always falling into his eyes. He would often affect an
abstract pose, but did not maintain it long in Thornton's presence. Thornton was sure he was a *Wunderkind* and predicted a
startling future for him. The name of his discovery, he divulged to
his friend, was Orson Welles.[8]

Though Thornton had traveled to Europe in the spring and
summer of 1931, he did not witness that particular performance.
He did, however, meet someone he had long admired—the Viennese director Max Reinhardt. Reinhardt lived outside Salzburg,
one of Thornton's favorite cities. His home, Leopoldskron, was as
much a reflection of his dramatic art as were the settings for his
plays. It was "so beautiful, so romantic, so perfect in every detail,"
a guest remembered, "it might have been created on a stage by
Reinhardt's orders. It had been a chateau of the old archbishops
of Salzburg. . . . It was Reinhardt's joy to have the great lofty
rooms lighted only by candles—hundreds of candles which shed a
tender, luminous glow on all the old, rare, beautiful things which
he had collected to furnish the rooms. Always there was an effect
of mystery and enchantment. The candles gave Leopoldskron a serene, dignified beauty which was immediately felt by nearly everyone who entered its doors."[9]

Reinhardt's attraction for Thornton was his thorough knowledge of theatrical tradition and his willingness to draw upon all
types of staging—circus ring, apron stage, and even the box set—to
create a desired effect. He had created a Chamber Playhouse
which staged intimate productions, yet could be as comfortable
with productions in a Greek amphitheater. He was well known for

the use of elaborate stage effects and for his measured, careful pacing.

Thornton was acutely sensitive to a play's setting and direction. Furthermore, in his own writing, he frequently drew upon and reworked plots from past authors. He was impressed with Reinhardt's scholarly approach to theater, and a warm and respectful friendship began.

A few months after he returned from Europe, Thornton began working on another play, but this time it was not one of his own. He agreed to translate André Obey's *Le Viol de Lucrèce* for Katharine Cornell. The play had been written in the style of a Greek tragedy, complete with chorus and commentators, and offered a creative opportunity for both translator and cast. There were, however, some questions about the text that Thornton wanted to discuss with Miss Cornell, and he arranged to see her in Chicago, where she would be performing in May.

That summer, Thornton spent June and July at MacDowell working out the intricacies of his version of the play. The original plot, upon which Obey had drawn, was set in Rome; but Obey had updated the play and set it in France. His change in time presented some problems to the translator. The dialogue could range from the simple, straightforward talk of a country peasant to the more elaborate speech of an early Renaissance noble. Of all the roles, those of the servants posed the greatest challenge to Thornton; but he liked the play enormously and saw it as some intricately woven tapestry, delicate in feeling and tone.[10]

The play opened in Buffalo on December 12, 1932, with Cornell in the role of Lucrèce and Brian Aherne as Tarquin, the man who violates her. The local reviewer found the play "superb theater. . . . Magnificently played and staged, it holds close attention from its beginning to its tragic end. It has its moments of eloquence and beauty." The star "never appeared as winsome as she does in the first scene. . . . In the succeeding scenes, Miss Cornell never rose to greater emotional heights. . . ."[11] But a few days later, when the company performed in New York City, the response was not as warm. Even Thornton's friend Stark Young was disappointed, and some of his criticism was directed at the translator. "You have a sense of complex implications that are constantly defeated by a thin simplicity in literary manner. The dramatic moment is perpetually being dropped by this tone of extra-pellucid style-writing. . . . There are, also, too many banal contrasts in phrase, though the worst banalities lie in the too obvious simplifications at many points in the writing." At the climax of the play, which depends upon Lucrèce's monologue to sustain it, Young thought that Wilder had reached the lowest point in his translation. "Nobody could say this speech," he wrote. "What we should have here is either to speak in rich images, a sensuous and austere movement in ideas and ornament, a compelling texture in the style, or else to speak directly and purely, the statement bared to its bones. The speech falls between these two qualities and remains only feeble, uncertain and unglamorous." The actors were hampered by having to "say little things very simple or tame or pseudo-modest and merely literary."

But the sets and costumes, Young thought, were admirable. Robert Edmond Jones had designed lovely Renaissance clothing for the cast. The main setting, while it might have benefited from "either more polish or more color" was still effective.[12]

John Anderson, in the New York *Journal*, echoed Young's views. ". . . *Lucrèce* seemed stilted, too conscious of all its own art, and quietly, but firmly, tiresome." He added, however, that the cast had the benefit of "the best of Mr. Wilder's English at their command in some very vivid passages." Brooks Atkinson, in the *Times*, found the play "no more than a polite commencement study." The acting, especially Katharine Cornell's Lucrèce, was superb, but "the literary qualities . . . are no match for such acting. The thoughts are trivial. Although the phrases are carefully mitred, they lack passion and beauty. . . . What Miss Cornell needs . . . is Shakespeare. André Obey out of Shakespeare and faithfully translated by Thornton Wilder is only a watered down pretense."

Thornton, unhappy over the reception given by these major critics, disagreed over the causes of *Lucrèce*'s apparent failure. "The flaw I see," he told an interviewer, "was the setting and costuming. It was a shy, intimate, quiet play intended as a sort of tapestry in the French renaissance. But the producers put it on in a setting like the Grand Central Terminal." Nevertheless, he bowed to the general opinion about the play. "I am one who believes in the unconscious discrimination and collective judgment of the American masses," he said. "And when a play like 'Lucrèce' fails I don't say that it was too good for the public."[13]

Besides his work on *Lucrèce*, his teaching at Chicago, and his own writing, Thornton was a frequent lecturer. What had at first been a painful experience soon became more enjoyable. It was a way of seeing his country and meeting people—characters who might, in one way or another, appear in his novels and plays. "A lecture tour," he told a reporter, "is an ignoble experience which consists of a series of changing events about 11 o'clock in the morning and its only compensation is that you see America."[14] And he added to another interviewer, "A writer's business is to have his eyes rest on as many human beings as possible. I have stayed in the motels of America and have been rewarded with many wonderful encounters."[15]

The American scene was especially important for his next book, in progress in 1933, which had a very different setting from his previous works. He was dealing now with his own world, and he was finding it difficult to bring to that world "the same kind of imaginative life one has extended to those removed in time and place."[16] The book would be a picaresque story about a traveling salesman, a mixture of Don Quixote and a Bible Belt evangelist, who becomes involved in various lives and adventures in Main Streets and small towns across the country. "I am trying to make likable, or at least sympathetically understandable . . . the kind of man and the type of thinking that New York sophisticates particularly scorn," he said.[17]

"The action is episodic," he explained, "but the episodes are not unrelated; each has its bearing on the development, the education, of the hero.

"He is introduced as a book salesman, traveling in the southwest; an admirer of Gandhi; and to some extent an imitator of him—keeping days of silence, practicing voluntary poverty. His geographical wanderings are accompanied by mental and spiritual development; it remains to be seen just how far he will get."[18]

He had planned to wait until he was forty or fifty to do what he called his "real work" about real America. But he decided, at thirty-six, to go ahead with that theme. "My new novel will deal with life today. Not perhaps in the way the left-wingers would wish it to, but in *my* way."[19]

Wilder thought that America was ready for both the theme and the simplicity of the hero's personality. The arts had discarded their veneer of false sophistication and were ready for down-to-earth, homey writing. He saw even in his students at Chicago a rejection of the stylized writing that was exalted in the twenties. "They have outgrown the shrill, facile abuse of the Mencken school. They have outgrown the imitation Parisian sophistication which was considered a sign of maturity. Shall I mention names or not? Yes, I will, Cabell and Van Vechten. They have outgrown the photographic, documentary novel which is the less interesting half of Sinclair Lewis' comic genius." Even in film he saw "a veering away from the great glamorous prima donnas" to the more interesting character actors.

However much he was attracted to the revitalization of "urban folk arts," he took great amusement in the living world of Hollywood, where he was invited in October 1933. On October 25 he dined at the sumptuous Pickfair. That same morning he had spoken at the Breakfast Club, where the audience received with deference the man who had attended Oberlin, Yale, and Princeton. The night before, he had dined at the Hollywood Writers' Club, meeting Emil Ludwig and Will Rogers. Rogers' homespun humor and quiet, good-natured manner endeared him to Thornton immediately. And the diversity of characters he met in Hollywood convinced him that America was, as he had always said, an incredible country.

Though Thornton had been considered "too literary" to work on screenplays, he was now asked by Samuel Goldwyn to adapt Tolstoy's *Resurrection* into a film to be titled *We Live Again*. The story, in which a Russian prince impregnates a servant girl, starting her on the road to prostitution, was to star Anna Sten and Fredric March. Thornton accepted the offer, but not with great enthusiasm. The difficulty in his working on screenplays, he said, was that he did not want to write dialogue for someone else's story. He would rather work on a screenplay that was entirely his own. "I really would like to do something for the screen but only under my own terms."[20]

The month after his Hollywood trip, Thornton sailed for Hawaii, where the Quill, a student arts organization at the University of Hawaii, wanted "to do honor to a great living author," having previously celebrated such writers as Robert Louis Stevenson, Mark Twain, and Charles Dickens. Thornton had not been in Hawaii since his father's years in China, when the family was required to make brief stopovers on each Pacific crossing. Still, his memory of the islands was clear. He was sure he could draw a map of the principal streets and roads. His image of Diamond Head and of the beautiful beaches was still vivid.

From the time the *Lurline* docked on November 2, Thornton had a full schedule of luncheons, interviews, dinners, and lectures. The islands were idyllic, he thought, especially the lush flora, which included a single tree of unique species and genus. He was delighted by the warm reception he received everywhere, and delighted by his visit to the father of one of his friends. When she found out that he was going to be in Honolulu, Ruth Gordon gave Thornton a note to her father and asked that he call on him. Captain Clinton Jones had been a sailor before he married and settled in Quincy, Massachusetts, where his daughter was born. After his wife died, he retired to Hawaii, where Thornton visited him in his tidy little bungalow. The conversation at first was a bit strained—Captain Jones was a reserved New Englander—but finally he stood and brought down from a shelf a heavy book wrapped in a large scarf. It was a scrapbook of his daughter's press clippings and reviews, from those of her early performance in *Peter Pan.* Each article was carefully aligned and the whole was titled in exquisite calligraphy. Thornton shared the captain's belief in Ruth Gordon's talents, and he shared his hopes for her success.

As always, Thornton's presence was different from what most people expected. "Wilder is late thirty-ish, I should say," a reporter wrote. "And not as schoolmasterish as I had been led to believe. He is about five feet eight, medium weight. His eyes are blue, something of that quality novelists call, oddly enough, steely. . . . His eyes smile a lot, and so does his mouth, which is

98    THORNTON WILDER:

generous. It is surmounted by an elongated toothbrush mustache, on the grey side. . . . His teeth are large and very white.

"His hair, I regret to report, is pretty thin. The scalp shows through pretty far back. . . . He talks faster than Floyd Gibbons, than whom he could resemble no less.

"His mind shapes so speedily that mere teeth and tongue and vocal chords [sic] cannot keep up with it. So he usually slurs the last few words of a sentence and rushes on to the next. It is disconcerting at first but one gets used to it and concentrates hard on the tail ends of his sentences."[21]

His platform personality was more polished than it had been a few years before and his lectures more cohesive and professional. He delivered three major talks: on the novel, biography, and theater, besides speaking to clubs, classes, and informal gatherings.

"Some Thoughts on the Novel" was more than a personal defense of his own writing. Instead, he spoke objectively of fiction as an aesthetic form, and of the author's aesthetic responsibility. "The beauty of a thing as a whole, as a sheer work of art, is grateful news in a world that is chaotic," he told his audience; "that arresting quality of perfection caught and held for a moment, brings reassurance that all is not lost." The perfection of a novel depended on the author's ability to foresee the end from the beginning, to select each event and anecdote with the whole in mind. Certainly the particular selection makes it impossible for a novel to duplicate reality; but in its transcendence of reality, the novel becomes art.

Even more removed from daily reality is poetry, Wilder went on. "In literature the poet is permitted to impart eloquence and wit to his creatures. In that world one is permitted to say adequate things at the right moment." Thornton continued by reading the opening lines of a few great books, advising his listeners that any fine work must be read with faithful concentration—especially poetry. ". . . The unit measure of our attention for poetry is not more than twenty-five minutes. Great poetry must be surrounded by silence."[22]

His lecture on the theater again dealt with a subject about which he had strong views. He believed that theater in America had not yet come of age, but that all the requirements existed.

"We have the designers, the actors, the audiences; not yet the great dramatists. But perhaps the air is now stirring with the fulfillment of such promise." Though he did not present himself as that great dramatist, he did offer thoughts on drama that reveal his own attraction to the form. A play possesses a unique vitality, he said, because it takes place in the "pure present." Instead of being manipulated by an omniscient author, it depends on the collaboration of actors and audience, taking place, in a real sense, in the mind of each viewer. "The theater is the art of a hundred collaborators," he said, including not only the playwright's sources, but everyone else involved in the producing and the viewing. Never did he doubt that America could rise to a great age in literature. "One of the signs of a great age," he said, "is that the theater is its reigning art. When the theater and poetry are combined, as in Elizabethan drama, the greatest art form, next to music, appears."[23]

Before sailing home on the twenty-second, Thornton took part in the ceremonial planting of the "Wilder tree," and set aside a few hours to meet with some English students and answer their questions about writing. The students' concerns ranged from "How do you make a story interesting?" (forward moving action, they were told) to "What made Eugene O'Neill the foremost dramatist of his day?" (O'Neill, being the son of an actor, grew up learning how to keep an audience in their seats, Thornton said.) He also imparted some personal facts: he liked to take long walks, listen to music, and play solitaire.

He did a little of each in the winter of 1933–34 and added some crossword puzzles, the reading of Keyserling's *Südamerikanische Meditationen*, the writing of his novel *Heaven's My Destination*, and the preparing of two lectures for the University of Chicago, to be delivered apart from his ordinary classes.

That summer he again went to Hollywood, to fulfill his agreement with Goldwyn to write *We Live Again*. He was able to see many of his friends—Dorothy Parker and her husband Alan Campbell, Ruth Gordon, Marc Connelly, Helen Hayes; met Marlene Dietrich and Billie Burke; but found work on the script tedious. Moreover, Goldwyn was a difficult man to work for. Just before shooting the final scene, he decided he wanted an entirely new ending written. Thornton and two other writers—Leonard Praskins and Paul Green—worked late into the night and finally came up with an emotional scene that depended on close camera work. Then, as they were about to end their session, they were informed that the star, Anna Sten, had a blemish on her nose and would not permit the camera closer than eight feet. The scene was shot at that distance, much to the writers' dismay. But Goldwyn loved it. It was, he told Thornton, the best scene in the play, and Thornton was heralded as a great screenwriter.[24]

He was not sorry to leave California, despite the interesting old sections of towns he visited and the nights spent at the Mount Wilson Observatory. But he did not head directly for Chicago, where, on September 28, he would begin teaching in the fall semester. Instead, he stopped off in Taos, New Mexico, to visit the irrepressible Mabel Dodge Luhan.

Mabel, a native of Buffalo, had escaped that claustrophobic environment and later married an architect, Edwin Dodge. They moved to Italy, where Dodge restored a Florentine villa to his wife's exotic tastes. When he died, she returned to New York, presided over an eclectic salon, took a stream of lovers, and made frequent trips to Europe. In 1918 she moved to Taos, settled into an adobe house, and exchanged her husband, the artist Maurice Sterne, for a Pueblo Indian, Antonio Luhan. The unexpected was common with Mabel. Once, when Thornton visited her in the company of his sister Isabel, they found the poet Robinson Jeffers and his wife, Una, were also guests. Jeffers began to pay considerable attention to a beautiful young pianist who was visiting and Mabel, always ready to kindle a flame, encouraged him. His wife, however, became so distraught that she tried to kill herself, a crisis Mabel found more exciting than disturbing.[25]

Nearby was another friend, the poet Witter Bynner, who lived in Santa Fe. Thornton was from time to time a house guest of Bynner and his companion, Robert Hunt. On a wall in Bynner's home there hung a gallery of self-portraits by writers and artists, including one of Thornton. In turn, Bynner provided a portrait in poetry of his friend, which he called "teacher."

Teacher of boys—and yet afraid the rule
Of lordliness in class should come besides
To be a habit and he play the fool,
He has a look which what it half confides
It more conceals. He flutters on the verge
Of telling you, first with his eyes and hands,
Then nearly his tongue; and yet the urge
Is less than something else which countermands.
Therefore his conversation turns to dreams
And their interpreting or to some such case
Of Freudian theory. A flicker gleams
Of almost rabid fervour on his face
And in his voice there's an excited tone—
Toward other people's cases than his own.[26]

# TEN

THORNTON resumed his teaching duties, taking time out to visit the Chicago World's Fair and the Art Institute, where a superb El Greco was being exhibited. He was also staging Handel's *Xerxes* for the music department, a project that required his presence at all rehearsals. His next book was on its way to publication, and he was enthusiastic about his new publisher, Harper & Bros. His first acquaintance with his editor, Cass Canfield, had been in 1927 when he received from the publisher an announcement of the Harper Prize Novel Contest. Thornton, curious about the contest, went to see Canfield. "He asked questions . . . , thanked me for giving the answers and thereupon departed hurriedly." A few weeks later, he telephoned Canfield and asked him to visit him at Lawrenceville. In their talk there, he said that when he had received the announcement, he had been thinking about which publisher to choose for his next book, because he had decided to leave Boni. Now he had made his decision —and wanted Harpers to handle his work. In August 1934 he received word from Canfield that *Heaven's My Destination* was accepted; in Taos he completed the final chapter and submitted the finished manuscript to his editor.

The atmosphere at "the great university" was exciting that fall. Jacques Maritain offered several lectures. Thornton was asked to introduce Edna St. Vincent Millay when she spoke on November 12; and the entire college community was eagerly anticipating the arrival of another literary figure—Gertrude Stein.

From mid-October, scarcely a day went by without an announcement or article in the university's *Daily Maroon* about Gertrude Stein's forthcoming visit. "Probably not since the Prince of Wales visited the campus in 1924 has the student body entered so wholeheartedly in the reception of a celebrity to the cloistered walls of this co-educational monastery," the paper reported shortly before she came. She arrived on November 7, in time to see a production of her own *Four Saints in Three Acts*, set to music by Virgil Thomson. Though she had just taken her first airplane flight—a prospect that had frightened her—she arrived beaming, and consented to pose for photographs, "although her secretary, Alice B. Toklas," the paper noted, "could not be persuaded to pose with her." They settled down at the Drake Hotel at first, then were invited to stay as house guests of Bobsie Goodspeed, a friend of Thornton and the Hutchinses. It was not long after their arrival that they met Thornton, to everyone's delight.

"We might have known him long ago," Stein wrote, when she found out that Thornton had been in Paris many times. "Would that have been as nice as knowing him now," she asked. "This I do not know."[1] Their meeting marked the beginning of an unusual friendship, and one that was to be among the most important in Thornton's life.

Stein had recently risen to popularity after the publication of *The Autobiography of Alice B. Toklas* in 1933. Although known by an esoteric circle of writers and artists in Paris, she did not enjoy the respect and esteem already accorded to Thornton. Instead, she was considered by most to be more a curiosity and an eccentric than a brilliant artist. It was well known that Hemingway had sat at her feet, along with other aspiring young writers who came to Paris for solace or inspiration. Yet Thornton was not to play the role of adoring apprentice. Though Gertrude was sixty and he only thirty-seven, he had already been celebrated for six years since winning his Pulitzer Prize for *The Bridge of San Luis Rey* and was well acquainted with the joys and annoyances of being a literary lion.

The publicity created around Gertrude led many to expect a powerful and difficult personality. She was, in fact, enormously motherly, warm, and jovial; with Thornton she could be relaxed and unaffected, even childlike in her sudden enthusiasm. Hers was the type of personality to which Thornton responded best. She was maternal without being domineering; she was down-to-earth, a totally democratic woman who was interested in everyone and wanted to know everyone. Only the discriminating eye of her friend Alice Toklas prevented her from cultivating certain friendships. But Alice completely approved of Thornton. He was polite, well mannered, well bred, a gentleman. Besides, he was a respected writer, a Pulitzer Prize-winner who, even by association alone, would help Gertrude's image.

Though their personalities were compatible, it would seem from a glance at the writings of each that their literary interests would place them far apart. But despite the differences in their styles, both writers were grappling with similar problems and had similar interests. One was the problem faced by a modern writer in creating a believable reality. "There is no real reality to a really imagined life any more,"[2] Gertrude wrote. And Thornton agreed that the "really imagined life" was a real challenge. No one, he told her, would have doubted that Hardy's Tess might have been seen walking down a shady English lane. But modern readers were incredulous, and modern writers had to come to terms with that disbelief. Readers, after all, were inundated with "events." "Nowadays," Gertrude noted, "everybody all day long knows what is happening and so what is happening is not really interesting, one knows it by radios cinemas newspapers biographies autobiographies until what is happening does not really thrill any one. . . ."[3] How to thrill, stimulate, and provoke the reader remained a great problem.

Gertrude responded by fragmenting her work and presenting a collage of dialogue and actions that united, in her own mind at least, into a whole. "There is no reason why chapters should succeed each other since nothing succeeds another, not now any more. In the old novels yes but not now any more. . . ."4 Thornton, however, was above all a teacher. As he wrote later to Gertrude, he thought he was, in some ways, hopelessly mired in the nineteenth century, at least as far as literary style. He would not have been able to resort to the cryptic language and idiosyncratic references with which Gertrude was comfortable. Instead, he tried in his themes—the eternal and the timeless, as opposed to the ephemeral and the mundane—to depart from the mere telling of anecdotes.

There was another problem, too, that each of them faced, and that was the problem of identity. The duality that Thornton presented in *The Cabala* and more obviously in *The Bridge of San Luis Rey* was something Gertrude understood. Though the source of her preoccupation with identity did not come from her having been a twin, she had gone through a long, agonizing period of trying to deal with her own sexual identity, reconciling her lesbianism in a society which dictated that such things be hidden. The maleness and femaleness of any individual, the difference between a person's public and private personality, were themes that recurred in many of her works.

Thornton, who did not bring his own sexuality to his works, kept such personal discussions out of his friendship with Gertrude as well. Once Samuel Steward, a mutual friend of Gertrude and Thornton, asked him if Gertrude and Alice were lesbians. Thornton "was totally fussed; 'Oh,' he said, 'I suppose they were in the first place, I don't know, but all that is certainly over now.'" Gertrude, when she was told what Thornton had said, replied, "'Poor Thornie. How could he know? He doesn't know what love is.'"

But Thornton was very much aware of love in the most broad, philosophical terms. While Gertrude's works are full of eroticism and references to her sexual life with Alice Toklas, Thornton's one abiding theme in all of his novels is love and the precarious links of human bondage.

Certainly his relationships with those closest to him—his mother and his sister Isabel especially—were deeply loving, if not outwardly demonstrative. And in his friendship with Gertrude it is difficult to determine where respect and camaraderie ended and love began.

But the friendship that would eventually blossom and deepen began on an immediate liking for each other's stories and gossip, laughter and joviality.

Gertrude was to have given two lectures in the university's Mandel Hall, one on November 27 and the other on the twenty-eighth. But the University of Chicago did not take seriously enough her mandate that her audiences be limited to five hundred, and tickets were sold far in excess of that number. Gertrude saw no alternative but to cancel her talks. She did, however, agree to appear before a selected audience of English students, speaking on "Poetry and Grammar" at the International House on November 28, and on "Pictures—What They Mean to Me" on December 1. She also appeared before the Arts Club of Chicago, where her talk was "The History of English Literature." She liked the city, especially its center at night and a small grocery store where she and Alice bought pears each day. She liked walking on the windy streets and meeting people who recognized her and would stop and talk. Like Thornton, she considered no one a stranger. A passer-by with an odd-looking package would be asked question after question about whatever he was carrying. ". . . I like to know the name and occupation and what their father did or does and where they were born about any one," she said.[5]

But as agreeable as Gertrude could be, she could also be difficult and argumentative if she chose. The first time she met Robert Hutchins and Mortimer Adler she was clearly not impressed. They had just come from one of their Great Books classes, and explained the program to their guest. Gertrude was upset—first, because the books were all in translation, and second, because all dealt with "sociological or government ideas." Government, she told them, was "the least interesting thing in human life, creation and the expression of that creation is a damn sight more interesting. . . ." As she became more excited, she focused on Adler, and began lecturing him on what she thought were truly great ideas, not all of which made sense to the professor. " 'On the contrary, Miss Stein,' " Adler told her, " 'there is more on one

Amos Wilder, c. 1884
(*Courtesy, Yale University Library*).

The Wilder family, c. 1906, Hong Kong
(*Courtesy, State Historical Society
of Wisconsin*).

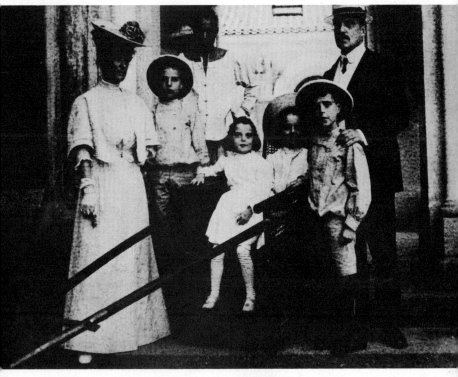

RIGGED FOR HIS NEW ROLE

Cartoon from Wisconsin
*State Journal:* Amos Wilder
off to Hong Kong *(Courtesy,
State Historical Society
of Wisconsin).*

Charles Wager
*(Courtesy, Oberlin
College Archives).*

Thornton Wilder, c. 1920
(*Courtesy, Yale University Library*).

Thornton Wilder (far right, second row)
and Clyde Foresman (far left)
with boys of Davis House
(*Courtesy, The Lawrenceville School*).

Davis House at Lawrenceville
(*Courtesy, The Lawrenceville School*).

Thornton Wilder and three Lawrenceville students,
bound for Europe, 1928 (*Courtesy, Clark Andrews*).

Thornton Wilder planting the Wilder tree, University of Hawaii
*(Courtesy, The University of Hawaii).*

Robert Hutchins
*(Courtesy, Berea College).*

Alexander Woollcott *(Photo by Richard Carver Wood; Courtesy, Hamilton College Library).*

Ruth Gordon *(Courtesy, Theatre and Music Collection, The Museum of the City of New York).*

Max Reinhardt and Thornton Wilder *(Courtesy, Center for Modern Theatre Research at SUNY-Binghamton).*

Peterborough, New Hampshire: "Our Town"
*(Courtesy, The Peterborough Historical Society)*.

Thornton Wilder in *Our Town*, College of Wooster
*(Courtesy, The College of Wooster)*.

Gertrude Stein (*Photo by Samuel Steward; Courtesy, Samuel Steward and The Bancroft Library, University of California at Berkeley*).

Alice B. Toklas (*Photo by Samuel Steward; Courtesy, Samuel Steward and The Bancroft Library, University of California at Berkeley*).

page of Adam Smith's *Wealth of Nations* than in all of Milton's
*Paradise Lost*. Statistics tell more than poetry.'

"'Nonsense, young man,' she replied. . . . 'There is more on
one page of *Paradise Lost* than in all of the *Wealth of Nations!*'"[6] Gertrude, not caring that she was the guest of honor at a
dinner, not bothering about the others at the table, continued
with more and more agitation until, suddenly, a maid announced
the arrival of the police. "Adler went a little white," Gertrude
recalled, "and we all stopped and then burst out laughing."[7] Gertrude was to be taken through the city in a homicide squad car,
hoping to glimpse some Chicago life firsthand.

Unfortunately it was a rainy night and, as the sergeant explained, there was not much happening on a rainy night. There
had been only one homicide—"a family affair and everybody
could understand everything." Gertrude wanted a mystery or a
crime with a character like Baby Face Nelson. She did, however,
get a tour of the city beyond the university and the homes on
Lake Shore Drive.

Before her Chicago stay was over, she had agreed to return, invited by Thornton to speak to some of his students, and even by
Hutchins and Adler to attend their classes. This time, Thornton
would turn over his apartment to the two ladies and they would
be able to feel completely at home.

In October, for the first time since he had been teaching at the
university, Thornton had decided to move out of the dormitory
where he usually lived, and set up a home of his own. His apartment on Drexel Avenue, which he said was bland but comfortable, had a very small but efficiently appointed kitchen, which
Alice Toklas appreciated more than Thornton did. He usually ate
in restaurants, especially small, dingy places in run-down sections
of the city, where he could observe the odd characters who made
up the clientele. It was to these restaurants that Thornton enjoyed taking his students, including one he befriended in the fall
of 1934, Robert Stallman. Stallman, an aspiring poet, had arrived
in Chicago from the University of Wisconsin, where he had
worked his way through school drying dishes and working in a
bookstore. But in 1934 he had contracted a case of shingles, which
had hospitalized him and prevented him from supporting himself.

Thornton was always sympathetic to the troubles of talented students and, not for the first time, arranged to help. One day Stallman was called into the president's office and informed that a stipend would be available for him—forty dollars a month. The money was secretly provided by Thornton.

A few years earlier, he had done the same thing for a student from Berea, whom he had met in New York. The young man was also hospitalized, and Thornton knew that his funds were very low. Then, too, he had arranged to provide a stipend for him through the college.

Stallman's income was eventually supplemented by his own efforts. For seventy-five cents an hour, he delivered papers for Robert Hutchins, often to the apartment of Elsie White, heiress to the White Star Line fortune, who lived in a suite at the Drake Hotel. Miss White tantalized the university by promising to leave a large sum of money to one or another of the school's departments. In an effort to sway her to their disciplines, professors besieged her and sent piles of professional papers and convincing reports. She was an eccentric, but one whose kindness extended to the young messenger. One day she asked, "Would you mind if I aided you?" and presented him with a check for several hundred dollars.

Thornton, known as T.N. to his student friends, met with Stallman on Fridays, taking him to cafés beneath the elevated train and including him in his occasional parties for his students. On one of their afternoon walks, Stallman remembered a characteristic occurrence. An elderly woman approached them, asking to be directed to a certain address. Thornton, instead of pointing out the direction, left Stallman standing while he guided her several blocks to the exact house. "It was his nature always to go out of his way for others," Stallman knew.

Though he was not enrolled at the university, Stallman did attend some of Thornton's lectures and found especially memorable a session on Dante where Thornton "paced the floor with Dante's *Inferno* in one hand. . . ." He always spoke without notes, and his pacing, rather than being a distraction, served to add momentum to his talk.

As mentor, Thornton gave Stallman more than immediate help.

With his recommendation, Stallman was accepted at the Bread-loaf Writers Conference for the summer of 1935, and there met such writers as Robert Frost, Bernard De Voto, John Mason Brown, and Howard Fast. Another recommendation came from Gertrude Stein, whom Stallman met when she returned to the university in March.

Though he found Gertrude amiable, Stallman had a less favorable opinion of Alexander Woollcott, who had come to Chicago at Thornton's request to meet the famous expatriate. ". . . Woollcott was saying something as we walked down the Midway from T.N.'s apartment," Stallman remembered, "and when I injected a few words into his momentarily halted speech, he turned on me with 'Young man, I have always managed to finish my own sentences.' Then he swung his cane and talked on uninterrupted."[8] Woollcott's reaction to Gertrude Stein was equally characteristic. She saw him again in New York at a luncheon given by Bennett Cerf. ". . . At table we were talking and I said something in contradiction and Alexander Woollcott said Miss Stein you have not been in New York long enough to know that I am never contradicted."[9] But Gertrude liked Woollcott more than Stallman did, mostly because they had in common a great love for poodles.

"Thornton had arranged everything," Gertrude wrote about her second stay in Chicago, "chosen those who were to come all the time and those who were to come part of the time, and it was all interesting."[10] The thirty students selected for ten meetings with her were not only English majors, but "those interested in philosophy and history and anything, which made it much more varied. . . ."[11] Besides the seminars, Gertrude delivered four lectures on narration, which were later published by the university as *Narration*, with an introduction by Thornton.

"We soon discover," he told readers, "that we are not to hear about narration from the point of view that the rhetorics usually discuss the subject." Gertrude, in her "homely language" and "colloquial usage," would attempt to answer "a deeply lodged and distinctly stated question," which reminded Thornton of that which Dante asked his guide:

I prayed him to bestow on me the food, for which he had already bestowed on me the appetite.

In bringing to her discussion of narration ideas from psychology, philosophy, and metaphysics, Gertrude could often be abstract. "She assumes," Thornton wrote, "that the attentive listener will bring, from a store of observation and reflection, the concrete illustration of her generalization." What interested Thornton most were her ideas on "the psychology of the creative act as the moment of 'recognition' and the discussion of the relations between the artist and the audience. . . . Miss Stein has said that the artist is the sensitive exponent of his contemporaneousness, expressing it while it still lies in the unconscious of society at large," he explained.

Thornton's interest in the sources of a writer's inspiration reflected a personal concern. A few months before Gertrude returned to Chicago, his fourth novel had been published—a book that was greatly different from the three that preceded it. Unlike *The Cabala, The Bridge of San Luis Rey,* and *The Woman of Andros, Heaven's My Destination* was comical, often satirical, more like a folk ballad than an allegorical tale. Thornton admitted that it was his most autobiographical work so far. "I came from a very strict Calvinistic father," he said, "was brought up partly among the missionaries of China, and went to that splendid college at Oberlin at a time when the classrooms and student life carried a good deal of the pious didacticism which would now be called narrow Protestantism. And that book is, as it were, an effort to come to terms with those influences."[12] It was the first time he had set his story in America, the first time he had written about the present. His inspiration to do both came in part from Michael Gold's attack five years before. Many reviewers realized what lay behind the theme of the book, and Edmund Wilson was even moved to write to his friend John Dos Passos that Thornton had "taken up the challenge flung down by Mike Gold. . . ."[13]

The story, as Thornton explained, is of an American Don Quixote, George Marvin Brush, a salesman of religious textbooks, who travels around America during the depression and often ends up rather depressed. "George, the hero . . . , is an earnest, humorless, moralizing, preachifying, interfering product of Bible-belt evangelism," Thornton said once.[14] But George had another side, too. "I'm George Brush!" Thornton would laughingly exclaim to friends.[15]

If, in Thornton's mind, George contained the spirit of Don Quixote, the reader is not always convinced. George is too self-righteous, too naïve, too exasperating to endear himself the way the Spanish hero could. And where Don Quixote had a foil in Sancho Panza, George is a loner, pitted against practical jokers and thin comic-strip characters, superficially buffeted, but all too ready to pick himself up, dust himself off, and continue. Even his bouts of depression, understandable as they might be, are only superficial. And we are left with the uncomfortable feeling that George may not be too intelligent.

George's sense of morality leads him to emulate Gandhi. He takes a vow of poverty, returns his bank interest, practices days of silence. Getting raises makes him nervous: "I think everybody ought to be hit by the depression equally," he maintains. Still, earning more allows him more to give away.

The book is structured around George's misadventures, his collisions with the "normal" people of America. He was born in Michigan, grew up on a farm, but wanted to go to college. Since his family disapproved, he took his future into his own hands and worked his way through Shiloh Baptist College. In his sophomore year, he underwent a momentous change: a woman evangelist came to speak on campus, and George was instantly converted. Even when he went back to her trailer and discovered that she was a drug addict, he was not swayed. And he was intent on spreading his lofty principles wherever he went, to whomever he met.

Usually George is not treated with sympathy, although at times his seriousness and earnestness save him. A few characters—the motherly woman who runs a boardinghouse, and the sister of the young woman George marries—seem genuinely to like him. But they treat him more like a boy who needs protecting than a twenty-three-year-old man. The involved story of his marriage is hardly believable, but forms a thread throughout the book. A few years before we meet George, he had "ruined" a farmer's daughter. From then on, he considered himself married to her and spent considerable effort trying to locate her again. When he finds her, she is a waitress in a Chinese restaurant and has no interest in him or his proposal. Characteristically, he perseveres until she consents, and a loveless union is legalized. It is short-lived, however; when George resumes his travels to sell books, she makes it known that she wants to return to her family and live apart from him.

George does get depressed by the people he meets and by life in general. "It's the world that's crazy," he exclaims once. "Everybody's crazy except me; that's what's the matter. The whole world's nuts." And though he believes completely in God—quoting Bible verses and denouncing Darwin's theory of evolution—he wonders "but why's he so slow in changing the world?" His deepest depression comes near the end of the book, at the same time he learns that a certain Father Pasziewski, a Polish priest who never appears but is often mentioned, has died. The priest had known about George, showed an interest in his life, and prayed for him on Fridays. He leaves him a small bequest: a spoon, and a message that perhaps George could "use a spoon some way." The priest's death revives George's mission, and a few days later he is back on his adventure-filled road.

Instead of seeing Thornton as the model for George, many readers thought of Gene Tunney. But Tunney, it seems, was the inspiration for only one scene, that of George doggedly trying to memorize *King Lear* as he shaves.[16] Though George "had read the play ten times without discovering a trace of talent in it . . . ," he had been told by a college professor that the work was great, and so decided to commit it to memory.

Most reviewers tried to see George as a symbolic character, which Edmund Wilson described as a "type of saint, . . . and therefore a universal character." Wilson, who thought the book "much Mr. Wilder's best novel," ended up "respecting and liking" George. Thornton, he said, "has created in his central character . . . a more complete and living person than in any of his other books." The story was told with a deft lightness and a comic touch "with the result that Mr. Wilder's vision of an imperfect and suffering humanity comes through a great deal more tellingly than in his earlier books." Thornton created "something more even than an excellent picture of an American variety of religious experience."[17]

Wilson's opinion was echoed many times. The book was chosen as the January selection of the Book-of-the-Month Club, and Henry Seidel Canby wrote an enthusiastic flyer for it. In his review in the *Saturday Review* he called *Heaven's My Destination* a work "which the eighteenth century, subtler than we in designating the purposes of literature, would have recognized as moral apologues, skillfully disguised as story telling, and indeed enriched by incidental and contributory stories which are admirable story telling." As he had done before, Thornton again showed a "consecration to perfection, the conscientiousness, and the absolute excellence of . . . a Collins, or an Addison."[18]

Even R. P. Blackmur, who had some reservations about the book, found it "a lively, entertaining novel of picaresque incident. . . ." But Blackmur was quick to see that although Thornton had changed the time and place for this book, he had not altered his choice of theme. ". . . He has merely matured his technique, dropped meretricious ballast, and shifted his angle of vision. . . . Certainly it is with the representation of goodness, conceived in terms of the Christian insight and posed in conflict with the world, that Mr. Wilder has always been concerned. Goodness, not intelligence . . . , not passion . . . , not the rational life . . . , is the predominating theme. It is goodness, too, taken not merely as a quality of resource but as the final vocation of life, and it is the special goodness of the Christian insight; which is to say that, as with the great novelists, the theme is made omnivorous and inclusive."[19] Certainly Thornton's epigraph for the book, a quotation from *The Woman of Andros*, supports Blackmur's idea. "Of all the forms of genius," Thornton wrote, "goodness has the longest awkward age."

Thornton's assertion of his likeness to George Marvin Brush seems difficult to accept. But in some aspects they were similar: both had a determined optimism that they thought would carry them through any difficulty. Both had faith, and even if George pressed his beliefs too dogmatically, it was evident that his faith was sincere. And both could become depressed because the world seemed so slow to change, because life suddenly was not as it should have been—because everything seemed futile. In the early spring of 1935 Thornton's usual bright spirits flagged. He wrote to

Witter Bynner that overwork had caused a small breakdown;[20] to Alexander Woollcott he jokingly described himself as trembling whenever he met someone who denied that there was any difference between poetry and prose;[21] suddenly he had to stop work and retreat for a moment to put his life in perspective. He arranged for a year's leave of absence from the university, but only gradually could he formulate a plan for his free time.

Thornton ascribed George's recovery to an act of divine providence. Perhaps he, too, felt an unexpected revelation, because by May he had recovered and regained his former enthusiasm. He was bound for Europe, he wrote to his friends, with at least three ideas for stories or novels and a few more for some works of nonfiction. His confidence in his writing talent revived, and among his ideas for books was a Christmas collection for which he would write stories and one of his talented students, John Pratt, provide illustrations.[22]

He was looking forward to his trip abroad and planned to leave on June 28, a few days after his older brother, Amos, was to be married, at forty, the first of the Wilder children to do so. This time, Thornton was not traveling alone. His companion was another of his students, Robert Davis, whose knowledge of philosophy and psychology Thornton respected immensely. Gertrude Stein had met Davis when she was in Chicago and invited him to join Thornton in visiting her at Bilignin. The two also planned to hike through Austria and Provence, to attend the Salzburg Festival, to visit with Max Reinhardt. . . . From New York, Thornton wrote to Woollcott that he was so happy he felt like falling to his knees at Rockefeller Center and saying a prayer in gratitude for his blessings.[23]

Before sailing on the *Ascania*, the pair spent a few days in Newport, Rhode Island, which Thornton remembered vividly from his Fort Adams days. It was the first time Davis had ever seen the ocean, and he was so excited that he even tasted it to make sure it was salty.[24] Thornton found Davis a stimulating companion with whom he could discuss metaphysics and psychoanalysis, especially Freud's theories, which interested Thornton greatly.

The two spent a few weeks in Paris, a city that Thornton had never liked. For him it was a three-dimensional picture postcard, with none of the charm of Vienna or Munich. Then they went to Bilignin, where Gertrude Stein and Alice Toklas spent the summers. Though Thornton often felt tied down as a guest, politely acquiescing to his hostess's wishes and not feeling free to wander as he wished, his stay with the two women was euphoric. Gertrude at times was working on a book whose improbable title was to be *The Geographical History of America Or The Relation of Human Nature to the Human Mind*. Both Thornton and Robert Davis were to appear in its finished version, but the main thesis centered around Gertrude's thoughts about literary masterpieces and the mind of the artist.

She and Thornton talked about the *Iliad*, the Old Testament, the plays of Shakespeare, *Robinson Crusoe*, and Jane Austen as Gertrude mused on the distinction between Human Nature and the Human Mind. It was only the Human Mind, free of external encumbrances, that could create a masterpiece. Human Nature was bound to a personality, to memory, and to an audience. It existed in time and had to respond to a sense of time. The Human Mind, however, could transcend time—past, present, and future; it could transcend place, whereas Human Nature was influenced by geography. "Flat lands are an invitation to wander," she wrote, "as well as a release from local assertion."[25]

Gertrude argued with Thornton about Hamlet, maintaining that he was not a realistic character because "the psychology in Shakespeare is no psychology at all. A young man whose father was just murdered, would not act like Hamlet, Hamlet was not interested in his father, he was interested in himself, and he acted not like a young man who lost a loved father but like a man who wants to talk about himself, that is psychology if you like but anybody in any village can do that.

"Now in a master-piece what does anybody do they do what they do that is they say what they know and they only know what they are as they know what they are, there is no time and no identity, not at all never at all ever at all."[26]

Their talks continued as they roamed up and down the hills of Bilignin. ". . . Thornton pleasantly eagerly and in a way said everything . . . ," Gertrude wrote. "We talked about time and the passage of time about the dogs and what they did and was it the same as we did. . . . These were the things we talked about going up and down and Bob Davis sometimes said something, of course he was not articulate like Thornton nor articulate like I am but every now and then and we always listened to him naturally we listened to him always listened to him when he said something. And so it was a pleasant time there in Bilignin a very pleasant time."[27]

Thornton thought Gertrude was no less than a genius, an opinion he maintained throughout his life. But her metaphysics was so deep that it was often difficult to understand her. She was not only a philosopher, he thought, who must reinvent the language, but also an artist. "When the metaphysician is combined with the poet we get such unusual modes of expression as the myths in Plato, the prophetic books of Blake and the difficult highly-figured phrases in Keats's letters"—and the "'metaphysical metaphors'" of Gertrude Stein.[28] The difficulty in her language was compounded with her humor and love for wordplay. The result, he said, was "an inevitably private language" that was, for some, impenetrable.

Gertrude's portrait of Wilder in *The Geographical History of America* is elusive but, Thornton said, accurate.[29] "In china china is not china it is an earthen ware. In China there is no need of China because in China china is china," she began.[30] Thornton explained that he had related to Gertrude his experiences as a child in China, and told her how much daily life seemed rooted in antiquity. Exquisite pottery was put into daily use, not set aside as museum pieces. "China in America is not an earthen ware," she knew.

Her comments about his personality also show great insight. "It is no doubt a resistance to yield to all," she wrote. Thornton frequently admitted that he always tried to be "obliging." Friends knew that he would readily do favors, read manuscripts, write letters of recommendation, and otherwise help when needed. But saying "yes" was a way of not yielding his own inner peace. He did not want the pressure and distraction of distressing relationships. "He has no fears. / At most he has no tears. / For them very likely he is made of them,"[31] Gertrude went on, implying that his outward sensitivity belied an inner strength.

In his relationship with his family—especially with his father—Thornton puzzled Gertrude.

> *Thornton Wilder is.*
> *Sometimes some one is as if he were an only son.*
> *But is he a son at all.*
> *May be he never has been.*[32]

She was clearly impressed by his talents as a writer, although he said once that Gertrude had never read any of his works.[33] Apparently she trusted her intuition, though, because she exhorted him to direct his energies into drama. "Now make a play," she wrote, "with human nature and not anything of the human mind."[34] He knew what qualities a masterpiece must have; he knew that "nature and music is not that." And he could, she was sure, separate himself from time, identity, and his audience to create such an exalted work. "It is so difficult to have anything to do with masterpieces," she admitted. "Yes Thornton."[35]

The entire visit, Thornton wrote to his friend Robert Stallman, was a most memorable experience. Gertrude would often take him and Davis on rides along winding country roads, until the vista of Mont Blanc would suddenly appear. Then they would proceed on foot, tramping through fields of wildflowers. Or they would sit on the terrace of her home, Thornton affectionately petting Gertrude's chihuahua, Pépé, "because as he said Pépé passed and existed from one caress to another."[36]

After ten days with Gertrude and Alice, Thornton and Robert Davis continued on their travels, hiking through the Alps in Austria and Italy. They were charmed by the colorful villages and impressive medieval churches, but took time from their sightseeing to work. Davis was reading Alfred North Whitehead's *Process and Reality*, and Thornton, with his ambitions now focused on six plays, began filling notebooks with ideas.[37] Still, though he well appreciated the beauty of nature, he admitted that his inspiration could come only from people, music, or poetry. He was enlivened when he finally arrived in Vienna after attending performances led by Bruno Walter and Toscanini at the Salzburg Festival.

There was a reunion and several new meetings in Vienna. Max

Reinhardt invited him to dinner and asked him to head a dramatic school he was planning to start in southern California, an honor Thornton declined. When Thornton found that another guest had never heard of him, he was a bit disappointed and vowed that he would try to become more famous. The guest was, after all, Thomas Mann. But on October 13 he was invited to talk with someone who had indeed both heard of him and formed a definite opinion. "Prof. Freud was told that I had expressed . . . a wish to see him," he wrote to Gertrude, "and he asked me to go yesterday to his villa in Grinzing. I was all alone with him for an hour and a half, and it was fine."[38] The seventy-nine-year-old physician was harsh with Thornton's novels. "I could not read your latest book [Heaven's My Destination]—I threw it away," he said. "Why should you treat of an American fanatic; that cannot be treated poetically." He admitted that his sister-in-law admired The Cabala, but said he did not. Thornton speculated that the reason was "a slighting reference to Freud" made by one of the characters.

They went on to talk about fiction in general. Freud believed that the principles of psychoanalysis could not be incorporated into fiction for several centuries. "Numbers of my friends," he told Thornton, "—Arnold Zweig and Stefan Zweig and Franz Werfel—have been using psychoanalysis in their novels; but it still comes out as clinical document, as schematic. Only in two or three hundred years will the Dichter have assimilated it at so deep a level that they'll know it without knowing they know it. And it will come out as pure novel."[39] Here Thornton disagreed. That "pure novel," he thought, had already been published in 1922: James Joyce's Ulysses.

The conversation turned to Freud's own background. "I am no seeker after God," he told Thornton. "I come of an unbroken line of infidel Jews. My father was a Voltairean. My mother was pious, and until eight I was pious—but one day my father took me out for a walk in the Prater—I can remember it perfectly—and explained to me that there was no way that we could know there was a God; that it didn't do any good to trouble one's head about such; but to live and do one's duty among one's fellow-men." But, he added, as he pointed to glass cases filled with Greek, Chinese,

African, and Egyptian images, ". . . I like god. . . . Just these
last weeks I have found a *Formulierung* for religion. . . . Hitherto
I have said that religion is an illusion; now I say it has a truth—it
has an historical truth. Religion is the recapitulation and the solution of the problems of one's first four years that have been covered over by an amnesia." He was, Thornton said, "a beautiful old
man. . . ."40

Vienna offered so many distractions that Thornton found it impossible to concentrate on his work. "Not only something Mediterranean flows through the air of this town," he wrote to Gertrude, "but something Oriental as well. The endless café-sitting,
the headwaiters who are indifferent as to whether one has ordered
or not, the relaxed idea of time. . . ." He could not get used to
the pace, and moved to a hotel about forty-five minutes away,
where he thought he could walk in solitude—and work.41 He was
already at the Hotel Schloss Cobenzl when he received the completed manuscript for Gertrude's *Geographical History of
America*. His enthusiasm was boundless. "What a book!" he
wrote to her. "I mean what a book! I've been living for a month
with ever-increasing intensity on the conceptions of Human Nature and the Human Mind, and on the relations of Master-pieces
to their apparent subject-matter. Those things, yes and identity,
have become cell and marrow in me and now at last I have more
about them. And it's all absorbing and fascinating and intoxicat-
ingly gay, even when it's terribly in earnest. . . ." His letter disclosed another reason for his feeling of excitement. Suddenly he
knew he wanted to return home. He no longer needed to be away
from the States. His depression had fully passed and he was looking forward to working again. He was, after all, "crazy about
America. . . ."42 But before he left, he begged Gertrude to meet
with him once more.

She and Alice Toklas had already returned to their home in
Paris, where Thornton headed even though, as Gertrude knew,
"Thornton does not like Paris. He says he does not and he is right
he does not. . . . But Thornton and I liked walking around even
so, and we walked around the last evening, he was going away to
America the next day and I walked home with him and he walked
home with me and we talked about writing and telling anything

and I said I had done things I had really written poetry and I had really written plays and I had really written thinking and I had really written sentences and paragraphs but I said I had not simply told anything and I wanted to do that thing must do it. I would simply say what was happening which is what is narration, and I must do it as I knew it was what I had to do. Yes said Thornton."[43] Gertrude would one day interpret that "yes" as an agreement to collaborate on a book, but for the meantime she was satisfied with his approval of *The Geographical History of America* and his agreement to write an introduction for it. He would not, however, go along with her publisher's idea of annotating the book with his interpretations on the page facing her text. There were long passages, he told her, that he did not fully understand.

He left Europe feeling very happy, but a bit uneasy, too, at the threat of war. He had urged Gertrude and Alice to return to the United States, even offering to find them an apartment on Washington Square, a neighborhood he thought would suit them. He blithely disclosed to Alexander Woollcott that he, with his political acumen, thought there would be no war—but his deeper feelings were just the opposite. He left, too, knowing that he was returning to a difficult family situation. On October 23, 1935, his father had undergone an abdominal operation at St. Raphael's Hospital in New Haven. His condition was only "fair," and it was evident to the family that he was dying. With his brother married, Thornton alone would have to sustain his mother and Isabel through a trying time.

# ELEVEN

---

THORNTON'S brother, Amos, and his wife, the former Catherine Kerlin, came to New Haven for a somber Thanksgiving. His father was still hospitalized, paralyzed after a series of strokes and now weakened from his operation. The family expected his death at any moment, and its imminence placed a great strain on Thornton's mother and his sister Isabel, the only daughter still living at home. Though no one imagined that Amos would survive into the New Year, he did, and Thornton was obliged to fulfill his commitments with only long-distance communication to the house on Deepwood Drive.

Early in February 1936 he began another of his lecture tours, this time to North and South Carolina, Virginia, Georgia, Oklahoma, Utah, and California. He was tired of the rigor of the tours but said they gave him a chance to see people, to look into new eyes and find new characters for his books. Somewhere among 126 million Americans, he thought, there would be inspiration.

He stopped off to see some friends in Tennessee and inadvertently left behind an envelope containing his lecture schedule. But the itinerary caught up with him in Washington, D.C., where he

spent a weekend getting reacquainted with the city, which seemed
to him more small town than nation's capital. While he was there,
he attended a play in which George M. Cohan was performing and
took a bus tour of Annapolis to learn a bit of history.

By the beginning of March he had left the South and was traveling across the desert on the Los Angeles Limited; and by April
he was back in Chicago, preparing to resume his teaching there.
He was planning to return to the university on the same basis as
before he took the year's leave of absence, and agreed to teach
during the summer of 1936. But his writing was drawing him
away from teaching. He remembered Gertrude's command to
write a masterpiece; he had many ideas for plays and wanted to
give them form and shape; he had become fascinated with Lope
de Vega, the prolific sixteenth-century Spanish playwright who
wrote some eighteen hundred works. By mid-June he had made a
decision: he wanted his freedom. He resigned from what he consistently and continually called the greatest university in the world
and vowed to devote himself to writing.

He was in Chicago on July 2 when he received word that his father had died in his sleep at dawn. He left for New Haven and
joined his family at the simple service held on the afternoon of
July 4. For his mother and Isabel, he knew the burden of the last
year, and especially the last months, was over. For himself, he felt
the sudden lifting of a weight that he had borne for nearly forty
years. "Thornton Wilder writes to us these days and says he is
shamelessly happy, and now he has no father," Gertrude Stein
wrote, adding, "Fathers are depressing."[1] No matter how far he
seemed to have come from his father's domination, Thornton always felt the influence of Amos's didacticism. "My father and my
ancestors went about grandly telling others where their duty lay,"
Thornton wrote later. "I hope that will never be said of me."[2]
Even in his writing, he blamed any pedantic style on his father's
lack of aesthetic sense; Amos, he thought, knew nothing about
art.[3]

Amos, in fact, wanted none of his children to be writers, and
yet each one of them turned to writing at one time or another in
his or her career. His older son, a minister, came closest to
fulfilling Amos's expectations for the choice of a profession. After

graduating from Yale, Amos spent two years at Mansfield College, Oxford, and three years as a pastor in Conway, New Hampshire. He earned his doctorate from Yale in 1933 and accepted a chair of Ethics and Christian Evidences at Hamilton College in Clinton, New York, and later a position as Professor of New Testament Interpretation at Andover Newton Theological School in Massachusetts. Yet besides works such as *Eschatology and Ethics in the Teaching of Jesus,* Amos published his own poetry: *Battle Retrospect, Arachne,* and *Healing of the Waters.*

Charlotte, a teacher at Smith College, would go on to publish two volumes of poems, *Phases of the Moon* and *Mortal Sequences.* In her first book, she recalled her mother standing in the kitchen of their home, looking out at the moon and saying, "As I grow older, . . . more and more I come to love *the moon.*" Her daughter, then, looked at it in wonder: "huge, spherical, incandescent-white; over the velvet-black woods, in space: strange, bleak and pure." Charlotte's father evoked a different image. ". . . My arch-enemy tyrant," she wrote, "O my bruised / outraged ancient: I come back, to walk with you, / the persistent obligation of these. . . . . . . . / dispassionate catacombs." Charlotte attained a frankness in her writings which her brother Thornton did not approach. "Readers made acquainted by modern science with aspects of the psyche heretofore uninvestigated," she wrote, in *Phases of the Moon,* "need hardly be told that complete abstinence from sexual experience—over a protracted span of time—results in states of consciousness curiously remote or violent: the former marked by a pervasive sense of detachment, and fundamental ennui: the later, by attitudes of acute defendedness. When spontaneous emotion, banked against outlet . . . is first permitted to issue—often in response to welcoming perceptiveness in a person of the same sex—there comes, associated with it, an uncontrollable volume of angry and bitter feeling . . . irrationally projected against the other; bewildering to the one suffering it, inasmuch as the genuine emotion is compounded solely of devotion and gratitude."

Isabel, too, was a writer, with several novels published in the thirties. *Heart, Be Still,* which appeared two years before her father's death, expresses in part feelings similar to Charlotte's. The

story deals with a young woman, Celia, who has devoted her life
to serving her father—with ambivalent feelings. " 'My father, my
father'—that was Celia's life. As she stood looking back at him
this night, she thought: It's the same between us to-day as when I
was five, ten, fifteen. Now I'm twenty-two, and it's still the same.
There's nothing in the world I would want except for life to go on
like this forever. . . ." Celia's complete acceptance of her life is
jarred by a forthright young man, Gibbs, who "kept asking what
she was going to do with her life—die at the typewriter, preparing
her father's notes, or taking a breakfast tray to her mother?" But
Celia feels "she had no talents to cultivate. There was nothing she
could do if she had to." She is afraid that her father's domination
—benign as it may have been—has kept her from attaining emotional maturity. "If I'm still a child, at twenty-three, whose fault
is it?" she asks him. "If I don't know anything, can't do anything, whose fault is it?" She manages, however, to suppress her
feelings, which often border on the violent. "She learned how to
cry without making a sound. Stark grief knows no screams and
loud torments; instead, it racks the body. By writhing and turning,
by twisting the arms over and about the head, by contorting the
face into horrible shapes and, lastly, by fighting for breath like a
strangling man, it is possible to find an outlet for overwhelming
despair. Then, complete physical exhaustion brings the spasm to
an end; next comes relief."

In *Heart, Be Still* and another novel, *Let Winter Go*, Isabel
suggests that love, a lasting relationship, might offer release from
the fear, loneliness, and repression her heroines feel. ". . . I'll tell
you what it is to live alone," Celia imagines herself saying to a
friend. "And how it is never to love, to be loved. You can't understand that, I know. Not even one who has had love and turned in
bitterness and disgust from more, can realize what it is never,
never to have had it. . . . I stand by my bed at night, afraid to
get in, because I'm overwhelmed by a vision of all the nights
ahead in which I see myself lying on that narrow mattress alone
. . . It's not just lying alone. No, no! It means walking and thinking alone. That's terrible, you know . . . Walking and thinking
alone. No one is supposed to have to do that all his life. . . ." In
*Let Winter Go* a friend asks the central character, Alicia Rowe,

"Aren't you ever going to let yourself fall in love, Alicia? . . . Somehow I know by instinct and by conviction that for a woman, for any woman at all, this is much, much better. It's the only thing for us. My love has taught me that. I've learned that our great need is to use ourselves and be used."

But Isabel's heroines echo the sentiments in Charlotte's poem "There is a country . . ."

> There is a country I have never seen, and to
> which I may never go:
> although from time to time, I have plucked the rose
> of it . . . have tasted the bubbling and limpid water;
> it has whirled round me in a living moment; and
> in my dream, the root of it has pierced through the
> enblissful tissue of my heart . . .

Despite his children's obvious writing talent, Amos had voiced other plans for them. Charlotte was to be a doctor and Isabel a nurse. The youngest, Janet, almost fulfilled Amos's wish for her to be a scientist by studying zoology.[4] But even she, as an undergraduate at Mount Holyoke, published a poem in the student magazine. "Another darn writer in the family," Amos commented.[5]

In September, after his classes were over, Thornton returned to New Haven to keep his mother company and help sort through his father's papers. He found her recovered from the initial shock of his father's death and thought she seemed optimistic about the future. As she sat darning socks or mending, he read to her from a history of the Boxer Rebellion, a lovely book, he described, which simply and gracefully dealt with the life of the Empress Dowager.[6] And one day, as he was looking through Amos's letters from the years he served in China, he found something that amused him greatly. In a letter to Alexander Woollcott, Thornton playfully suggested that the letters must be included in any future printings of *Heaven's My Destination*. They concerned Amos's problems about the marketing of liquor in China and included his protests to the Assistant Secretary of State, Theodore Roosevelt, and William H. Taft. Thornton found the government's replies, the letter of "instruction" that reminded his father of his consular duties, and Amos's threat of resignation.[7] Apparently, Thornton had not known then of the situation, and certainly when he was writing *Heaven's My Destination* he had no idea that his George Brush, in his self-righteousness and upright morality, was more like his father than he might have wished.

The following month he began his new life of freedom with a real vacation. He spent several weeks at Bluebeard's Castle in St. Thomas and, for the first weeks at least, thought everything was nearly perfect. Of course, he was irritated by the noonday heat and by the banal conversations of most of the other guests, with whom he drank cocktails each afternoon. The nights were some-times uncomfortable, too, since there was such an incessant noise of donkeys braying and dogs barking that one pair of guests, who happened to be Edna St. Vincent Millay and her husband, Eugen Boissevain, tried to bribe the chief of police to do something about it. But the scenery was heavenly, the fragrances soothing, the colors magnificent. Thornton claimed he saw thousands of different shades of blue in the harbor, and each evening at eight he dined beneath mahogany trees on a terrace overlooking the softly lit city and the bay beyond. He worked a little, he said, but most of all he enjoyed walking for hours each day—along the beaches, through the village, into the jungle—alone. He was tired of having to make conversation, tired of being sociable.[8]

But by mid-November, after he had moved to the Hotel St. Antoine in St. Lucia, his feelings had changed. The heat was now more enervating than before, and he felt especially annoyed by the humidity. He found that he had to change clothing several times a day to keep comfortable. Though the island was admit-tedly beautiful, he was becoming claustrophobic from having to sleep under a mosquito net and irritated at the enormous numbers of insects he found everywhere. He had enjoyed St. Thomas more, but after a month there had found no new paths to take. He might have stayed for a longer time in Martinique, where he spent only one day and found a lovely bookstore. But perhaps, he suggested, the problem was not so much in the place as in him-self. He was not a good traveler, he wrote to Woollcott, but still he could not resist the lure of far-off places. If he felt homesick at the moment, he knew that in a few months, a year, he would want to be off again. He might have agreed with Emerson: "We owe to our first journeys the discovery that place is nothing." For Thornton, too, the wonders of nature or charm of a village were not as rewarding as listening to Mozart or looking at a Van Gogh. And no matter how he had felt in October, the loveliness of the oleander and hibiscus could not compensate for a conversation with a good friend. He had had enough of being alone; he was lonely, and by the end of November he was home.

He spent the beginning of December at Berea, visiting with his friends the Hutchinses and lecturing at the college. By the middle of the month he was in New York, where he visited Edward Sheldon, the bedridden playwright whom he had met some years before.

Sheldon, blind and paralyzed, was a source of inspiration for writers, actors, and actresses over several decades. He lived in a penthouse on East Eighty-fourth Street in Manhattan, where he received visitors in a large room in which he lay immobile. He always wore a half-mask to hide his eyes, and his cheeks were always ruddy and healthy because he spent hours on the rooftop terrace. "The way the bed was draped contributed to the uncanny, I am tempted to say occult, impression that Edward Sheldon made on the unaccustomed visitor," Glenway Wescott wrote. "A Persian rug, or it may have been just a heavy brocade, was drawn quite smooth and flat across it, and hung foursquare to the floor, with not the least mound or hump or other indication of the crippled body stretched out under it."[9] The atmosphere of that room, however, did not stop visitors from coming; in fact, it was Sheldon who often sent telegrams canceling an engagement with one friend to see another. Playwrights read him their latest works, actresses rehearsed their parts, directors came for advice, all came for encouragement—for "wisdom, courage, the example of how to ignore defeat," the actress Ruth Gordon wrote.[10] "Sheldon's attention to human phenomena was like a sponge," Thornton had said; and he knew that Sheldon was spending his life trying to be useful to others.[11]

He shared the news of his plays with Sheldon. At the time,

Thornton was working on several different pieces, two of which would eventually appear as *The Merchant of Yonkers* and *Our Town*. The latter, tentatively called *Our Village*, had, in its beginning versions, some of the spirit of *The Happy Journey to Trenton and Camden*. Also, it could evoke Edgar Lee Masters' *Spoon River Anthology*. But it was hardly begun. Even by late spring only the first act was completed. Another first act that Thornton felt showed promise was a comedy, *Homage to P. G. Wodehouse*. But the play, which was supposedly finished, did not fully please him. The comedy needed work, and Thornton planned to spend the summer at MacDowell polishing it.

In February and March 1937 he went on another lecture tour, first to Florida, where the sunshine was most welcome, and then to snowy Iowa City. For the first time, Thornton seemed less than enthusiastic about the masses who came to meet him. They treated a writer as if he were somehow apart from the rest of humanity, not quite a member of the same species. He found solace by reading Boswell's *Tour to the Hebrides*, an account of his journey to Scotland with Johnson, and by writing letters to his more literate friends.

His plans for the summer were suddenly changed in May when he was invited by a representative of the Carnegie Foundation to serve as American delegate to the Eighth International Conference of the Institut de Coopération Intellectuelle, sponsored by the League of Nations, in Paris. He was to sit on a committee concerned with the special problems contemporary writers faced and would be conferring with such renowned authors as Paul Valéry, Thomas Mann, and E. M. Forster. Even his passage on the *De-Grasse* would be paid. Thornton was considering a trip abroad in September—wanderlust once again—but decided to leave earlier to become part of the conference.[12] The change would mean he could spend only a few days at MacDowell, and he could not go at all to visit Alexander Woollcott at Neshobe in Vermont; but it did not mean that his work would suffer. After he fulfilled his obligations in Paris, he would go on to visit Gertrude Stein and Alice Toklas in Bilignin, then return north to Salzburg, and finally to Zurich. In Salzburg he planned a reunion with another close friend, the famed English hostess Sibyl Colefax. Thornton had met her during his 1928 trip to Europe, and at her teas found such illustrious figures as Arnold Bennett, André Maurois, Noël Coward, and John Gielgud. Lady Colefax, sophisticated, worldly, and admiring, gave Thornton the same kind of encouragement that he received from his mother, and offered the kind of stimulating conversation he had with Gertrude Stein. They shared a love for Mozart, and Thornton knew that Lady Colefax's presence at the Salzburg Festival would make the experience especially enjoyable for him. He planned to escort her to all of Toscanini's performances.

At the end of June he took up residence in the Veltin Studio at MacDowell, writing and reading. He decided to read the unabridged version of Gertrude Stein's *The Making of Americans*, her first "novel," published in 1925. Gertrude's chronicle of a family contained oblique portraits of her own parents and siblings and even included her friends. The style, however, was anything but realistic. Gertrude's repetitious prose spiraled and drew itself out, sometimes taking on a biblical quality, sometimes intimating the difficult phrasing of her future writing. Her family was all families; its particular time could have been any time. She had more to say about the nature of men and women than about her protagonists, the Herslands and the Dehnings. But for all its attempt at universalizing the family, the book was staunchly American. "It has always seemed to me a rare privilege, this, of being an American, a real American," Gertrude began, "one whose tradition it has taken scarcely sixty years to create. We need only realise our parents, remember our grandparents and know ourselves and our history is complete.

"The old people in a new world, the new people made out of the old, that is the story that I mean to tell, for that is what really is and what I really know."[13] The sentiments of Samuele, leaving Rome and heading for New York, were in sympathy with those of Gertrude.

Thornton must have appreciated, too, Gertrude's portrait of a "depressing" patriarch. Her own father had been a difficult man, as domineering as Amos, but he had died when she was a child. She had been raised by her oldest brother, Michael, upon whose understanding and sympathy she could always rely. Still, she re-

membered her fear and resentment of her father, and began her
book with an appropriate anecdote:

> Once an angry man dragged his father along the ground through
> his own orchard. "Stop!" cried the groaning old man at last, "Stop!
> I did not drag my father beyond this tree."

But she knew, too, that with age her resentment had dissipated.

> It is hard living down the tempers we are born with. We all begin
> well, for in our youth there is nothing we are more intolerant of
> than our own sins writ large in others and we fight them fiercely in
> ourselves; but we grow old and we see that these our sins are of all
> sins the really harmless ones to own, nay that they give a charm to
> any character, and so our struggle with them dies away.[14]

Thornton thought Gertrude as important a writer as Whitman,
and *The Making of Americans* as much a landmark as *Leaves of
Grass*.

His stay at MacDowell was not filled with the pleasant company and conversations of previous years. He felt isolated at times
and found himself playing solitary word games as a diversion. His
mind was more on his trip than on his work and finally, on July 3,
he sailed on the S.S. *DeGrasse*.

The trip was enjoyable enough, except when one passenger repeatedly had arguments with the waiters over the size of his por-
tions and when Thornton was asked to speak at a captain's dinner. Sibyl Colefax met him in Paris and they attended a
production of *Julius Caesar* and one of Giraudoux' *Electre*.
Thornton admired the dramatic new lighting of Notre Dame,
visited the Louvre and the palace at Fontainebleau. The conference began on July 20, and Thornton met Paul Valéry and E. M.
Forster, both of whom impressed him greatly. He had a less favorable opinion of Jules Romains and Georges Duhamel.

From July 30 to mid-August he stayed with Gertrude. She was
then musing about money, the topic of a series of short pieces she
would soon write, and she showed him her manuscript for *Everybody's Autobiography*, the story of her life beginning where *The
Autobiography of Alice B. Toklas* left off. She was also working

on a short piece called "Ida," which eventually would be expanded into a novel. The theme is identity, and the question Ida asks herself is "am I one or am I two." It was a question with which Thornton was familiar. One Ida was a fairly conventional character who even won a beauty prize. The other was a more detached personality who "had a prize too she had a prize for not remembering any one or anything." The piece has a happy ending, however: "Ida was no longer two she was one and she had every one."[15] There were wonderful conversations with Gertrude, and wonderful meals provided by Alice or taken at local inns and restaurants. The only difficulty Thornton had was finding words of praise for the paintings of Francis Rose, some of which Gertrude had recently acquired. For all his enjoyment of his visit, though, Thornton felt at times oppressed by the solicitous attentions of his hostesses. Had Gertrude been aware of his feelings, she would have completely understood. When she had stayed in his apartment in Chicago, she, too, felt herself "a prisoner of love."[16]

Thornton stayed overnight in Zurich before he proceeded to the music festival at Salzburg. Besides Sibyl Colefax, he also saw Max Reinhardt, with whom he was now very close, Erich Maria Remarque, and actress Marion Mill Preminger.

His real work began in Zurich, where he stayed at a small hotel five miles from the city. His room had a balcony overlooking the lake, and he hiked each afternoon for his mail, a cocktail, and some fruit. The atmosphere was perfect for concentrated work: he was the only guest at the hotel. He was working mainly on two plays: his comedy, which he had already completed, and *Our Village*, now called *Our Town*, which had only its first act.

The comedy was based on a nineteenth-century farce by Johann Nepomuk Nestroy, *Einen Jus Will Er Sich Machen* ("He Wants to Have a Fling") which itself had been based on another play, John Oxenford's *A Well Spent Day*. It borrowed also from Molière, a scene from the first act of *L'Avare*. But despite its early sources, the play was set in New York in the 1880s and in spirit was very much Thornton Wilder. The plot deals with an eccentric and lovable matchmaker, Dolly Levi, and her stodgy, stubborn client, Horace Vandergelder. Instead of finding him some

docile young woman to wed, the widowed Mrs. Levi decides to
marry him herself. A subplot follows the romance of Ambrose
Kemper, a struggling young artist of whom Vandergelder disap-
proves, and Vandergelder's niece, with whom Kemper is in love.
Dolly, of course, manages to right all problems, ensnares Vandergelder as her husband, and offers a bit of good advice to anyone
who will listen. Thornton dedicated the play to Max Reinhardt
"with deep admiration and indebtedness" and meant to have
Reinhardt direct it in America.

The other work was, uncharacteristically, not based on older
sources, though Thornton did say once that Emily's farewell to
her family and friends was similar to a speech of Achilles, and
that the stage manager's speeches were inspired by passages from
Euripides. Instead, the play was drawn from his own life and experiences: the village, from Peterborough, New Hampshire, where
the MacDowell Colony is located; the characters, from his friends
and family. This play was dedicated to Alexander Woollcott and
contained a reference to Woollcott's life: Mr. Webb, the newspaper editor, is, like Woollcott, an alumnus of Hamilton College.

While Thornton was working on *Our Town,* he received a visit
from a friend of Gertrude, Samuel Steward. Steward, a young
writer, had come from Bilignin carrying a note of introduction
and remembering Gertrude's description of Thornton:

Poor Thornie, he wants to take care of the whole world. I remember Sylvia Beach once said about him, he reminded her of a
man taking everyone in the whole world on a Sunday school picnic
and trying to get them all on the train at the same time. He's a
funny mixture, his background and bringing up, I suppose. He likes
the gypsy world of the theater, that's his green go-ahead light, but
then that New England part of him turns the light red just when
he is about to kick over the traces and have a really good time.[17]

Steward arrived at the time when Thornton was having trouble
with the play. He "was stuck at the end of the second act," Steward remembered, and decided that the best thing to do would be
to take a walk. Unfortunately he chose a rainy night. ". . . I kept
hollering about my feet being wet," Steward said, "and wanting

an umbrella, and now I see that act three opens with a crowd of
people under umbrellas in the rain in a graveyard. Thornton's
nice, even though he nearly gave me pneumonia waltzing me
around in the wet to show me where Dadaism began with the
reading of laundry lists into poetry—and we had to stay up all
night until the bells began to ring because he wanted me to hear
them in the morning the way Max Beerbohm described them.
And of course we had to see the house where Nietzsche 'in great
loneliness,' so he said, wrote Zarathustra. . . ." The two also
drank a great deal of Pernod and cognac that night. But the next
morning, while Steward was still asleep, Thornton rose and wrote
the entire third act.[18]

With Reinhardt committed to directing *The Merchant of
Yonkers*, which he planned to begin rehearsing in the fall of 1938,
Thornton had only to find someone willing to bring to the stage
his unconventional drama. He found that person in Jed Harris,
whom Thornton knew well through Ruth Gordon. Harris was
considered one of the most spectacular directors on Broadway—
young, imaginative, and daring. He had staged Thornton's translation of Ibsen's *A Doll's House*, with Gordon as Nora, which was
acclaimed as "one of the finest Ibsen revivals we have had in this
neighborhood [Broadway] in years."[19] And Thornton's translation
was equally praised. "Thornton Wilder," Brooks Atkinson wrote,
"has pruned away most of the stiff Nordic fripperies that were frequently distressing in the Archer version."[20]

Harris said he thought *Our Town* "was one of the preciously
few masterpieces of the American theatre. . . ."[21] Thornton was
convinced that he understood the real meaning of the play and
did not see it merely as the story of a small town, its simple inhabitants, and their daily life. He thought that Harris understood his
intent, the central theme of the play: "What is the relation between the countless 'unimportant' details of our daily life, on the
one hand, and the great perspectives of time, social history and
recurrent religious ideas on the other?"[22] The play's lack of scenery, its unusual treatment of time and sequence, its use of a stage
manager to communicate directly with the audience—all these innovations did not trouble Harris. On the contrary, he saw the play

as pointing the direction to a new and exciting theater in America. Rehearsals were to begin in the late fall, and the play—with the hopes of its author deeply bound up in it—would open in the new year.

# TWELVE

———◆———

GERTRUDE was correct when she told Samuel Steward that Thornton liked "the gypsy world of the theater." He was excited by every aspect of a play's production, from casting to lighting; he involved himself completely in rehearsals, nervously waited out first nights at pre-Broadway openings, anxiously listened for the applause—where it occurred being as important to him as its intensity—and intently read the next day's reviews. He enjoyed the company of actresses and actors, calling them "gifted children who live somnolently by day in order to dispense their gift at night."[1] He even enjoyed the sense of urgency that surrounded a production, the tenseness of the final days of rehearsals. He loved the reality of theater—and he loved its illusion.

More important, he felt that through theater he could make his greatest contribution to the literature of his own time. His aesthetic notions about playwrighting were greatly different from those of his contemporaries, and he wanted to translate those theories into actual plays. For Thornton, American theater was still very much in the nineteenth century, aspiring toward "verisimilitude" instead of reality. "The box set encouraged the anecdote . . . ," he wrote. "The unencumbered stage encourages the truth operative in everyone. The less seen, the more heard. The eye is the enemy of the ear in real drama. All the masters knew this. Plays of all great ages were performed on a stage with a minimum of scenery and with the public on three sides. We have to kick the proscenium down. . . . The box set, the curtain, the practical door and the window were all mistakes of the nineteenth century, carried on by us in the twentieth."[2] Even costumes, he said, were not necessary to stimulate the audience's imagination. "I look forward to the time when actors will be able to play not only without scenery but without specific costume—perhaps using a sort of Guild uniform—and thus the imagination of the audience can clothe the actors in their fitting garb as well as the stage with its fitting scene."[3]

Looking back to the history of theater, Thornton saw that in the great ages of drama there was the least scenery. "Aristophanes' 'The Clouds'—423 B.C. Two houses are represented on the stage, *inside* one of them we see two beds. Strepsiades is talking in his sleep about his race horses. A few minutes later he crosses the stage to Socrates' house, the Idea Factory, the 'Thinkery.' In the Spanish theatre Lope de Vega put a rug in the middle of the scene—it was a raft in midocean bearing a castaway. The Elizabethans, the Chinese used similar devices." The theater told lies; the theater used conventions—but only to present "the truth that dictated the story—the myth."[4]

The playwright's theme, however, must not be didactic. As Thornton knew, plays had been written as political propaganda, moral instruction, mass education. But he believed that the real function of theater must be to provide "the most immediate way in which a human being can share with another the sense of what it is to be a human being. . . . A dramatist is one who from his earliest years has found that sheer gazing at the shocks and countershocks among people is quite sufficiently engrossing without having to encase it in comment. It's a form of tact. It's a lack of presumption. That's why so many earnest people have been so exasperated by Shakespeare: they cannot isolate the passages wherein we hear him speaking in his own voice."[5]

The stage, for Thornton, was a place where the time was always "now." Whatever occurred on that stage was necessarily *"what is. . . .* We live in *what is,"* he said, "but we find a thousand ways not to face it. Great theater strengthens our faculty to face it."[6] In a novel, anecdotes that supposedly took place in the past are told by an omnipresent author. But in a play there is the strong vitality of the present. "A play visibly represents pure existing," he wrote, in language which is reminiscent of Gertrude Stein.

For Thornton, the theater presented an irresistible challenge:

> The gathered audience sits in a darkened room one end of which is lighted. The nature of the transaction at which it is gazing is a succession of events illustrating a general idea—the stirring of the idea; the gradual feeding out of information; the shock and countershock of circumstances; the flow of action; the interruption of action; the moments of allusion to earlier events; the preparation of surprise, dread, or delight—all that is the author's and his alone.[7]

Perhaps theater's greatest attraction for Thornton was its reliance on collaboration between the author, actors, and audience. "Painting, sculpture, and the literature of the book are certainly solitary experiences," he wrote; "and it is likely that most people would agree that the audience seated shoulder to shoulder in a concert hall is not an essential element in musical enjoyment." But for a play, he continued, there must be a crowd. Otherwise there could be no pretense, no excitement, no spirit of the festival. "Life imitated," he thought, "is life raised to a higher power."[8] There was in theater the element of rite and ceremony—of magic.

With such deep feelings about the nature of drama, it is no wonder that Thornton invested a great deal of emotion in the production of his first full-length play, *Our Town.* He had no doubt that it was great. He had no doubt, either, that it would in some ways revolutionize the theater. But he quickly became unhappy over the play's progress.

Harris's interpretation reduced his theme to a superficial story of Grovers Corners, where the milkman makes his morning rounds, teen-agers stop for sodas after school, and one Emily

Webb marries a certain George Gibbs, dies in childbirth, and returns in spirit to relive a day of her life on earth. The play came
across as moving, nostalgic, and unaffected; and though Thornton
wanted it to be moving, he intended it to be powerful and, in a
sense, shattering. He felt that his theme had been victimized by
his plot. And the plot, unfortunately, can be read simplistically.

In the archetypal town of Grovers Corners, a small, white New
England village like those pictured on calendars and Christmas
cards, live Dr. and Mrs. Gibbs; their children, George and Re-
becca; and Mr. and Mrs. Webb with their children, Wally and
Emily. "It's a very ordinary town, if you ask me," Mr. Webb, the
town's newspaper editor, comments. "Little better behaved than
most. Probably a lot duller." Emily, who wonders if she is pretty
enough to attract boyfriends, falls in love with George, and
George with Emily. They marry, she dies, but her spirit cannot
rest among those hovering above the church's graveyard. She asks
to have one last day on earth, her birthday, but still a day in
which nothing out of the ordinary occurred, to remember for eternity. What she discovers is the distance between human beings,
their lack of communication with one another, the hollowness of
most relationships. "Oh, earth, you're too wonderful for anybody
to realize you," she exclaims, reiterating a sentiment in Thornton's *Bridge* and *Woman of Andros*.

The play offers some homey thoughts and lines that might
come from a friendly preacher imparting his wisdom to his beloved congregation. "I don't care what they say with their mouths
—everybody knows that *something* is eternal. And it ain't houses
and it ain't names, and it ain't earth, and it ain't even the stars
. . . everybody knows in their bones that *something* is eternal, and
that something has to do with human beings," Thornton tells us.
That "something" sustains the townspeople and will continue to
sustain humanity for as long as it exists. "There are the stars—doing their old, old criss-cross journeys in the sky," the Stage Manager muses toward the end of the play. "Scholars haven't settled
the matter yet, but they seem to think there are no living beings
up there. They're just chalk . . . or fire. Only this one is straining
away, straining away all the time to make something of itself. The
strain's so bad that every sixteen hours everybody lies down and

gets a rest." And he urges the audience to go home and rest, too. Thornton watched as they left the theater, eyes red, cheeks stained with mascara.

But he was bothered because the audiences would have had to dig deeply to understand his real meaning. Certainly he meant to tell a tender story, certainly he meant to give a realistic picture of the village and villagers. But it was not just the life of that village he wanted to portray; instead, he wanted to show "the life of a village against the life of the stars." He wanted to juxtapose the Gibbses and the Webbs against the multitudes of all who will have lived. "The recurrent words in this play," he wrote, ". . . are 'hundreds,' 'thousands,' and 'millions.' Emily's joys and griefs, her algebra lessons and her birthday presents—what are they when we consider all the billions of girls who have lived, who are living, and who will live? Each individual's assertion to an absolute reality can only be inner, very inner. And here the method of staging finds its justification. . . . Our claim, our hope, our despair are in the mind—not in things, not in 'scenery.' Molière said that for the theatre all he needed was a platform and a passion or two. The climax of this play needs only five square feet of boarding and the passion to know what life means to us."[9]

Indeed, it was from the staging that sensitive viewers knew they were not seeing a simple drama. It was, Mary McCarthy wrote, "essentially lyric, not dramatic. The tragic velocity of life, the elusive nature of experience, which can never be stopped or even truly felt at any given point, are the themes of the play—themes familiar enough in lyric poetry, but never met, except incidentally, in drama. Mr. Wilder, in attempting to give these themes theatrical form, was obliged, paradoxically, to abandon almost all the conventions of the theatre. . . .

"Mr. Wilder's play is, in a sense, a refutation of its own thesis. *Our Town* is purely and simply an act of awareness, a demonstration of the fact that in a work of art at least, experience can be arrested, imprisoned, and preserved. The perspective of death . . . gives an extra poignancy and intensity to the small-town life whose essence he is trying so urgently to communicate. . . . The perspective is, to be sure, hazardous: it invites bathos and sententiousness. Yet Mr. Wilder has used it honorably. He forbids the spectator to dote on that town of the past."[10] While some in the audience might easily have become homesick and wonder if their response was lacking in sophistication, McCarthy was astute enough to realize Thornton's intent. "I remember," she commented, "how uneasy I felt when I decided that I liked Thornton Wilder's *Our Town*. Could this mean that there was something the matter with me? Was I starting to sell out?"[11]

Thornton believed that such a question would not have been possible if Harris had not made some serious errors in directing the play. First, though Thornton felt that most of the cast performed beautifully in their parts, he thought three characters were weakened because of miscasting. Frank Craven as the Stage Manager, Thomas Ross as Mr. Webb, and Arthur Allen as Professor Willard all lacked the strength necessary for their roles. They should have had a stoic New England manner about them; instead, they were too homey and soft. Moreover, he thought, Harris read the play as if it were a nostalgic period piece, and would sometimes drop lines to further that effect. Thornton, irritably sitting through rehearsals, would fight vainly for his lines to be put back. He wanted to see his play produced as he had intended it, he complained to Alexander Woollcott in late January.

Woollcott, who had seen the play grow from the germ of an idea into what he considered Thornton's finest work, was strong in his support, yet cautioned his friend not to overreact.

Stick to your guns. But not to the last ditch. After all, what matters most is that the play, as published, be the way you would have it. That is the form in which it will be read in years to come and from which, in years to come, revivals will be made.[12]

But apparently Thornton had already reacted too strongly. In Princeton, where the play opened on January 22 to excellent reviews, Harris was convinced that Thornton "detested" both the production and the director. "And his detestation reached such shrill heights on the opening night . . . that all further communication between us lapsed. The Author was not even remotely in my confidence while the show was in Boston."[13] And it was in Boston that the need for communication was most important.

The audience that came to the Wilbur Theatre on January 25, 1938, was less than warm about Thornton's venture. Playwright Marc Connelly was among the viewers and remembered that "Mrs. Alvan Fuller, the wife of Massachusetts' governor, had walked out during the performance. So had several others in the audience. The reviews of the play in the morning and afternoon newspapers were very discouraging."[14]

"It is generally not known," Jed Harris wrote, "that in the single week *Our Town* played in Boston before its opening in New York, it lost over ten thousand dollars. And for absolutely no better reason than [that] the critics in Boston were too stupid to appreciate what was being offered them."[15] The tepid reviews frightened New York theater owners, and Harris could find no one to book the play. "So I telephoned Gilbert Miller in Pittsburgh, where he was in the midst of a preliminary tour with a show starring Ina Claire. This was scheduled to open in two weeks at the Henry Miller Theatre, which, for the moment, was dark. What I proposed to Miller was that he should let me open *Our Town* at that theatre a week from Saturday night for a single performance."[16] Though Miller thought the idea was crazy, he consented to let Harris have the theater free for the single night. But Harris's difficulties were not over. On the afternoon of February 4, opening day, Harris was informed by the Stagehands Union that two extra men had to be added to the stage crew. He pointed out that, of the four already employed, only one had anything to do—and this was the house electrician who turned on and off the house lights. But the union official was adamant. "Your actors are moving furniture on the stage," he told Harris. "That's against our regulations. Only our men can move stage props." Harris tried to explain the roles of the Stage Manager and Assistant Stage Manager, but his adversary was stubborn. Finally, an hour before opening, the company manager succeeded in convincing the man to allow the play to proceed as written. Though two stagehands began to set out the furniture, and were removed only by the use of "a little force," it seemed as if the production would continue without mishap.

Frank Craven, in his role as Stage Manager, began speaking his lines; but Evelyn Varden, who was to play Mrs. Gibbs, suddenly collapsed in her dressing room. Her understudy prepared to go on, and a physician was called to attend to Varden. She was revived, but was so upset that she doubted she could perform. When Harris suggested that the opening be postponed, however, she rallied. "In a matter of minutes," Harris remembered, "Miss Varden's cue to go on would be heard. I had her on her feet near the entrance to the stage. She was leaning on me with all her weight. Her eyes were closed and she drew her breath at long even intervals, like a person in a deep, drugged sleep. Just before her cue came to go on, she opened her eyes and looked at me ruefully, then I gave her a gentle push and she walked briskly on the stage crying, 'Children! Children!' in her wonderfully clear stage voice. . . ."[17]

But the cast was doubtful that their performance would receive a better welcome in New York than it had in Boston. "Backstage," recalled Marc Connelly, who had been invited to the opening by Jed Harris, "the cast was dejected, convinced that Our Town would expire after three more performances. Nevertheless the spirited playing of the first act was in the best tradition of the theater." Judging from the comments he heard during intermission, even Connelly was not sure that New York sophisticates understood the play. "The plot jumped in every direction and went back and forth in time every which way," he heard members of the audience comment. "What little story it had to tell was forever being interrupted by Craven's coming out and talking to the audience. And except for a couple of grape arbors and some chairs and stepladders brought on after the play started, there was nothing to see except the theater's steam pipes on the back wall of the stage. They said that the critics had certainly been right in panning it [in Boston]." After the performance, Connelly was invited to join Thornton and Jed Harris in Harris's hotel suite. "Thornton was as exhausted as Jed," Connelly said. "When we began to talk about the play Thornton was unable to respond to my enthusiasm. 'I'm sorry, but my brain won't function after eleven.' As he left, Jed bade him good night with a caustic, 'All right, go to bed, you god-damned schoolteacher.' . . ."[18]

But whatever problems may have been encountered in finally bringing Our Town to New York, the reviews the next morning made it all worthwhile. Brooks Atkinson, in the New York *Times*, called it "a beautifully evocative play." Wilder, he wrote, "has transmuted the simple events of human life into universal reverie. He has given familiar facts a deeply moving, philosophical perspective. . . . 'Our Town' has escaped from the formal barrier of the modern theatre into the quintessence of acting, thought and speculation." The play was "one of the finest achievements of the current stage," and Wilder, who had won his fame as a writer of fiction, must now be considered an eminent dramatist. Atkinson was struck, especially, by the unique atmosphere that Thornton created. ". . . By stripping the play of everything that is not essential, Mr. Wilder has given it a profound, strange, unworldly significance. This is less the portrait of a town than the sublimation of the commonplace; and in contrast with the universe that silently swims around it, it is brimming over with compassion."[19]

Edith Isaacs, whose review appeared later in *Theatre Arts*, welcomed Thornton "to the thin ranks of our serious playwrights. . . ." He wrote, she said, "with the gift of humor, of simplicity, of moderation added to his recognized talent for story-telling and characterization." Thornton, she continued, "appears to search no deeper into character or motive than a man strolling down Main Street," yet he managed to create a story "that runs like a bright thread across the pattern of village life."[20]

But Thornton's former supporter Stark Young had reservations about the play's merits. "The prevailing tone of it is essentially literary," he thought, though he admitted that the scene where the dead sit on their graves waiting for Emily provided "a stage image that is unforgettable." The play as a whole was "a kind of factual reverie" of small-town life, but without "the bite, the unpredictable, the deep glimpse, the divine insight and the wayward taste" of Sherwood Anderson's *Winesburg, Ohio*. "All the assumption of homely effect is not so much a thing itself, the actual life and town, as something we see arise from dreams of it."[21]

Nevertheless, the play received accolades from important reviewers like John Mason Brown, who wrote that he surrendered "especially during the first act, to the spell of the beautiful and infinitely tender play. . . . Mr. Wilder's play is laid in no imaginary place," he concluded. "It becomes reality in the human heart."[22] The reviews were so positive that Harris had no trouble finding another theater—the Morosco—in which to continue the play's Broadway run. But the weekly receipts were, he reported, "on a very mediocre level." ". . . The show actually had more losing weeks than profitable weeks during its entire New York engagement. In mid-June, when the play had been running four months, it was losing on an average of five hundred dollars a week and it was necessary to ask the cast to take a cut in salary in order to stay open at all." The play did not offer the attractions of other Broadway shows: it lacked scenery, which some thought was a way of saving money; it was not a tuneful musical; it was thought to be somewhat morose—at least according to one notable viewer. Eleanor Roosevelt saw *Our Town* and said it had "moved her and depressed her beyond words. 'Our Town' . . . is . . . interesting and . . . original and I am glad I saw it, but I did not have a pleasant evening," she reported.[23]

And two others, of more concern to Thornton than Mrs. Roosevelt also did not enjoy the play: Thornton's mother and his sister Isabel. "You see," he explained, " 'Our Town' inevitably means our family, too. I remember my sister asking, 'Mother, am I pretty?' and when my folks sit there and see themselves say that very thing in the show, they find it harrowing."[24]

There were many, however, who did have a pleasant evening because they thought the play distinctive and important. And there was a period of four weeks in May when profits soared. The boom occurred after it was announced on May 2 that Thornton Wilder had won his second Pulitzer Prize "for the original American play, performed in New York, which shall represent in marked fashion the educational value and power of the stage, preferably dealing with American life." Thornton was awarded $1,000 and public sanction of his talent as a playwright.

Even before the announcement of the prize, Thornton had already left the scene and was deep at work on his next play, *The Merchant of Yonkers*, which Max Reinhardt was soon to direct. He was satisfied with Acts I and II, but needed still to polish the third and fourth acts. He could not concentrate in the East, where his fame had peaked; instead, he left for Tucson, Arizona, in April, not returning until May 8, 1938, with a nearly completed version of *The Merchant* in his hands.

During the summer he took a short and happy respite from writing—to act. Thornton had often said that a playwright should know the theater from all sides and advised newcomers to pitch in making scenery, working as stagehands, and acting in stock companies. Now he would have his chance to act professionally, many years after his amateur performances at Berkeley High School and Oberlin. He threatened that he was going to ask Jed Harris for a salary of $300 a week, which he would then turn over to the Actors' Fund. Though he was not entirely confident of his talents, he was sure of his interpretation of his own material; and his part was well suited: he would replace Frank Craven as the Stage Manager.

For Thornton, the experience was great fun. Again and again throughout his career he took opportunities to appear in touring companies and summer stock groups in one or another of his plays. He was affectionate and enthusiastic with the cast, and often gave a moving performance.

In July he took a brief trip again out West, this time accompanied by Isabel. His destination was Taos, where Mabel Luhan awaited him with stories and gossip. His letters to Alexander Woollcott were blithe and carefree until September 1938, when pressures began to weigh upon him. First, his sister Isabel was about to undergo a serious operation, and he was worried. Then, with Reinhardt arriving in one month, he still had to write a final speech in *The Merchant* and compose a few songs. Besides that, his house in New Haven had been badly hit by a hurricane; and to make matters worse, he had to break the news of Isabel's illness and damage to the house to his mother, who was returning from a trip to Scotland. Even his election to the American Academy of Arts and Letters, which placed him in the ranks of fifty eminent scholars, offered only brief cheer. He was too distracted to write, though he had recently begun another play, *The Alcestiad*, in October.

Professional pressures, too, were weighing on him. The character of Dolly Levi in *The Merchant of Yonkers* had been written with a specific actress in mind: Ruth Gordon. Mrs. Levi's gestures, her zany, lovable character, the sentiments she espoused on life and love, all awaited, in Thornton's vision, the comic genius of Ruth Gordon. But Gordon, who was then living with Jed Harris, found it awkward to work in a play directed by Reinhardt, especially when the rift between Harris and Thornton had never been healed. At first Thornton suggested Laurette Taylor for the part and asked Woollcott's advice on the matter. Finally he compromised on Jane Cowl, convinced that she would be able to play the role with verve and style. He was very pleased with Nydia Westman and June Walker in their roles, and with Joe Sweeney as Melchior.

Watching the rehearsals, however, was often painful, and Thornton promised himself that for his next play he would run away to the South Pacific. He was required to write a number of transitional passages, and he suffered with Reinhardt at the stubbornness of Jane Cowl. Cowl refused to take direction for the first weeks, and the disheartened author and director watched as she became more and more stilted in her part. Finally even she realized what was happening and, toward the end of November, begged Reinhardt to show her how to save the role

Thornton had no doubt about Reinhardt's talents, and in general his mood was buoyant as the play approached its opening. He thought the direction aptly fitted the play. The comedy was hilarious and the cast superb. Everyone loved Reinhardt, and everyone had great hopes for the play's success. On December 12, 1938, their hopes were dashed.

# THIRTEEN

———————◆———————

ON December 18 Alexander Woollcott arrived in Boston to help "the sorely beset Wilder get tight at the Copley-Plaza. The new Academician . . . —he has just succeeded to the chair left vacant by the belated death of Owen Wister, and all I have to say is, 'What is this country coming to?'—the new Academician is having trouble with the Boston try-out of his new play, a fine old-style farce rendered depressing to my notion by a humorless performance. So I was busy comforting him with strong drink. . . ."[1] The trouble at the Colonial Theatre began when the audience found the play ridiculously childlike. Reinhardt's direction, contrary to Thornton's pre-opening opinion, was seen as plodding and unsuited to what should have been a light farce. From the twelfth to the twenty-seventh, Thornton was fully occupied with making changes in the script with the hope of saving the play when it opened in New York on the twenty-eighth. Woollcott reported his progress to Gertrude Stein on Christmas Day.

The ineffable Wilder has just gone through what would be to a more normally constituted person the harrowing experience of hav-

ing had his second play turned into a good deal of a bore by unfortunate casting and heavy handed direction. He thought he was writing an adaptation from the Viennese but all unbeknownst to
himself his good American ancestry took possession of him and
what he really wrote was a pure Charles Hoyt farce of the 1885 vin-
tage. If this had been given to any American stock company prior
to 1900, it would have presented no problem and they would have
put it on the following Monday with great success. Under Reinhardt's hand it all went faintly Launcelot Gobbo. Or so it seemed
to me when I watched the try-out in Boston last week. Now it will
come to New York and I suspect be trampled upon. If all this
bounces off Wilder like a rubber ball thrown at Gibraltar, it is because his thoughts are really engrossed in Play Number Three and
he hardly notices what they are doing to him.[2]

Woollcott's prediction about the New York reception of the
play was correct. Rosamond Gilder, writing in *Theatre Arts*, said
that Thornton had "amused himself by ornamenting it [Nestroy's
play] with every farcical gadget in the storehouse: coincidence
and mistaken identity, screen scenes and closet scenes, overheard
conversation and confidential soliloquies, match-making and elope-
ments. Everything, in fact, except the bubbling comic impulse
which originally set these mechanisms in motion." The actors, furthermore, were not up to what was required of them. Jane Cowl's
gestures and costumes "ornamented if they did not explain the
role of Mrs. Levi."[3]

George Jean Nathan was even more caustic. "The production
of Thornton Wilder's *The Merchant of Yonkers* is apparently
predicated on the theory that outmoded situations and jests,
which in 1939 costumes and stage decor would promptly put an
audience to sleep, immediately become acceptably hilarious if
offered in those of 1880. Derived from a farce written . . . about a
hundred years ago and one that in the meantime had already been
paraphrased at least a hundred times, the current edition presents
the usual depressing spectacle which results from the sentimental
theatrical presumption that all you need do to convert a tiresome
old joke into a rip-roaring one is frankly and a bit wistfully to
admit it is a tiresome old joke."[4] After twenty-eight performances
at the Guild Theatre, *The Merchant of Yonkers* closed.

But for Thornton the plot was not hackneyed and the theme was not trite. He rightly saw that the failure of the play lay more in the direction and the miscasting of Jane Cowl as Mrs. Levi than in anything he had written. Max Reinhardt had turned Thornton's parody of turn-of-the-century companies into bela-bored European comedy. Jane Cowl was too haughty and glamor-ous for the disheveled and raunchy Mrs. Levi. Though the criti-cisms did not quite bounce off Thornton "like a rubber ball," as Woollcott had described, they did not hurt him as much as they might have if he did not fully believe in what he had written. No one seemed to understand, really, what the play was "about," and he took it upon himself to explain: "My play is about the aspira-tions of the young (and not only of the young) for a fuller, freer participation in life."[5] And it contained lines that only Thornton Wilder could have written.

The character of Mrs. Levi, which dominates the play, reflects much of Thornton's own personality. Mrs. Levi has a "large, shrewd but generous nature, an assumption of worldly cynicism" that hides her real amusement at life. She is a good-natured meddler, as befits her profession—or one of her professions—as matchmaker. Everyday life, she tells the artist Ambrose Kemper, is not interesting enough for her, so she frankly meddles, acts as an agent in other people's affairs. She observes, she contrives: she makes life more amusing. Her monologue in the last act is noth-ing less than one of Thornton's amiable sermons. Each person, she tells the audience, has within him the potential for great cru-elty. Each is, in his own way, a fool. But one must decide, at some time in his life, whether to live among the other fools and affirm the human race—or to live alone and condemn it. "As for me," she announces, "I've decided to live among them." She continues:

If you accept human beings and are willing to live among them, you acknowlege that every man has a right to his own mistakes.

Yes, we're all fools and we're all in danger of destroying the world with our folly; but the one way to keep us from harm is to fill our lives with the six or seven human pleasures which are our right in the world; and that takes a little money, not much but a little; and a little freedom, not much, but a little. . . .

Oh, my friends,—fellow-fools, fellow-monsters,—I want to live in a world where there is just enough money for us to enjoy ourselves in moderation, and just enough freedom for us to play the fool in moderation.

Along with the gregarious Mrs. Levi, Thornton created a minor character, Melchior, whose cynicism is charming. "Everybody's always talking about people breaking into houses, ma'am," he comments; "but there are more people in the world who want to break out of houses, that's what I always say." And contrasted with both is the stolid Vandergelder, who pronounces, ". . . Most of the people in the world are fools. The law is there to prevent crime; we men of sense are there to prevent foolishness."

Though Thornton was never reluctant to scrap a poor work, he knew that *The Merchant of Yonkers* could be saved. It needed a second chance and someday, he hoped, that chance would come. Meanwhile, Thornton himself needed a vacation.

At the end of January 1939 he was on board the S.S. *Siboney* approaching Veracruz, Mexico. Mexico was extremely picturesque, he wrote to friends. He visited Popocatépetl, saw the Aztec ruins and the Orozco frescoes, walked in Cuernavaca and Taxco. A fine description of the Mexican spirit had been written, he thought, by D. H. Lawrence in his beginning of *The Plumed Serpent*. But it was Thornton's perception of that very spirit combined with his feelings about the country's history that caused him to flee a short time after he arrived. Mexico, he decided, was a place he detested.

He could not sleep because of the altitude; he developed a bad cold from the ever-present dust; he could barely digest the food. But most of all, he could not work in a place where oppression was felt everywhere. He could not detach himself from the plight of the Indians, whose poverty and maltreatment sickened him. His own work seemed suddenly irrelevant. All around him he could see nothing but scenes from a bloody past.

In the middle of February he was back in the United States, in Corpus Christi, Texas, where he taught himself to read Spanish fluently and, for a bit of diversion, tried his luck at a local gambling place. He was known there as "Doc," and found that he was often a winner at dice—no doubt because of his Scottish ancestry, he thought. After his depression in Mexico, he was much relieved to be back in America. Even bad news about *Our Town* did not really upset him. Jed Harris, convinced that the play was not earning enough money to make it worthwhile continuing its tour, suddenly decided to close it. Thornton felt that Harris's move was partly directed at him, but his reaction was not one of animosity. He had other preoccupations: writing new works, reading books he always meant to read; and he refused to become involved in petty squabbles.

Writing, and the freedom it afforded him, was to be his permanent way of life, he decided. When Princeton University offered him a teaching position, he refused it; and by June he was off again—this time to Europe.

He visited first with Gertrude and Alice in Bilignin, where the days were so pleasant that he wished, he wrote to them later, to relive each one. Back in Paris, he went on a moderate shopping spree to buy clothing for his stay at the Manor House, in Mells, with Sibyl Colefax. He did not want to appear overdressed, he said, but rather as if he were used to fine things.

He reported to Gertrude about his weekend in Somersetshire, which he thought Henry James would have adored. The talk ebbed and flowed in an understated politeness. True feelings were deeply hidden beneath a shell of custom and manners. But all through the visit he could do nothing but think about the suffering that England had borne during the last world war. He would look out to the garden and imagine nothing else except the thousands of young men who died. "If they could read my thoughts," he wrote to Gertrude, ". . . wouldn't they be surprised to read in capital letters: You lived through the War."

On the day he left the Manor House, he was overtaken by a strong but not easily explained feeling, which he tried to describe to Gertrude:

That Sunday I fell in love with everybody in the house. . . . That strange phenomenon LOVE that pops up in the strangest places, that hurdles the most obstinate barriers, that refuses the most pressing invitations; there it was. It popped up again yesterday, too, at

Max Beerbohm's. And Sunday night at dusk there it was, as for a few minutes our car stopped in the roadway before Stonehenge. And here it is, as usual, on my shoulder as I write to you. I pass to him the pen and we both sign this letter.[6]

Before he returned home in mid-July, he had spent another hour with Freud, had dined with Jean Cocteau, and had visited with Louis Jouvet. Most important, he discovered a new book, one that fascinated and soon obsessed him: James Joyce's *Finnegans Wake*.

Returning to the States on the *Ile de France*, Thornton made a delightful new friend, the playwright Samuel N. Behrman. Behrman was equally charmed with the Pulitzer Prize winner, who described himself as "a schoolteacher who writes," and was impressed with his knowledge of theater—not only American, but French and Spanish, too. Yet Thornton was always unpretentious and eager to listen to his companions. "I have never known anyone," Behrman wrote, "whose feeling is so precise for the exact stance of whomever he happens to be talking to. Whatever the subject under discussion, he allows the other person full expression for his particular views, then expresses his own beliefs with absolute clarity without crushing his opponent's toes. . . . When he talks about something that interests him, his voice is intense, his words tumble over each other and he underlines his points with emphatic gestures."[7]

Soon after he returned, he began negotiations with Sol Lesser for the filming of *Our Town*. He met with Lesser in New York in September before visiting Woollcott. By the time he returned at the beginning of October, Lesser had already begun collaborating with Frank Craven on the screenplay. Lesser was co-operative about incorporating Thornton's wishes into the filming of his play, and Thornton did have definite opinions about film. He said that he hoped "some day . . . to have gained my own confidence and a company's confidence sufficiently to suddenly compose a motion picture that is a motion picture from the first moment on."[8] But he realized, too, that though *Our Town* was his play, it would be Lesser's film. As he explained to Lesser, he thought his own opinion "should often give way before that of those who know moving-pictures thoroughly."[9] But Lesser wanted Thornton's approval of changes, such as dating the story from 1919–1923. Thornton agreed that the change would take the setting out of the "horse-and-buggy pre-automobile days which may have been a part of the much-discussed 'nostalgia' which people found in the play."[10] Lesser, however, eventually decided to retain the play's original dates, which set the story beginning in 1901. Thornton was worried over the wedding scene because Lesser planned to film it realistically. ". . . Your wedding scene won't be interesting enough, and . . . it will reduce many of the surrounding scenes to ordinary-ness," he objected. Wedding scenes were usually interrupted or "showed the bride hating the groom . . . or some other irregularity." On stage his scene worked, he wrote to Lesser, because of the lack of scenery, the use of the Stage Manager as the minister, the second thoughts of the bride and groom. "You have none of these. . . . Here is a village wedding and the inevitable let-down when it all runs through *as expected.*" He cautioned Lesser that the play succeeded for its "new bold effect in presentation methods," which he might do well to translate on the screen.

Eventually Thornton agreed to rewrite the wedding scene, having each character's thought revealed to the audience.[11] He was happier, but not completely satisfied, with the results. "My demurring is just between you and me, Sol," he wrote, "not as to whether it's a good treatment and a faithful transcription—that it already is—but whether for your joy as well as mine, it is a movie that beats other movies—and which the public and the critics will receive as a deep movie experience. For that I feel that there is still some more work to be done."[12]

Lesser agreed, and the work to be done involved a major change in plot. He thought that the character of Emily Webb must be substantially changed, that her marriage to George Gibbs must be sensed differently by the audience, and that her return after her death to relive her twelfth birthday should be, instead, a return to her fifth wedding anniversary. Emily, whom Thornton portrayed as a typical village girl with just a touch more strength and intelligence, would now become a woman much brighter than her husband, who unknowingly tries to dominate him and make his deci-

sions. She would sometimes be impatient with George and fail to
appreciate his fine qualities. When she returns to earth, she is
shocked at her insensitivity and is overcome by an enormous desire to live. Lesser thought the changes, drastic as they were,
"would give the picture more appeal for the forty millions," and
not basically change Thornton's philosophical intent.

But Thornton was, at last, upset. "I feel pretty concrete about
trying to dissuade you against showing Emily returning to her
fifth wedding anniversary and regretting that she had been an un-
wise wife," he wrote. He had purposely laid a foundation for her
return to her twelfth birthday, he told Lesser, and all that effect
would be lost. Also, he did not want to see Emily turned into a
"school-marm" or anything but the simple girl he intended her to
be. "The balance of the play reposing between vast stretches of
time and suggestions of generalized multitudes of people requires
that the fathers and mothers, and especially the hero and heroine,
be pretty near the norm of everybody, every boy and every girl."[13]

Lesser was not the least irritated by Thornton's disapproval. On
December 4, 1939, he cabled Isabel asking what sort of car Thornton might like for Christmas. Isabel's reply was that her brother
didn't know how to drive—but still, he always said he would pre-
fer a Chrysler convertible with a rumble seat. On Christmas Day,
Thornton was, apparently, surprised by the sumptuous gift. He
and his sisters, who joined his mother in New Haven for the holi-
days, were delighted by all the gadgets, dials, and lights "and a
top that goes up and down without anybody losing their temper."
He was "astonished," he wrote to Lesser, and sent "a thousand
thanks."[14]

Sometimes Lesser's questions about *Our Town* were concerned
with minute details. For example, Thornton had described the
gravestones of Civil War soldiers as having flags on them. But his
description was vague, and even Thornton could not recall
whether he had actually seen such stones or merely imagined
them. He went to the churchyard of Grace Church in Manhattan,
but could find nothing appropriate. Finally he wrote to a New
Englander he knew, a fellow writer from MacDowell, asking for
help. Fortunately the woman could find a stone, copy its design,
and send it on to Thornton.[15]

Since he had been completely unconcerned with projecting an exact replica of a small New England town, Thornton's details sometimes lacked veracity. He often wondered, he said, why no one noticed that Mrs. Gibbs and Mrs. Webb are blithely stringing just-picked beans in May.

By early January much of the script had been finalized. Lesser's only question to Thornton was whether or not each person's self-preoccupation should be made more obvious "to the forty million. . . ." He suggested that perhaps when the milkman is seen delivering milk, the Stage Manager might comment, "Howie, you know, does one of those services that we just naturally take for granted." Thornton was not too enthusiastic about that particular suggestion, but did understand Lesser's concern. "I should suggest that the idea is not so much suggested by the service a Milkman renders—the American Mind assumes that what you get money for cannot be classified as benevolence—but by some picture of a person's not noticing another's need or claim or call. (Chekhov's plays are always exhibiting this: Nobody hears what anybody else says. Everybody walks in a self-centred dream.) Children perpetually feel it as a rebuff:

" 'Mama, mama, look what I found—isn't it *wonderful?*'

" 'Yes, dear, now go and wash your hands.' "[16]

Shooting was supposed to have been completed by the end of February, but at the end of March, Lesser again wrote to Thornton—this time because he thought he was in "a jam." He had to decide whether or not to let Emily live. "There are two schools of thought here, as naturally there would be. But I find myself bouncing from one side to the other. . . ." If Emily lived, the film would differ substantially from the original play, Lesser admitted. "Those who are purists and who loved the play will be outraged, but to those countless others, like myself, who have during the running of the picture come to love Emily as well as the other characters, it is a most satisfactory and logical conclusion." Surprisingly, Thornton agreed. In a film, he thought, the relationship between the characters and the viewers changed from what they were on stage. Those relationships became more concrete; Emily was more real; and her death would seem "disproportionately cruel. . . ."[17]

The last decision was made, and the filming was completed. Sol Lesser was sure he had made a successful film, and when it opened in Boston on May 24, 1940, with Martha Scott and Frank Craven re-creating their Broadway roles of Emily and the Stage Manager, he was proved correct. The opening was a gala event at which Lesser and Frank Craven spoke, along with composer Aaron Copland, who wrote the score for the film, and Mrs. Edward MacDowell, at whose Peterborough estate Thornton did so much of his work. Even the governor of Massachusetts, Francis P. Murphy, attended; and unlike a previous governor's wife, he stayed. Thornton came, too, at Lesser's request, after having spent a vacation in the South.

In the preceding months his life had included more than corresponding with Lesser about the film. He had moved to Manhattan in November 1939, renting an apartment at 81 Irving Place. "I like it ever so much," he told an interviewer. "I roam around a lot. I rise early and take the Staten Island ferry. Long hikes are a life-time hobby with me. I like to take the subway to the Heights and walk on Riverside Drive as dawn comes up. In fact, I hope to be a New Yorker." But he did not see himself becoming involved in the literary or publishing circles in the city. "One of the problems of the writer is keeping the moments of writing free of any consideration other than the act itself—free of speculation about audience approval or disapproval, free of consideration as to monetary rewards, free of the image of critics or friends. Living in a community of fellow writers, one inevitably becomes aware in some corner of one's mind [of] a lot of pressures of self-consciousness that are extraneous."[18] A community of writers, drawing upon one another's suggestions and art, could be successful in a great age—"the Elizabethan taverns, for instance"—but otherwise could serve only as a distraction.

Even if he had wanted to immerse himself in literary New York, he was hardly there long enough to do so. A month after he moved, he took a brief vacation in Atlantic City, staying at the Claridge Hotel and working on a great new interest: annotating *Finnegans Wake*. And by early March 1940 he had given up his apartment and returned to the family home in New Haven. A few weeks later, he began taking driving lessons, with the plan to travel across country to the Southwest, stay for several months, and return East by the end of June.

Instead, he went South. In the middle of April he, his mother, and Isabel drove to Williamsburg, Virginia, stopping off in Washington, D.C., and Charlottesville. He drove on to Savannah and St. Augustine, until he arrived in Winter Park, Florida. He enjoyed Florida with its endless souvenir shops and gas stations, its stuffed alligators and live snakes. When he returned he went North, spending more than a month at the MacDowell Colony. He was assigned the room that E. A. Robinson once used, to Thornton a great honor. But it was more than the room that gave him his inspiration for his next play: it was the war. Though he had always professed a belief in the endurance of the human race, he could not turn away from the real urgency of the world at war. His role as an artist seemed more important than ever, and his new work more meaningful than any he had ever written.

"In the slow education of the human race to living side by side with one another in understanding and peace there are two forces," he had said not long before. "The force of those that are endowed for a practical, immediate activity in the correction of injustices. And the force of those who feel the only thing they can do is to compose as best they can works which, through the attempt to present illustrations of harmony and of law, are affirmations about mankind and his ends.

"The race needs both the practical worker and the believer that the ends are valid." George Bernard Shaw, he said, was an example of "the practical pamphleteer." But his was not the only way to influence humanity. "The great poet describing an apparently impersonal suffering is saying something about the dignity of man which ultimately finds its way into legislation and into concrete humanitarian work. A poet is a triumph of common sense, but on a time scale of centuries. A pamphleteer works in decades."[19]

His new play would, in style, depart even further from convention than had *Our Town*. And in theme, it would deal with his own world—a world in turmoil and great difficulty—understood in the light of the history of the human race. He no longer felt it necessary to draw only upon the drama of the past. "For years I shrank from describing the modern world . . . ," he explained. "I was alarmed at finding a way of casting into generalization the world of doorbells and telephones. And now, though many of the subjects will often be of the past, I like to feel that I accept the twentieth century, not only as a fascinating age to live in, but as assimilable stuff to think with."[20]

He left MacDowell with the first act completed and returned to New Haven for a few months of intensive work. In October and November he brought his manuscript to Quebec, a city he thought gracious and lovely. In an interview he repeated his feelings about the integration into his own writing of an artist's sensibilities about the war. "So vast is the struggle and so vivid is its relationship to us all, that, for the present, one would scarcely venture to make any episode or phase of the war the subject of a novel or play," he said. "One's narrative would sound hollow under the shadow of these realities. . . . However, there are a great many ways whereby, indirectly or by allusion, one reaches that part of the mind which is never free from hopes and thoughts in this great struggle." Of his own new play, he said little, except to describe it as "a strange mixture of laughter and sadness."[21] It was not to be his only war effort; but it was to be the most controversial, most startling, and most daring work he ever produced. And he would call it, he decided, *In the Nick of Time*.[22]

# FOURTEEN

———————◆———————

IN October 1940 Thornton took a short trip to Madison, Wisconsin, to deliver a lecture on "Religion and Literature" at the First Congregational Church. Madison's favorite son had an attentive audience. When he spoke about the current crisis, he admitted that the question might arise: "But why is it worthwhile to talk . . . of poetry and literature in a world of such distress to our fellowman?" He explained that he hoped his talk might inspire one or two in the audience to "have a vision. Two hundred years from now, your one or two will have grown into larger groups. In 500 years, the message of the vision will become commonplace, and enacted into law. Eight hundred years hence it will be the tacit assumption of the man on the street."[1]

In the same way, his new play might inspire a vision, but it would not be he alone who spurred the inspiration. His play was deeply indebted to the writing of James Joyce, and especially to *Finnegans Wake*. One reporter who interviewed him in Madison noticed that he carried a copy of the book "with more words of marginal notes than appear in the text."[2] His letters to some friends carry an ongoing commentary on his progress in decipher-

ing the puns and decoding Joyce's abstruse language. Some, like
Edmund Wilson, disagreed with certain of his views. ". . . I
think you're exaggerating the importance of the anal element—
which has always been present in Joyce (Bloom's preoccupation
with Molly Bloom's rear)," Wilson wrote to Thornton. "Don't
you think, after all, that he means to present it as merely mixed
up with all the other elements of the human situation?" He cautioned Thornton against too narrow an interpretation of Joyce's
use of the alphabet and said that for himself "the central thing in
*Finnegans Wake* is the family situation. . . . This is really . . .
the thing that ought to be fully worked out."[3]

Thornton believed that Joyce had used the technique of the
inner monologue with far greater success than had Proust. And the
depth of Joyce's understanding of history and myth was, to
Wilder, astounding. "Those who have deciphered even a small
part of the work have glimpsed the grandeur of the plan: the
sleeper reliving the history of mankind and identifying himself
with the heroes and sinners of the world's myth literature; his
thoughts influenced by the stars that pass over his head and
couched in a language which reproduces the talking-on-two-levels
characteristic of sleep; a language in which all the tongues of the
world have coalesced into a pâte . . . ; the sleep wrestling all
night with the problem of original sin, with the sense of guilt
acquired from offenses which his waking self knows nothing of.
Towards dawn, his enemies mastered, identifying himself with
Finn, the ancient Irish hero, he awakes to a new·day in the eternal cyclic revolutions of lives and civilizations. Finn! Again
wake!"[4]

Joyce's "confessional," Thornton felt, incorporated the most sophisticated psychological sensibilities and beautifully translated
the work of Freud and Jung into fiction. Like all great writers,
Joyce knew that in dream symbols were the revelations of the subconscious. And to reveal the extent to which everyone is archetypal, he drew upon himself, his own responses and his own subconscious. "It is a wonderful experience to unburden the heart in
confession," Thornton knew, "but it is a very difficult thing to do.
The subject longs to tell his charged secret and longs not to tell
it."[5] Even if Thornton had wanted to write his own "confes-

sional," he knew he could not. His sense of privacy would inhibit him; he had been brought up to believe that one's innermost feelings were not to be publicly aired. And, in truth, he thought that although it was courageous, it was not really necessary to dissect one's own personality in order to create a believable Everyman. Modern writers had long been facing the problem of the validity of an individual's experience. Each individual's "existential thing," his emotions, is at the same time real and absurd. Within the boundaries of one's existence, those emotions swell in importance. But in historical time, they diminish to insignificance. "It is absurd to claim that 'I,' in the vast reaches of time and place and repetition, is worth an assertion."[6] He believed that readers, too, had lost interest in anecdotes or in an examination of one particular individual. Instead, there was renewed interest "in the great types."

Joyce went about his writing as if he were an archaeologist, much as Thornton had done since his days in Rome. Twentieth-century writers, said Thornton, were aware, as writers had never been before, of the multiplicity of lives. The printing press, he thought, and its resulting mass media had caused a change in perspective. And juxtaposing the individual against billions of others changed the writer's consciousness. "We are less interested in the anecdote, in the 'plot.' . . . As Gertrude Stein said, 'If you read any of the four greatest novels of the twentieth century for *what happens next*, you might as well throw the book away at the beginning. . . .'" For Stein, those four books were Proust's *Remembrance of Things Past*, Joyce's *Ulysses*, Thomas Mann's *The Magic Mountain*, and of course her own *The Making of Americans*.[7]

There was another quality besides the universality evident in Joyce that Thornton greatly admired: a comic spirit. In a world where misery and destruction seemed so prevalent, where each individual often felt hopeless and despondent, the comic spirit offered some relief. Beneath the comic veneer of *Don Quixote* or *The Misanthrope* was "agonizing material," Thornton wrote. "The comic spirit has saved them from the precipices over which they hang: defeat and despair."[8] His own new play certainly stemmed from his personal despondence over the war. It had been

written, he said, "under strong emotion." He had hoped to finish
the play by the end of February 1941, when he was scheduled to
represent the United States on a State Department tour of Colombia, Ecuador, and Peru. On January 13 he left New Haven for
Alexandria, Virginia, where he was intent on doing nothing but
writing. But, instead, he found himself interrupted by trying to
learn Spanish well enough to converse fluently with the various
writers and artists he was about to meet.

The war intruded into his thoughts in ways other than the
theme of his new play. He donated manuscripts for auctions to
raise funds for the war effort in Europe. It was not the first time
he had allowed his own papers to be used for political purposes.
During the Spanish Civil War the final draft of *Heaven's My
Destination* was sent to help those fighting for the republic in
Spain.[9]

His departure date, set for February 28, seemed once threatened
to be postponed when visa and ticket complications sent him back
to New York. But at noon on the planned date he sailed for Bar-
ranquilla, Colombia, to be a "good-will ambassador" of his country. On shipboard he found congenial companionship in Sherwood Anderson and his wife, Eleanor. Unfortunately Anderson
took ill, much to Thornton's concern. He sent a note to Eleanor,
recommending several physicians in Colombia and the Herrick Institute in Panama, should a doctor be needed; and he urged her to
take advantage of his friendship for any service he could perform.[10]

His trip was described by the State Department as "a distinct
success." In Colombia the film of *Our Town* was shown to an appreciative audience and was preceded by Thornton's talk "about
his novels and dramas and other literary subjects." When he
learned that there was to be a national competition for a prize
play, he contributed to the award, a gesture "which received most
enthusiastic comment from the local press." Thornton was equally
enthusiastic about his trip—the places he saw and the fellow
writers he met. Finally, thirteen years after the publication of *The
Bridge*, he found himself visiting Peru.

But a more satisfying and important trip took place in the early
fall. He was invited to a conference of the International Committee of PEN and would be able to witness the war firsthand, since

the conference was taking place in London. He left on September 6, 1941, and hoped, in the month he would spend abroad, to be permitted to go to France and visit his friends Gertrude Stein and Alice Toklas.

Thornton truly admired the English spirit, a "guarded equanimity," as he called it in an article, "After a Visit to England." Their spirit, though, did not come from naïveté about the country's true position in the war, nor from a deeply imbued "stiff-upper-lip" attitude. "It arises from a deep consternation, on the one hand, and from a sense of communal responsibility, on the other." After France fell to the Germans, it became clear to the British that their own position was very weak. But instead of becoming angry or panic-stricken, they retained a calmness and strength that Thornton sometimes found amazing. He was impressed with each person's unstated "sense of responsibility for the mental temper of his neighbor."

Often he was asked if the destruction he saw—the bombed neighborhoods and the smoldering buildings—was more or less than he had expected. He found the question difficult to answer. If he said less, the questioner might be offended: he knew, after all, that he had suffered greatly. But if he answered more, the questioner became worried: perhaps he was being naïve in showing any hope or spirit at all. Thornton was often asked, too, "Isn't it like Pompeii?" and he knew he was expected to answer, "Yes." But he could not help but disappoint his questioners. The English had been able to maintain their civilized and well-mannered society even in the midst of their ruins, and their resilience set them far apart from the population at the ancient site.

Thornton was not sure of the roots of the English spirit. He had noticed before the penchant for understatement that was characteristic of English conversation. But he felt that this alone did not sustain the population. Besides, they had an enormous pride in their country and in their airmen, a tradition of will power that gave them endurance, and "in many minds a smoldering resolution to remold the structure of society after the war."

After he returned to the States, Thornton wrote to a friend whose family lived in England expressing his belief that the war had taken a turn for the better and that no matter what difficulties the English had yet to endure, he did not doubt their ability to successfully resist German attacks. But privately he knew his own spirit had been assaulted by his experience in England. For solace he turned to Spinoza and the study of Latin, claiming that the order of thought in both assuaged some of the pain of everyday living. Sometimes, he said, he wished he could shut off the world and live in solitude. But such an act would have been impossible for him. Instead, he decided to take a role that would involve him directly in his country's war efforts. Early in 1942 he enlisted.

On New Year's Day 1942 he reported to Alexander Woollcott that he had finished work on his new play, now called *The Skin of Our Teeth*. He began to send it to some friends he hoped would want to direct it, and while he waited for their responses, kept himself busy writing scripts for government movies. The work for the government was done in good spirit, but it was not the kind of assignment he hoped would come from his volunteering. He was counting on his friend Archibald MacLeish, the Librarian of Congress, to find something more worthy of his talents. In February he was somewhat more excited by the government's request that he write the screenplay for a full-scale film reminiscent of *Our Town*, but updated to the present war. In it, it was suggested, he could show how one small village adapts to the war.

His scriptwriting occupied him while progress on the production of *The Skin of Our Teeth* moved at a frustrating pace. ". . . We begin to get reactions on the play," he wrote to Edward Sheldon in February. "And to my consternation arrived word that it was 'defeatist,' 'pacifist' and 'anti-war.'

"Apparently through New England 'tightness' and dread of preachiness, I had understated or smothered all the implications that were real to me: man's spiral progress and his progression through trial and error." Thornton was discouraged enough to rewrite the third act, "modifying . . . some of the bolder of the theatric novelties, and perhaps attenuating some of the legitimate 'hardness' of the Weltanschauung.

"I also came upon the fact that Act II, whose subject is a homage to marriage and the home . . . lacked any moment of the congenialities possible to the family situation; the children were represented as purely exasperating and the mother as nagging. So that was altered. So I hope that now there's a text that won't repel readers and auditors. . . ."[11]

Finally he found both a producer and director whose reactions were enthusiastic: Michael Myerberg and Elia Kazan, who had been recommended by one of Thornton's former students, the playwright Robert Ardrey. Thornton's biggest disappointment was in not having Ruth Gordon play the role of Sabina, the play's comic seductress. Thornton had confided to Alexander Woollcott that the part had been written expressly for her, but Thornton's preference was overruled by the producer. At first Myerberg offered the part to Helen Hayes. But after consulting with Edward Sheldon, Miss Hayes turned down the part. In a letter to Alexander Woollcott, she explained her reasons.

I am very fogged at this point in my career. . . . Have you read Thornton's play, *The Skin of Our Teeth*? I think it is one of the great plays of our time. His mysterious producer, Mr. Myerberg, sent it to me with a suggestion that I play Sabina. Of course there's only one person to play that part—the person for whom I suspect it was written—Ruth [Gordon]. I wouldn't dare attempt it, since I'd be haunted by the thought of the way she'd speak every line. It's very distracting, though, to have to turn down a good play.[12]

Still, Thornton was confident that Myerberg's search would end with an able star, and for the present, at least, he was satisfied.

At the beginning of April he was often sitting at the bedside of Alexander Woollcott, who was recovering from a serious illness. And finally, on May 6, he received a call from Archibald MacLeish summoning him to Washington to talk over a possible assignment. He was looking forward to participating in the war at last when he received an unexpected telegram a few days later from Alfred Hitchcock. Hitchcock was planning a film about a murderer and his involvement with a small-town family. He offered Thornton $15,000 to spend six weeks acting as a consultant and screenwriter for the film. Thornton, however, was not sanguine about the project. The plot seemed contrived, and he thought he would not be able to write convincingly. He knew that MacLeish's offer would mean his imminent entry into one of the armed forces, a prospect that was very important to him. But equally important was Hitchcock's offer of remuneration.

In the past months, Thornton's family expenses had increased because of the hospitalization of his sister Charlotte, who was suffering from a mental breakdown. Unsure of the potential success of *The Skin of Our Teeth*, Thornton felt he could not refuse the opportunity to earn several thousands of dollars. As much as he would have preferred not to work on a film that interested him so little, he agreed on a compromise: he would go to Hollywood for five weeks, for which he would ask $10,000.

By May 17 he was in Hollywood, staying at the Villa Carlota, planning soon to meet with Hitchcock. He also intended to see Robert Ardrey, Sol Lesser, Max Reinhardt, and Fredric March. His feelings about the film changed soon after he met Hitchcock, whose respect for the writer made him especially amenable to suggestions. The film, *Shadow of a Doubt*, deals with the relationship between a young woman, played by Teresa Wright, and her mysterious uncle, played by Joseph Cotten. It takes place in a small town in California where Uncle Charlie arrives to visit his sister and her daughter, known as Young Charlie. It soon becomes evident to the young woman that her uncle is one of two men suspected of being a murderer, and despite her love for him, she realizes that he is the guilty one. When he becomes aware of her suspicions, he tries twice to kill her, but finally is pressured into leaving town and returning to New York. However, he lures her on board the train before it pulls out of the station and makes one last attempt to push her off the platform. But he falls, instead, and is killed by a passing train.

Before Hitchcock called Thornton, he already had the basic story outlined by another writer in a nine-page draft. But Hitchcock did not want to work with the screenwriters who might have been supplied by his studio. In England, he said, he had been used to working with fine writers and now, in America, he wanted to work with someone he respected. Because of Thornton's reputation as a playwright and the reception of *Our Town*, Hitchcock was convinced that he was the right person for the assignment. His feelings for the film, in fact, were colored by the pleasant experience he had working with Thornton. Each morning he and

Thornton would meet at the studio to discuss the plot; sometimes they amazed themselves by the intricacies they suggested. In the afternoon, Thornton would return to his rooms to make notes and work on one scene or another. "He never worked consecutively," Hitchcock remembered, "but jumped about . . . according to his fancy." When one problem seemed to be how to begin the film, Thornton suggested an opening similar to that used by Hemingway in one of his short stories, "where a man is lying in bed in the dark, waiting to be killed." Hitchcock was surprised. "I, who fear being influenced by anyone in my work," he said, "was astonished that a great writer should not be afraid of another writer's influence." Though he decided on another beginning, he was impressed by Thornton's modesty and lack of vanity. Besides the actual writing, he depended on Thornton's advice for the choice of a town where the filming could take place. ". . . Wilder and I went to great pains to be realistic about the town, the people and the decor. We chose a town and we went there to search for the right house. We found one, but Wilder felt that it was too big for a bank-clerk. Upon investigation it turned out that the man who lived there was in the same financial bracket as our character, so Wilder agreed to use it." Unfortunately the owner of the house was so excited about the film that he had the house completely repainted. Hitchcock's crew had to "paint it dirty again," and repaint it when the filming was completed.[13]

Thornton's five weeks were all he could spare for work on the film. His training for the Air Force Intelligence Corps, the branch of service to which he was assigned, began immediately after his work with Hitchcock. When the director felt the screenplay needed some additional work, he found his favorite screenwriter no longer available. Thornton suggested that Robert Ardrey be asked to help, but Hitchcock wanted some comic touches, and Ardrey was a serious dramatist. Instead, Sally Benson was called in. Hitchcock admitted later that he had been "touched by his [Thornton's] qualities" and would have liked to work with him on another screenplay. But Thornton was already involved in the war, and he would not meet Hitchcock again for many years.

While Thornton had entered the Army for ostensibly altruistic reasons, he found life as a soldier unexpectedly comfortable. As the once-dutiful son of a domineering father, he found he could adapt easily to the rules and regulations. Though he realized he was making only a small contribution to the total war effort, he felt that the urgency that the war gave to every action put his life into a new perspective. Only those moments of intensive work and those few times shared with close friends now seemed important.

Thornton was to have been excused from participating in a training course, but then found it necessary to enroll for preparation as an officer. His course began on June 27, 1942, with classes alternating with field practice. He boasted to Alexander Woollcott that he led his class in ardor during bayonet practice. His secret was saying the name "Jed Harris" as he charged.[14] Though he was nervous about passing the various tests required of him, he earned a perfect score in "Company Administration," and proudly reported his achievement to Woollcott.[15] Still, he was not sure he would be successful as an officer. He was too sentimental, he thought, and he was often on the verge of tears at one thing or another, including the playing of taps, which he thought beautiful.[16]

He admitted a feeling of profound accomplishment that all his efforts were directed toward one goal. Distractions were virtually nonexistent. Still, he felt a deep longing for some of his friends, and a deep attachment to them. Alexander Woollcott, however, was despondent that Thornton's stay in the Army would cause an irreversible rift in their friendship. ". . . The only person I can't write to at all is you," he told Thornton in a letter, "partly because I have far too much to say and to ask and to hear, partly because I am too acutely conscious of the widening gulf between us. I remember too well from the summer and Fall of 1917 how dim and . . . how distasteful all my civilian friends seemed. When compared with the men who slept in the adjoining bunks on the transport or stood in front of or behind me in mess line, the oldest and dearest friends I had back home seemed like paper dolls. . . ."[17]

Woollcott needn't have worried. Thornton wrote devotedly every few days with news of the Army or, sometimes, of the faraway outside world. In August he learned that Myerberg had finally found an actress for the role of Sabina. Fredric March,

Florence Eldridge, and Florence Reed had already been signed. Now Tallulah Bankhead would join them. "I was about the last actress considered for the role," she said, and her acceptance pleased Thornton. The play would now go into rehearsals, with an opening scheduled for early November.

Totally occupied with his duties as an Army intelligence officer, Thornton's wistful dream of being in the outlands during rehearsals for his play was partly fulfilled. He could still be reached by letter, of course, and he soon learned that Tallulah Bankhead's acceptance of the part of Sabina was less than happy. From the first, her animosity toward Michael Myerberg was evident to everyone. "Myerberg was an erratic, tactless man" she thought, "lean as Cassius, who had been fiddling around the theater for a dozen years with little success."[18] Furthermore, she knew that Myerberg had come to her as a last resort. She complained constantly about his "bickering, his petty tyrannies, his genius for arousing hostility," and even accused him of causing her ulcer.[19]

The ill-feeling between Bankhead and Myerberg might have been mollified by the director, but the actress had no great respect for Elia Kazan either. Though she admitted that he was "alert and eager" and "reacted to the problems presented by the Wilder comedy courageously," she was often dismayed at his direction and would have liked Wilder there to guide him. "Kazan and I had minor differences of opinion about the interpretation of Sabina during rehearsals," she said. "Such differences are productive, as often as not, of sharper performances. When the contending parties do not see eye to eye—actor and director—it is generally agreed free discussion of their differences clears the air."[20] But during rehearsals for *The Skin of Our Teeth*, the discussions produced, instead, a tension among the cast that made work difficult.

Though Tallulah was the cause of the tension, she was also one of those who suffered most. During the out-of-town openings, she was stricken with sharp pains that were eventually diagnosed as symptoms of a gastric ulcer. Placed on a strict diet of milk products and bland cereals, she soon became alarmed that her seductive Sabina was bulging in the wrong places. Only the admonitions of an unyielding physician convinced her that she must submit to the discipline of the treatment.

Though the role was written for a vastly different actress, and though Tallulah was at odds with the producer and director, she felt strongly about the merits of the play itself. It was, she thought, a "brilliant and controversial comedy that . . . defied all the canons of the theater, confused the literal-minded. It was a gay delight to those with imagination as it was to those who rejoiced in nose-thumbing at tradition."[21] Her own imagination led her to defy the producer to make sure one of Thornton's scenes was played to its full potential. Sabina and her employer, Mr. Antrobus, must engage in "some amorous antics in an Atlantic City cabana." The cabana was supposed to be in the orchestra pit, but the entrance to the pit in one theater required the two to go down a flight of stairs and past those seated in the first row. "The space granted Sabina and Mr. Antrobus for their folly was so cramped as to preclude the full potential of the desired fireworks." She thought the two aisle seats should be removed, but Myerberg was not about to lose those highly priced tickets. Tallulah was not defeated. "I resorted to direct action," she said. "Armed with a carpenter's kit, I invaded the auditorium of a dark afternoon, while stage hands were wrestling with lights and properties, and started to remove the offending chairs. With that Myerberg capitulated. The seats were removed. Antrobus and Sabina were able to validate their ardors in satisfactory fashion."[22]

*The Skin of Our Teeth* opened at the Plymouth Theatre in New York on November 18, 1942. It was, thought Lewis Nichols of the *Times,* "the best pure theatre" of the forties. Thornton's story "of man's constant struggle for survival, and his wonderment over why he so struggles, is presented with pathos and broad comedy, with gentle irony and sometimes a sly self-raillery." Wolcott Gibbs of *The New Yorker* agreed that the play was "by far the most interesting and exciting . . . I've seen this year. . . . Fredric March and Florence Eldridge, as Mr. and Mrs. Antrobus, achieve just the proper combination of the normal and the supernatural; they speak with the unmistakable accents of suburban America, but it is also easy to believe that they have been married for five thousand years."[23] *The Skin of Our Teeth,* thought *Time*'s reviewer, "is like a philosophy class conducted in a monkey house." The plot concerns the eternal survival of Every Family as represented by Mr. and Mrs. Antrobus, their son, Henry (né Cain), and daughter, Gladys. They are assisted in coping with their daily trials by their maid, Sabina, the archetypal seductress, whose exasperation with the play's lack of convention is sometimes conveyed directly to the audience. Walls lean, bits of scenery rise and fall, a long-suffering stage manager must convince Sabina to continue her role. . . . Some viewers wondered if the effects were not contrived by the director, Elia Kazan, whose nickname, "Gadge," came from his willingness to try any innovation. But it was Thornton who called for whatever details he wanted, drawing on the old stock companies he remembered from his childhood in California, vaudeville, musical comedies, plays he had seen in Germany in 1928, and his own lively imagination. "*The Skin of Our Teeth* is a cockeyed and impudent vaudeville littered with asides and swarming with premeditated anachronisms. Dinosaurs collide with bingo; the Muses jostle the microphone." Thornton had created "spectacular stagecraft" with a message that was always understood. "Perfectly clear . . . is Wilder's optimistic conclusion that mankind, for all its bad luck and narrow escapes, is indestructible."[24]

Indeed, it was the message, rather than the "highjinks" and "academic, if not collegiate" humor, that impressed Stark Young. ". . . The underlying theme, that of man's struggle and survival, climbing, falling, destroying himself, being destroyed, surviving by the skin of his teeth but passionately and stubbornly and touchingly alive, is a profound and ancient theme. From it arrive passages in the play that are moving and elevated. The conception of the Cain motif, rash figure of blood and destruction but kept yet in his human frailty, is a notable piece of imaginative creation. And . . . to quote all those superb passages from great thinkers is certainly to invite the gods to supper."[25]

Thornton was especially gratified by Rosamond Gilder's review in *Theatre Arts*. "When the breath of creative imagination blows through the theatre, what exhilaration to the lungs, what refreshment to the spirit! Doors may bang and scenery fly about; audiences may be outraged, infuriated, delighted, but the theatre is once more alive. Thornton Wilder's *The Skin of Our Teeth* is not only a tribute to the indestructibility of the human race . . . ; it

is also a giddy proof of the theatre's own imperishable vitality."[26]
Thornton suggested to Edith Isaacs that he would like one day to
do a piece for the magazine annotating his new play. He would
not try to explicate it, he said, but only to tell other playwrights of
his intent in writing it.

Another opinion that more than interested him was conveyed
privately in a letter from Alexander Woollcott. While most critics
hailed Tallulah Bankhead's performance as "inspired," with "a
gusty, irresistible humor that is almost sufficient, in itself, to jus-
tify Wilder's theatrical jump over the moon,"[27] Woollcott could
not conceal his disappointment, though of course, he thought the
play brilliant.

> Having seen *The Skin of Our Teeth* and thought about it and read
> it, I know what I think about it. I think no American play has ever
> come anywhere near it. I think it might have been written by Plato
> and Lewis Carroll in collaboration, or better still by any noble peda-
> gogue with a little poltergeist blood in him. I had not foreseen that
> you could write a play that would be both topical and timeless,
> though I might have remembered from *The Trojan Women* that it
> could be done. . . .

> One thing I *am* sure of. Tallulah does not know how to play Sabina
> and cannot be taught to. She has some assets as an actress but she
> is without any comic gift. . . . In the first act I found her afflict-
> ing. In the second and third acts I was quite reconciled to her. It
> was not until I read the play that I saw how in every scene and
> every line it aches for Ruth Gordon. It will be played many times
> and by many women. It will never be really played until Ruth plays
> it. March is good. Florence Reed is surprisingly good. Tallulah is, I
> think, a misfortune—how great a misfortune only those can say who
> know the play.[28]

When Woollcott had seen the play during its pre-Broadway
performances, he had wired Thornton, hoping that he could obtain a leave to help smooth out a "slight muddle" here and there.
But Thornton's leaves were granted sparingly, and Woollcott
seemed to miss him more than the cast of the play. "Present and
pending American shortages will doubtless be good for us all," he
wrote to Marie Belloc Lowndes in September. "Of those to which

I have already been subjected, I mind only the acute shortage of Thornton Wilder."[29] And Thornton returned the sentiment when he wrote a few months later, "Nothing so lifts a soldier's morale as getting a letter from home and nothing so depresses him as reading it."[30]

Though Thornton realized that his friend was in failing health, he was not prepared for the news of his sudden death on January 23, 1943. Many did not understand the depth of their devotion to each other. Once, at a gathering shortly after Woollcott died, Thornton called the guests together to listen to a eulogy he had prepared. His emotions were bared and his love for Woollcott unconcealed. Yet to some the praise of a man whose impatient wit had offended a great many people seemed out of place. Finally, after an embarrassed silence, the host of the gathering, William James's son Billy, could not help but ask, as gently as he could, if the eulogy did not quite fit the subject.[31]

In a letter to Woollcott's biographer, Samuel Adams, Thornton tried to explain his feelings. "I agree with you completely," he wrote, "that all the essentials of 'ethical responsiblity' were the heart of Aleck's life, but that it had no 'canal' into the traditions of religious or philosophical thinking. Four or five summers ago . . . I remember him saying that he envied, yet was cut off from any resources on which some of the people he most admired seem to draw (he instanced Father Duffy) and he proposed making some inquiry in Christian 'source books.' . . . He never mentioned such a need again. Those last years were so filled with affirmation of an interpretation of destiny—for him—and that, rightly, was his resource."[32]

One of Woollcott's last pieces was a comment on *The Skin of Our Teeth* in which he called the play "a bulletin issued from the sickroom of a patient in whose health we are all pardonably interested, a bulletin signed by a physician named Thornton Wilder."[33] In some ways, Thornton was Woollcott's personal physician, raising his spirits with his usual optimism and encouraging him to write. In a letter to his friend written shortly before he died, Woollcott jokingly told of a meeting he had with a visitor who commented, "I do not see how you have the time and energy to accomplish all you do." To Thornton, who was often chiding Woollcott for not publishing more, the comment would be amusing. To Woollcott the comment was simply ironic: his visitor, he revealed, was Eleanor Roosevelt. This note ended, like so many others, with the words, "I need and miss you."[34]

In losing Alexander Woollcott, Thornton lost a strong supporter and a friend who could serve as a buffer against criticism and attacks. And even at the time of Woollcott's death, Thornton was caught in the most devastating scandal of his career.

# FIFTEEN

---◆---

TWELVE years after he was attacked for elitism in the pages of *The New Republic*, Thornton again found himself the center of a controversy, this time inspired by an article that appeared in the *Saturday Review* in December 1942. The charge was no less than plagiarism, and his accusers were Joseph Campbell and Henry Morton Robinson, who had spent the previous three years working on *A Skeleton Key to Finnegans Wake*.

". . . One fine day," Campbell said later,

I read in the paper, which I used to read in those days, that Thornton Wilder had a play going, *The Skin of Our Teeth*. I'd done all my theatergoing in the Twenties, but somehow I thought I'd like to see that play. We got tickets. First row balcony, center. Hey, one quote after another from *Finnegans Wake*! "Do you have a pencil?" I start copying it down on the program. So in the morning I phone Rondo [Henry Morton Robinson] in Woodstock. "Rondo, *Skin of Our Teeth* is *Finnegans Wake*." "Oh?" "Something oughta be done about it." Monday he phones Norman Cousins and he says yes, so we wrote a piece and Cousins published it as *The Skin of Whose Teeth?* And it really rang a bell all over the country.[1]

*The Skin of Our Teeth,* they decided, was "not an entirely original creation, but an Americanized re-creation, thinly disguised" of Joyce's famous novel. "Important plot elements, characters, devices of presentation, as well as major themes and many of the speeches, are directly and frankly imitated, with but the flimsiest veneer to lend an American touch to the original features." To Thornton, who had spent considerable time dissecting Joyce's work, it came as no surprise that anyone who knew Joyce could relate his play to the novel. What did shock and distress him was the uproar the accusations caused in the literary world. "It is a strange performance that Mr. Wilder has turned in," Campbell and Robinson commented. "Is he hoaxing us? On the one hand, he gives no credit to his source, masking it with an Olsen and Johnson technique. On the other hand, he makes no attempt to conceal his borrowings, emphasizing them rather, sometimes even stressing details which with a minimum of ingenuity he could have suppressed or altered."

To the two writers there could be only one answer. Thornton was assuming that his audience was as yet illiterate of Joyce's novel and would not discern his borrowings. "He realized fully that *Finnegans Wake* has not yet been assimilated by the larger public, and that the chances of explicit protest during the run of the play were slight. For in Joyce's work the themes are multidimensional and queerly interwoven, developing bit by bit throughout the obscure text. Even the studious eye is baffled by their intricacy. Mr. Wilder, having mastered the elaborate web, has selected a few structural strands, reduced them in size and weight, and presented them, neatly crocheted to box-office taste. Many of the Joyce-Wilder correspondences are so subtle and extended that it would require a vast wall for their exhibition." But Campbell and Robinson proceeded to point out to the curious just what some of those correspondences were.

The setting and the personalities of the main characters, they found, were obviously alike in both works. In both, also, the seductress—Lily Kinsella in Joyce, Sabina in Wilder—was a pretty servant girl who liked movies and once had been raped. Thornton's Mrs. Antrobus echoed the words of Joyce's Mrs. Earwicker, and both mothers, coincidentally named Maggie (Joyce spelled it Maggy) loved their son, Cain.

In form, the two works were again similar, both drawing upon prehistory and circling into the present. "The last book of *Finnegans Wake* and the last Act of the play treat of the world's brave re-beginnings, following almost total catastrophe; they do not conclude, but circle back again to the start of all." Minor references are likewise dissected, including the repetition of the number 32 in Joyce's book and Wilder's beginning his play with an announcement that the sun rose at 6:32 A.M. A second article followed the first, and the accumulation of charges seemed to make Thornton's guilt inescapable.

The Campbell and Robinson accusation shocked many critics, but one had the boldness necessary to defend Thornton. Edmund Wilson, who had long known of Thornton's interest in Joyce and had followed his analysis of *Finnegans Wake*, aired his own views in *The Nation* on January 30, 1943. "The general indebtedness to Joyce in the conception and plan of the play," he wrote, "is as plain as anything of the kind can be; and it must have been conscious on Wilder's part. He has written and lectured on *Finnegans Wake*; is one of the persons who has been most fascinated by it and who has most thoroughly studied its text. . . . Joyce is a great quarry, like Flaubert, out of which a variety of writers have been getting and will continue to get a variety of different things; and Wilder is a poet with a form and imagination of his own who may find his themes where he pleases without incurring the charge of imitation." Wilson found no objection to Thornton's drawing upon Joyce, except where it might have distracted him from "his own ideas and effects. . . ." He dismissed Campbell and Robinson, but felt that Thornton might have written a greater play if he had allowed more freedom for his own sense of creativity instead of having "been somewhat embarrassed and impeded by the model of the Earwicker family."

Thornton's silence during the controversy exasperated many. Indeed, to some it was tacit admission of his guilt of plagiarism. But he had never denied, in past works, the influence of other writers and would not do so now. The sentiments of Goethe sustained him. "The world . . . remains always the same," Goethe had said long before; "situations are repeated; one people lives, loves, and feels like another. . . ." Artists repeat each other: Shakespeare has sources in Homer; Byron tried to pin down the sources in *Faust*; others tried to determine the sources in Byron. The artist can best defend himself by saying, "What is there is mine . . . and whether I got it from a book or from life, is of no consequence; the only point is, whether I have made a right use of it."[2]

"People are always talking about originality," Goethe continued; "but what do they mean? As soon as we are born, the world begins to work upon us, and this goes on to the end. And after all, what can we call our own except energy, strength, and will?"[3] The question of literary influences was irrelevant for Thornton, and he often admitted that he was more a borrower or reinterpreter than an innovator. He believed, as did Goethe, that there is "through all art a filiation. If you see a great master, you will always find that he used what was good in his predecessors, and that it was this which made him great."[4]

For several months the controversy continued, with much confusion. Most viewers and most critics were ignorant of Joyce's work. The articles had been persuasive and Thornton's silence somewhat damning. In April, when the New York Drama Critics Circle met to choose the prize play of the season, even some who were convinced of the merits of Thornton's play wavered in their feelings and voted for another work. Wolcott Gibbs, *The New Yorker*'s critic, made a public apology in his column for having failed to choose Thornton's play, but said that since Thornton had not countered the charges against him, he had had to vote for *The Patriots* instead.

Nevertheless, despite the unhappiness the articles caused, the furor was finally ended in May when, for the third time, Thornton was awarded the Pulitzer Prize.

Thornton meanwhile was applying his considerable writing talents to the editing of an air force manual, working six days a week in Washington, D.C., with little opportunity for leave. In the spring of 1943, however, his prospects brightened when he was sent to North Africa. His mother was worried about her forty-six-year-old son, though, and expressed her concern to one of his friends. Would he be able to get a good shoeshine in Africa, she wondered.[5]

Samuel Steward
*(Courtesy, Samuel Steward)*.

Robert Stallman
*(Photograph by Susan Newman;
Courtesy, Robert Stallman)*.

Jed Harris (*Vandamm photo; Courtesy, Theatre and Music Collection, The Museum of the City of New York*).

Elia Kazan (*Friedman-Abeles photo, Courtesy, Theatre and Music Collection, The Museum of the City of New York*).

Montgomery Clift
(*Photo by Alfredo Valente; Courtesy, Theatre and Music Collection, The Museum of the City of New York*).

Florence Eldridge, Frances Heflin, Fredric March, and Tallulah Bankhead in *The Skin of Our Teeth* (*Courtesy, Theatre and Music Collection, The Museum of the City of New York*).

Thornton Wilder in uniform
*(Photograph by Sam Rosenberg;
Courtesy, Theatre and Music
Collection, The Museum of the
City of New York).*

Thornton Wilder (second
from left) at banquet
for Robert Frost *(Courtesy,
Amherst College News Service).*

Mrs. Lyndon B. Johnson,
Thornton Wilder, Isabel Wilder
*(Courtesy, The Lyndon Baines
Johnson Library)*.

Thornton Wilder at
MacDowell Colony
*(Photograph by Bernice B. Perry;
Courtesy, The MacDowell Colony)*.

Thornton Wilder at The Williamstown Theater, rehearsal for *Our Town*
*(Courtesy, The Williamstown Theater Festival).*

Thornton Wilder with innkeeper John Fitzpatrick and Lawrenceville alumni
at The Red Lion Inn, Stockbridge, Massachusetts *(Courtesy, John Fitzpatrick).*

Tyrone Guthrie
*(Courtesy, Stratford, Ontario,
Shakespeare Festival)*.

Newport Harbor
*(Courtesy, The Newport
Historical Society)*.

Cliffs at Narragansett Bay
(*Courtesy, The Newport Historical Society*).

Carol Channing in *Hello, Dolly!*
(*Courtesy, Theatre and Music Collection, The Museum of the City of New York*).

After a year in Algiers and Tunis he was again transferred, this time to Rome, a city that delighted him under any conditions. When he had free hours, he visited the Sistine Chapel and the Villa Medicis and wandered through the city's beloved streets. For him, the soldiers who now walked on the ancient stones were only repeating a scene that had been played many times before. Rome was withstanding another invasion, only now the uniforms were those of Americans. Even the war, with its immediate dangers and risks, could be seen through his own peculiar telescope and taken calmly. By the fall of 1944 Thornton had been in the Army for two and a half years. Though he was forced to put aside much of his writing, and though he was separated from those he loved, he felt no regret at having volunteered for service. An obedient and hard-working soldier, he had been promoted from captain to major by the time he was discharged, and felt a boyish pride at his titles and his uniform. It was almost with a sense of loss that he announced his discharge in the fall of 1945.

But he quickly readjusted to civilian life. By December he was at work on a play and a new novel. The play, which he had begun years before, was based on the story of Alcestis. The novel, which soon became his dominant occupation, was inspired by his recent visit to Rome, his reading of *Ciceron et ses amis* and some of Catullus' poems, and his desire to write about power, politics—and art. Many of its characters were drawn from his circle of friends. Lucius Mamilus Turrinus was inspired by Edward Sheldon; Catullus, by the young man he had met more than twenty years before, Lauro de Bosis.

De Bosis, who had died in 1931, was certainly a romantic enough figure to inspire fiction. By the late 1920s he had already gained a considerable reputation as a poet in Italy, and in 1927, inspired by Lindbergh's crossing of the Atlantic, he published a prize-winning poem, *Icaro*, which contained prophetic last lines: "Men, listen to his inspired song; wherever in the world a human heart, armed against the Fates, burns with eagerness and love, there, for ever unseen, Icarus watched over him."

De Bosis' heart was burning with hatred for Mussolini and passion against fascism. An idealist since his youth, he had watched for several years as the dictator rose to power in his homeland,

and he determined to act in some way to stop him. In the spring of 1930 he made his first attempt. Every two weeks he sent out six hundred chain letters, asking their recipients to send six letters each. The letters explained "that all men of law and order should be in accord in preparation for the day when fascism should fall." He continued his project until the end of November, and in December, when he needed to travel to England, he left the work in the hands of two friends. In a short time, both were arrested, tortured, and imprisoned.

De Bosis was incensed and prepared at once to return to Italy to help them or share their punishment. But he was warned against rash action by his friends. Instead, he spent his time in England learning to fly; and then he went to France, where he took a job as a concierge at the Hotel Victor Emmanuel III. Between answering the switchboard and attending to guests, he composed a message to the King of Italy and studied intently a map of the Mediterranean. By the time he returned home, his plan was set as it was later documented in a letter left for posthumous publication, "The Story of My Death." In his plane, *Pegasus,* he planned to cross Italy and drop four hundred thousand leaflets upon its citizens, calling for an end to fascism. ". . . We are not going in search of chimeras," he wrote, "but to bear a message of liberty across the sea to a people that is in chains." He was certain that the flight would end in his death, but knew, too, that such tragedies were necessary. "I am convinced," he said, "that fascism will not end until some twenty young people sacrifice their lives in order to awaken the spirit of the Italians." He outlined his route in detail.

After having flown over Corsica and the Island of Monte Cristo at a height of twelve thousand feet, I shall reach Rome about eight o'clock, having done the last twenty kilometres gliding. Though I have only done seven and a half hours of solo flying, if I fall it will not be through fault of pilotage. My aeroplane only flies at 150 kilometres an hour, whereas those of Mussolini can do 300. There are nine hundred of them, and they have all received the order to bring down at any cost, with machine-gun fire, any suspicious aeroplane. However little they may know me, they must realize that after my first attempt I have not given up. . . . They are there waiting for me. So much the better; I shall be worth more dead than alive.

On October 3, 1931, he took off from Marseille and headed for Rome. On the way to the airfield he mailed his letter to a journalist he knew in Belgium, requesting that it be published if he failed to return from his mission. By eight o'clock, as he had predicted, he was circling low over Rome, blanketing the city with his leaflets. Then he headed for the sea, and disappeared.

Like De Bosis, Edward Sheldon was, for Thornton, a paradigm of courage. Despite his illness, his bravery and optimism astounded many of his friends. But Thornton never had the chance to read his new manuscript to him. Sheldon died on April 1, 1946. For Thornton, it was the beginning of several months of mourning.

In June, Mrs. Wilder and Isabel went to Nantucket, a place Mrs. Wilder especially liked. For nearly two weeks she enjoyed the sea and the change of scenery from New Haven. She saw many of her friends. Then, suddenly, she became ill, and on the morning of June 29 Thornton lost his most devoted admirer and dearest friend. Isabel Niven Wilder, he once said, was the most intelligent woman he had ever known. He had depended on her support and encouragement, her appreciation of his talents, and her love. Now, at seventy-three, she was dead.

The family gathered, Amos flying in from Maine, Janet and her husband coming in from Amherst, Massachusetts. Only Charlotte, then residing in London, was absent. A simple service was held in a Congregational church that had once been the parish church for Nantucket whalers.

Saddened first by the loss of a respected friend and then even more deeply distraught over the death of his mother, Thornton turned with great concentration to his manuscript. Much of what he was feeling, he wrote to a friend, was becoming part of his new book, *The Ides of March*.

In the character of Caesar, about whom the book centers, Thornton expresses many of his own feelings. Caesar is preoccupied by death, not only his own, which he clearly foresees, but those which he has witnessed and which have shaped his emotions. When he thinks of the past, he imagines those he has loved, now dead. "All of it, all of it, seems of a beauty that I shall not see again. . . . At the memory of one whisper, one pair of eyes, the pen falls from my hand, the interview in which I am engaged turns to stone." Often he was required to attend a dying friend. "To those in pain," he said, "one talks about themselves; to those of a clear mind one praises the world they are quitting. There is no dignity in leaving a despicable world and the dying are often fearful lest life was not worth the efforts it had cost them." He himself believed fully in the wonder of life, though he was well aware that the universe was blind and uncaring. As Lucius Turrinus, his maimed friend, once told him: "The universe is not aware that we are here." From Lucius, Caesar learned to view the world with detachment and resignation. "Hope has never changed tomorrow's weather," Lucius told the dictator when he was young, and Caesar forgot neither the words nor his shocked reaction when he heard them.

Yet with an acute consciousness of death, and with a resignation about life, Caesar could still celebrate the beauty of an individual's existence. Contrasted with "the dream of the void" which often overtook him was a vision of pure happiness. "I wish to cry out to all the living and all the dead that there is no part of the universe that is untouched by bliss." Though the short span of any life made it impossible to comprehend the larger meaning of human existence, Caesar was able to commit himself wholly to living. Those who called him rash and irreverent simply did not understand that he was acting as a man who would not bind himself with the strictures of following one set of ideas or one master. He was self-possessed, without even the weight upon him of truly caring about the opinions of his contemporaries. It was only pretense, he thought, to give others the impression that their praise mattered. He knew that he was indifferent to those around him, and often his indifference prompted their anger.

Caesar admitted that his own passion for life had begun when he was able to envision his own death. From that moment, he could discern those "who had not yet foreseen their death" from those wiser and more sensitive men who had. ". . . Only those who have grasped their own non-being are capable of praising the sunlight," he said.

Essentially, *The Ides of March* is a study in identity. Thornton set out to create a portrait of Julius Caesar as a complex personality, concerned as much with power as with his own mind. He portrays a sensitive thinker, a lonely man, a man who could feel great tenderness and pity. In contrast, he could also be cold and ruthless; he acknowledged himself as a tyrant. In creating his character, Thornton was again confronting two problems he had often discussed with Gertrude Stein: identity and the creation of a believable reality.

In the late 1930s Gertrude was at work on *Ida*, a novel that was expanded from her short piece of the same name. Thornton was at Bilignin during the time she was writing the piece and, in an effort to be an obliging guest, he read her still-incomplete manuscript. Gertrude wanted him to help with the narrative. She was having some difficulty and thought he understood her work well enough to collaborate. Thornton, though he understood the theme when she explained it, simply could not follow the complex prose. "Well just read it," she told him. "It's in plain English, why can't you understand it. It's simple." He tried again, but still much of the sense eluded him.[6] Gertrude, he thought, wrote on eight levels, and he understood only the first three. Yet his understanding of those three was enough to convince him that they were both exploring the same problems. In *Ida*, as in many other pieces, Gertrude was trying to create a portrait of a woman by showing "the intensity of movement" within her. "If you listen, really listen," she once said, "you will hear people repeating themselves. You will hear their pleading nature or their attacking nature or their asserting nature."[7] She was not interested in following her character through a carefully contrived plot. Many of her works, as Thornton noted, appear to be constructed before the reader's eyes. ". . . She does not, as other writers do, suppress and erase her hesitations, the recapitulations, the connectives, in order to give us the completed fine result of her meditations. She gives us the process."[8] Her writing, then, was analogous to *cinéma vérité* where the peripheral activity is often more revealing than the object of central focus. She wanted her style to convey a sense of im-

mediacy; and she wanted her analysis of a character, though fragmented and certainly not treated realistically, to show a distinct
basic nature.

In dealing with the character of Julius Caesar, Thornton hoped
to revitalize a man who had been buried beneath ages of histories
and fictional treatments. Furthermore, he wanted to create a living Caesar, credible and sympathetic to modern readers. To do so,
he turned to a contrivance that Gertrude Stein never would have
used: the compiling of fictionalized letters, diary entries, messages,
documents, to create a picture of a time long past. He was not attempting to be faithful to history, he wrote in a brief preface, and
he included events and characters that were not always contem-
poraneous. His was more a "fantasia" than a retelling of history.
Nor would he, as Gertrude had done, create his work before the
eyes of his readers. His prose was, as always, polished and precise,
qualities unfailingly noticed and praised by his critics. Yet Thornton believed that *The Ides* showed Gertrude's influence more
than any other of his works. She never acted as a critic. In fact, he
admitted, she hardly read anything he wrote; but her goals and his
were similar.[9]

Their emotional responses, too, were similar. Thornton called
her "an impassioned listener to life . . . ," just as many have described him. Yet she did not focus on the particular happenings of
an individual's life, but on something larger—"the struggle of the
human mind in its work which is to know."[10] She extracted a person's basic nature from the particulars of his or her daily life; she
abstracted her characters into Everyman or Everywoman. And
though her purposes were serious, she never lost her gaiety, her
sense of humor, her love of life. "Neither her company nor her
books were for those who have grown tired of listening," Thornton wrote. "It was an irony that she did her work in a world in
which for many reasons and for many appalling reasons people
have so tired."[11]

Thornton's months of mourning extended later into the summer of 1946 when, on July 27, Gertrude died. With her death,
Thornton lost a kindred spirit. And his feelings for her had been
reciprocated. She had once thought of naming him as literary ex-
ecutor of her estate, but changed her mind, regretfully, because

she felt the drudgery of carrying out the chore would take valuable time from his work. Nevertheless, at his suggestion, she sent all her papers and letters to his alma mater, Yale, for safekeeping during the war, and they remain there still.

At the close of 1946 Thornton was approaching fifty. His world had been diminished by the death of three of those spiritually closest to him. But even in his deepest despondency, he knew he could rally. As Caesar's friend Lucius had said in *The Ides*, the universe was blind to an individual's suffering. There was nothing to do but continue to create and to work. "The first and last schoolmaster of life," he wrote, "is living and committing oneself unreservedly and dangerously to living. . . ."

# III

*A narrow ring*
*Bounds our life,*
*And many generations*
*Are continually linking on*
*To the endless chain*
*Of their existence*

GOETHE
"Bounds of Humanity"

# SIXTEEN

---

EARLY in 1946 Thornton had boarded a Norwegian tramp steamer and sailed for the Yucatán peninsula in Mexico. One night, long after the Mayan ruins had been officially closed to tourists, he climbed to the top of a pyramid to gaze at the stars, much as he had done as a boy in the Ojai valley of California. They were, as he wrote in *Our Town,* doing their eternal criss-crossing in the sky, and were no less spectacular to him now, in his middle age, as they had been nearly forty years before. He thought he might one day write about the Mayans, with insights very different from those of archaeologists and other experts. If only he could take off a year, he wrote to his former Yale professor, Chauncey Brewster Tinker, he would devote himself to such an article.[1] But he wondered if such indulgences were fitting for a man nearing fifty.

For Thornton, middle age was a thoroughly comfortable time of life. He had always felt older than his contemporaries, he said, and in some ways had always felt fifty. Now, with his hair graying and his girth increasing, he looked the part of the benign neighborhood physician for whom he was often mistaken. No less than before, he felt it important to devote himself completely to his work and often worked on more than one project at once. Late in 1946 he completed a play for the Century Association of New York to be presented at its centennial celebration in April 1947. Thornton was less than pleased with the piece and once suggested that someone else take it over, working from his preliminary sketch. Indeed, the finished work is not one of his major contributions. *Our Century* presents three brief vignettes taking place in the lounge of the club. In the first scene, we see the club as the members' sons might imagine it; in the second, as a nervous new member perceives it; and in the third, as some envious wives might see it. The whole is slight and faintly humorous.

More important to him was his novel *The Ides of March*, completed in June 1947 and published on February 18, 1948. It would be his first novel in thirteen years, had been accepted as a Book-of-the-Month Club selection for March, and was eagerly anticipated by critics and Thornton's admiring readership. But its reception was disappointing.

He had hoped that readers would appreciate his distance as a narrator from his relating of events in classical Rome, but many objected that the documents, letters, and edicts gave the novel a stilted form. Some were not happy with his capricious handling of historical facts, others with the characterization of some of the secondary characters. His depicting of Julius Caesar, however, was generally praised. *The Times Literary Supplement* (London) saw Caesar as a man of enormous stature and great tragedy, one of "moral and mental pre-eminence. . . ."[2] J. M. Lalley, writing in *The New Yorker*, saw Thornton's Caesar as "a tireless and determined but benignly intentioned pedagogue who has somehow got the whole world for his classroom, only to have his heart broken by the perverse unwillingness of his pupils to be indoctrinated in sound, positivistic social principles." But Lalley was disappointed in Thornton's literary device. "The use of imaginary documents," he wrote, "has the advantage of permitting Mr. Wilder to substitute philosophical reflection for action, to exercise his admirable essay prose, and to indulge in a highly refined form of satire. . . . It is also a method that makes for tedium, and on the whole the tedium exceeds the wit."[3]

Richard Watts, Jr., in his article in the *Saturday Review,* likewise thought Caesar a powerful character about whom Thornton showed enormous insight. But he added, "The weakness is that, having established his Caesar as a great leader, a believable intellect and a living man, Wilder does so disappointingly little with him." His use of documents inhibited his ability to dramatize situations. Though Thornton evidently had profound ideas about the use and misuse of power, "they are not dramatized sufficiently or fought out in proper terms of human conflict." Watts did add, however, that Thornton's "study of the ideas of democracy, dictatorship, liberty and power," set as they were "against a classic background . . . makes them seem virtually timeless."[4]

The Canadian publication of his book brought Thornton a more satisfactory review. Here the critic seemed to understand precisely Thornton's aims. ". . . The reader . . . finds himself addressed as if he had an intimate acquaintance with ancient Rome, its geography, its public figures, its customs—as if, in fact, he were a Roman. Thus the reader, while he is removed from the scene of action, is at the same time transported into the period by means of a technique which description cannot equal in immediacy and authenticity. This assumption of the reader's knowledge does not cause confusion or irritation, as it might well do; owing to Mr. Wilder's skill it simply renders the reader capable of regarding the Janiculum Hill or the Appian Way as casually and yet as poignantly as Montrealers regard Sherbrooke Street.

"Mr. Wilder's combination and manipulation of materials make an experiment which evokes interested participation rather than excitement."[5]

Many of Thornton's friends were dismayed at the critical reception of *The Ides of March* and wrote him solicitous letters that often irritated him. He had lived with worse reviews, he responded, but he was disappointed when critics accused him of academic reworking of histories. He wanted his writings to be considered vital and exciting—and relevant to the contemporary world. But his disappointment was mollified by his work.

In January 1941 Thornton had attended a luncheon sponsored by the National Conference of Christians and Jews held at Longchamps restaurant in Manhattan. Among others attending were

Carl Van Doren, Dorothy Day, John P. Marquand, Edna Ferber, Henry Seidel Canby, and the then Librarian of Congress, Archibald MacLeish. At the time, the committee was interested in having writers contribute works that promoted tolerance; it was suggested that dramatizations be written of the lives of "minority heroes." MacLeish offered the facilities of the Library of Congress to any writer who proposed such a work.

Thornton's response to the committee's request came in 1948 with a script for *The Unerring Instinct*, a short, well-intentioned, but uninspiring play on tolerance. There are three characters: Leonora Thorpe, her sister-in-law Belinda Watson, and Arthur Rogers, a friend of Leonora and her husband. Thornton uses his customary device of having a character communicate directly with the audience. This time, Leonora explains a practical joke she played on her sister-in-law to show her prejudice. As if the plot were not simplistic enough, there is an added device of the use of three colored lights: red for fear, blue for despair, and green for malice, to show the audience Belinda's progressing emotions as Leonora tries to make her suspicious of anyone named Smith. The name, she tells her, derives from the German Schmidt, and anyone bearing that name was sure to have been a blacksmith or ironworker. Logically, descendants would likewise be *"strongwilled* and ruthless. . . ."

Soon Leonora convinces Belinda that all Smiths are evil, and Belinda unknowingly snubs a friend of her husband because Leonora introduces him as a "Smythe." The intense green light that Belinda has provoked is extinguished, and she admits that what she called her unerring instinct was merely the workings of prejudice. Leonora, though, doubts whether Belinda really changed. "Only one Belinda in ten ever learns anything," she tells the audience. "It's my nieces and nephews that I'm interested in." And then, with an apology to all the Smiths "who were for a moment disparaged in this play," she bids the audience good-night.

A more important occupation for Thornton in 1948 was his research into the early plays of Lope de Vega, a project he had begun years before. He acknowledged that there were at most thirty people who would be interested in his findings, but still he persevered. Five years later he would publish "Lope Pinedo, Some

Child-Actors, and a Lion" in the scholarly journal *Romance Philology* that was the result of his "effort to establish a chronology for a number—though not all—of the plays which Lope wrote between 1599 and 1606." His work took him to Madrid, where, in chilly, damp libraries, he contacted an earache and cold. At the Centro de Estudios sobre Lope de Vega, he transcribed and translated an important paper by Agustin G. de Amezúa, a renowned Lopista. Thornton admitted that much of his works depended on educated guesses, "combining conjecture with conjecture until their sheer multiplicity affords sufficient admiration for the poet's variety, for the unfailing felicity of his versification, for his dramatic resourcefulness, and for the fascinating complexity of his personal character."

In June 1948 Thornton returned to theater, as an actor in several productions of *The Skin of Our Teeth*. He opened the season at the Berkshire Playhouse in Stockbridge, Massachusetts, playing the part of Mr. Antrobus. For Thornton, the return to Stockbridge was a happy occasion. In 1939, when he had appeared as the Stage Manager in the Playhouse's production of *Our Town*, he fell in love with the Berkshires and revisited Stockbridge often, staying at the Red Lion Inn. His affection for the town was so well known that, years after *Our Town* was first produced, viewers mistakenly identified Grovers Corners as Stockbridge, Massachusetts. He believed that the kind of spirit prevalent in such small New England towns was necessary for regendering political interest that had flagged after the war. "We don't want to think," he said, "and our political apathy is defeating the democratic process." Writers "must mix the cement for others to build the walls." But it would be necessary to inspire, nationwide, the sense of responsibility that could be found in every small town meeting.[6]

From Stockbridge, Thornton went south to New Hope, Pennsylvania, where he repeated his role at The Bucks County Playhouse. The stage director, Franklin Heller, had heard rumors that Thornton was "an ardent, if somewhat limited, actor" and was not eager to direct him in his own play, especially when there would be only one week of rehearsals before opening night. He

would, he decided, take a week's vacation and allow someone else
to direct *Skin*.

But his meeting with Thornton was a more than pleasant experience. Thornton came to New Hope early, when Heller was
directing *Years Ago*, an autobiographical play by Ruth Gordon.
He was much impressed by Heller's handling of the play. "In
fact," Heller remembered, "he went so far as to say that it had
certain values which had not been realized in the original production and that he was going to call up Miss Gordon and Mr. Kanin
and 'insist' that they come to New Hope to see their play performed in my interpretation.

"I did not know then that this was characteristic of Mr. Wilder
to praise where he thought praise was due, and to do more than
just express himself in words. In fact, Miss Gordon and Mr.
Kanin did come to New Hope by limousine and did sit through a
matinee and, although they were not quite as enthusiastic about
what I had done as Mr. Wilder had been—that was understandable—they were, indeed, very complimentary. . . ."

Heller, grateful for Thornton's support, gave a large party in his
honor, inviting the casts of *Years Ago* and *The Skin of Our Teeth*
and many prominent personalities. George S. Kaufman and Moss
Hart were to come but, to Heller's disappointment, neither arrived. The party was a tremendous success. "Shortly after midnight, Thornton . . . took me aside and said he wanted to talk
and could I get everyone's attention," Heller recalled. "That was
easy, and Thornton sat down in a large chair and he said this date
was an anniversary of the day he had met Gertrude Stein . . . and
he wanted to talk about Miss Stein.

"He then proceeded to discourse about those famous days on
the Left Bank, the literary and artistic group which surrounded
Miss Stein and many amusing and enlightening sidelights. The
discourse became a dialogue and, sitting at his feet, literally, the
actors and others plied him with questions on many subjects on
all of which he was able to speak both entertainingly and tellingly.
Thornton warmed to the actors and they to him, and it was just
nifty. . . . The party broke up about 3 A.M. and would not then
except the actors had a matinee the next day, and Thornton was

to rehearse in the morning, and this party was talked about in New Hope for the rest of the season."

It was not long before Kaufman and Hart heard that they had missed a rare evening. ". . . The following Friday they invited Thornton to a party at Mr. Hart's home," Heller said, and though he himself did not attend, he was told what happened.

"Mr. Hart had all the cognoscenti of the Bucks County community at his house, like Oscar Hammerstein II, Joe Bryan III and numberless other people, but somehow the discourse never started, although there was some dialogue. Many efforts were made to entice Mr. Wilder into reminiscence such as they heard had taken place at our house, but it did not work.

"Thornton did, however, find that, in responding, he inevitably fell into quotations from obscure German poets in their original tongue. Medieval French historians in their language, many quotations from Latin and he may have spoken in English a little too.

"Shortly, he looked at his watch and announced that he had a matinee the next day and said he had to leave, and he was gone before midnight. After he departed, George S. Kaufman, who had not said a word so far, spoke up. 'You know,' he said, with that grimace so characteristic of him, 'that's the best educated actor I ever met.' "[7]

Besides acting, Thornton spent much of the summer of 1948 working on a new play, *The Emporium*, which was written with a specific actor in mind. The plot deals with a young man who is seeking a position in a "vast, mysterious" department store, but is rejected in favor of other, less qualified applicants. Inspired by Kafka's *The Castle*, the play was to have been staged under blazing lights, with no change of lighting to depict day or night. The young man was to have been played by one of Thornton's latest friends, Montgomery Clift.

Clift had performed the part of Henry (Cain) in *The Skin of Our Teeth* and in 1944 had acted in a revival of *Our Town*. The two men had in common a friendship with Robert Ardrey, literary agent Janet Cohn, and Libby Holman. Though they had met earlier, their friendship solidified in 1945 when Clift was performing in *Foxhole in the Parlor*, a play by Elsa Shelley that opened on Broadway in May. Thornton saw two performances and came backstage to praise the young actor. ". . . Such adjectives as he had for me," Clift wrote to a friend, ". . . right then and there I was convinced he was the greatest playwright on the continent!" To Clift, Thornton was "a real intellectual" possessing a great store of knowledge about the theater, and he treasured the times he could listen to Thornton talking "about philosophy— Kierkegaard, paintings—Gertrude Stein, Kit [Cornell] and Helen [Hayes] and what those two can or can't do and on and on into any hour of the night. . . ."8

Besides discussing theater, the two talked about a common concern—being a twin. Clift had a twin sister, and at times, he confessed to Thornton, he was confused about which twin he was. Thornton concurred that all twins were troubled about their identity and urged him to nurture his relationship with his sister.

In September 1948 Thornton sailed for Europe, where his itinerary included speaking at the university in Marburg, Germany, a town known as "a center . . . of traditional German militaristic valor." By that time Thornton had become a somewhat jaded speaker. He preferred meeting informally with students for wine or beer and asked that such an opportunity be given to him at the university. This particular evening was not on his scheduled tour, but Thornton agreed to go to Marburg after a telegram was sent to him by some members of the American Foreign Service. Writer Kay Boyle, then the wife of one of the officers, remembered what was written: "We need you here where everyone has forgotten how to think, not having for a long time been permitted to think. We need to be told again that poets are a little above kings and not at all below the saints, because nobody here remembers this any more."9

"His coming," she recalled, "and the things he said, were like a candle being carried into a dusk-filled room, bringing instant light, but at the same time causing the shadows of men to be flung, far larger than reality on the surrounding walls." He "spoke of works that had come out of the hearts and minds of men in other times and places, and he spoke of works that were still to be conceived of and achieved, thus opening a wide perspective of hope to all who listened, and bringing the illumination of intelligence to a scene that had seemed hopelessly obscured. He made the centuries seem one long chapter in the experience of men of every time and every nationality, and those who believed in the universality of what he said could suddenly lift their heads."[10]

After World War II, Thornton found himself an immensely popular writer in Germany. Hemingway, Faulkner, Steinbeck, and Saroyan were strong literary influences, but Thornton was "hysterically popular." As one observer noted, ". . . The Wilder vogue in Germany is . . . significant of the post-war condition of the German psyche which, after wallowing from 1933 to 1945 in brute political realities, now hankers as violently after the spiritual, the disembodied and the ideal."[11]

*The Bridge of San Luis Rey* became "one of the best beloved American books in German" after the translation by Herbert E. Herlitschka appeared in 1929. Thornton's fame grew with postwar productions of *Our Town* and peaked with *The Skin of Our Teeth*. After a performance in Munich in 1946, one critic wrote that the play was one of "those rare works of art which are like delphic centers of an epoch in which through the words of the poet the oracles of the spirit of the time themselves seem to find expression as through the mouth of a Pythia." To the Germans, *The Skin of Our Teeth* seemed to reveal their deepest, unspoken feelings. It seemed to many that the play should have been written by a German—or at least a European: someone who actually had suffered physically the chaos of the war.

The play inspired a controversy among critics and students. Some held that Thornton was expressing an optimistic viewpoint about humanity; others, that mankind's endless repetition of mistakes will someday be ended by catastrophe. We escaped this time, they thought he was saying, but only barely; next time we may not be as lucky. Where American productions tended to be raucous and joyful, German staging tried to draw upon the medieval mystery play or create a Faustian atmosphere. Thornton, interviewed in Germany, cautioned his audiences not to take the play more seriously than he intended it.

He was amazed at the Germans' response to *The Skin of Our Teeth*. Men and women who allowed themselves few luxuries crowded into frigid theaters to see the play time after time.[12] He was repeatedly asked if Henry Antrobus represented Germany.

"But really I was not thinking particularly of Germany," he explained; "I had in mind Ur and Chaldea." Only once did he find an adverse response. "In Berlin," he said, "the Russians closed the play down. They closed both 'Our Town' and 'The Skin of Our Teeth.' They closed 'Our Town' because they said it glorified the family. You will never guess what they found wrong with 'The Skin of Our Teeth.' They said it equated war with natural disasters like the Ice Age or the Flood, whereas anybody knows war is caused by imperialistic capitalism."[13]

# SEVENTEEN

---

I N late June 1949 the bicentenary of Goethe's birth was celebrated in Aspen, Colorado. Seminars, concerts, and lectures
were held for two weeks and participants included Albert
Schweitzer, Stephen Spender, José Ortega y Gasset—and Thornton Wilder. Robert Hutchins, the chairman of the festival, explained the choice of Aspen as a suitable site. The planners had
sought "a small, peaceful, simple, and somewhat remote community free from the distractions of a large city, to which people
would have to make a pilgrimage because they wanted to be there;
in a larger metropolitan center visitors could have dropped in casually, more or less out of curiosity."[1] Thornton thought the setting truly beautiful, from its pine valley to its snow-capped mountains. Eero Saarinen had designed a huge tent in which lectures
and concerts were held. Even the bar of the Jerome Hotel, in
which Thornton spent a good deal of time, was charming, with
walls covered with posters from old plays.[2]

Thornton felt a deep affinity with Goethe and an admiration
for him that increased as he prepared himself for the festival by
rereading many of Goethe's works. Thornton, like Goethe, loved

the theater. Both held great respect for Lope de Vega and Menander and a special affection for French theater. But both were
discouraged in their artistic inclinations. "My father was altogether of a didactic turn," Goethe had written in his *Autobiography*, "and in his retirement from business liked to communicate to others what he knew or was able to do." His father
would have preferred that he study law, and when Goethe returned to supper after attending the theater he had to suffer his
father's "constant reproaches, that theaters were useless, and
would lead to nothing." Nevertheless, he received support and encouragement from his mother and especially from his sister Cor-
nelia, until her early death.

Both brought to literature a great breadth of knowledge from
other fields, and their excitement could be piqued by any number
of interesting oddities. Both felt awe at the wonders of nature.
"There is in nature an accessible and inaccessible," Goethe had
told his companion Eckermann. "Be careful to discriminate between the two, be circumspect, and proceed with reverence."

Shortly before the conference began, Thornton wrote to a
friend, the naturalist Rudyerd Boulton, about a fascinating lecture
he had attended in Austria. The lecture dealt with the behavior of
bees and detailed the peculiar dance bees enact when transmitting
information to other members of the hive. The information was
"danced" with such accuracy that attempts to manipulate the
bees' behavior repeatedly failed. For Thornton, such glimpses of
scientific inquiry were proof of the wide range of knowledge still
to be uncovered, and he believed that the nonscientist must seek
out and respect such knowledge. "Thoreau despised and dreaded
Science," he wrote; "to inquire too narrowly into the laws of nature seemed to him to threaten those increasingly infrequent visi-
tations of irrational joy. 'If you would obtain insight, avoid anat-
omy,' . . ."[3] Goethe would have disagreed, Thornton knew. Even
late in his life, he still derived much pleasure from his study of
vertebrates, of botany. The awe he felt for nature was translated
into his writing and inspired his vision. Yet science, Thornton
believed, must be tempered by literature and art and a thoughtful
philosophy about humanity. "Goethe, the last great man-of-all-
mankind who was also a distinguished scientist, warned us against

this uncurbed specialization, urging that education of scientists should particularly include all the needs and capacities of human society. It is too late to do anything about this now beyond recognizing it. Our educational systems are now in a race to produce more and more laboratory workers with blinkers on them."[4]

For Thornton, Goethe, perhaps more than any other writer, spoke directly to modern man. "He has words . . . for us all. The whole world has been disordered and may be plunging to its ruin. This poet, scientist, philosopher, and man of affairs has a host of messages of the highest importance for our time.

Among them:

He restores the diminished dignity of man by his emphasis on the unity of the living being with the entire creative expansion of all nature. (He refused the doctrine that the "World is wicked," that man is alone in a soulless universe, that man is the victim of a closed mechanistic determination.)

He offers an ethics to scientific investigation, an ethics which is not a muzzling but a directive and which throws a powerful light on the manufacture of atomic weapons of war and on the threats of extermination by biological means.

He illustrates in a thousand ways that we learn the nature of life not by speculation but by fulfilling our immediate duties.

He teaches us that we become strong by reasoning, by selecting, by defending our objectives. This doctrine of renunciation surprises hasty readers who think that "Faust" is a summons to experience everything, yearn for everything, grab everything.

. . . He was not only the great poet but the wisest, most far-seeing prophet voice for the instruction and enrichment of twentieth century society.[5]

At the convocation, Thornton translated for Albert Schweitzer, who came directly from Lambaréné, and for Ortega. On July 5 he delivered his own address, speaking about Goethe and the human spirit. The modern age, Thornton said, was suffering, not from political, economic, or social ills, but from "a difficulty of the human spirit," and it was the task of those gathered together in celebration of Goethe to "search out in ourselves the depths of the spirit that sustained the optimism of Goethe."

"Our time is a moment—if a dark moment—in the life of the Goethian spirit," he continued. Goethe believed in a universal man which transcended "the partial, the provincial, and the passing." It was necessary to revive that belief if art, and even everyday life, was to be improved. "We try here to undeceive and fortify ourselves. We turn here to Goethe and search him, the better to turn to and search ourselves, and cry *More Light! More Light!*"

He hoped that the festival would restore Goethe to his proper place in our literary heritage. "The tragedy of Goethe," he told an interviewer, "is that he belonged to a race that disgraced itself. . . . Because of that, his philosophies have largely been ignored—philosophies that are applicable to twentieth century living and that could possibly have spared mankind the spiritual miseries he is suffering.

"Goethe was highly critical of the faults of the German people in his own writings. Literary geniuses, too, are largely removed from any racial association by their genius.

"Just as Shakespeare is not truly British, Goethe is not truly German."[6] Goethe, he added, was "a delayed time bomb, a repeating time bomb. . . ."[7]

After the festival, Thornton visited at the ranch of Walter and Elizabeth Paepcke, who, with Hutchins, were among the planners of the convocation. There he began a friendship with the Paepckes' youngest daughter which lasted until his death. Thornton made friends easily with young people, and showed them an affection and respect that they found rare among adults. Later, "Uncle Thorny" advised the Paepckes to send their daughter to Radcliffe College instead of "one of those horrid Women's Nunneries" like Smith or Mount Holyoke.[8] When he had performed in *The Skin of Our Teeth* in Stockbridge, he became friends with eight-year-old "Mousey" Miles, the daughter of director William Miles. He would invite her for a soda at Benjamin's, a pharmacy and soda fountain that he might have created for *Our Town*. Once he asked her to choose something from the magazine rack and cheerfully bought the little girl copies of *Popular Science* and *Popular Mechanics*. Thornton showed children a warmth he was

too shy to reveal to adults. When he left Stockbridge, he patted
Mousey on the shoulder, saying, "Keep me green, Mousey. Keep
me green."9

His involvement with young people did "keep him green," and
in 1950, when he was invited to deliver the Norton lectures at
Harvard University, he knew he would have the opportunity again
to meet with students and be stimulated by conversations with
them, as he had at the University of Chicago.

He was enthusiastic, too, about many aspiring playwrights,
actors, and writers. As his own fame grew, he made himself more
and more accessible to students and amateur theater groups.
Often, when he was invited to speak at a college or university, he
would do so only on the condition that he be able to meet informally with students afterward. It was from them that he derived
real pleasure. It was not surprising, then, that he consented to
play the Stage Manager in a production of *Our Town* at Wooster
College in Ohio.

He came to Wooster directly from Europe, where he had visited his friend Alice Toklas in Paris, bringing her a huge bouquet
of white lilacs and, to her great delight, a Mixmaster. Since Gertrude Stein's death in 1946, Thornton remained close to Alice,
and she often turned to him for emotional support and for advice
in her efforts to publish Gertrude's large *oeuvre*. In 1947 he had
written an introduction to *Four in America*, published by Yale
University Press, which greatly pleased Alice. He also served as an
adviser in the preparation of the press's edition of Gertrude's
works. Among Gertrude's friends, Thornton earned Alice's unqualified respect. She would defer to his opinions and even admitted being a little afraid of him.

His visits—sometimes alone, sometimes with Isabel—were fes-
tive occasions for Alice. Flowers, gifts, dinners in elegant restaurants, evenings at the theater were all reported in detail to friends
and gratefully acknowledged, usually to Isabel, since Alice knew
that Thornton was embarrassed by lavish displays of emotion.

When his appearance at Wooster was publicized, all seats in
the school's auditorium were sold out immediately, and even prestigious alumni were turned away. Thornton was much praised for

his performance. "Mr. Wilder doesn't act; he just talks. And with his apparently spontaneous remarks, he creates that friendly intimate atmosphere that comes with congenial conversation. This atmosphere infuses the entire play, and blends with the characters who come and go in the fanciful streets of the New Hampshire village."[10] Thornton, another viewer noted, "gave a sincere interpretation of the action, breezy at times, humorous at others and, in the final act, achieves a solemnity that drove the play's final moral points home with an uncomfortable directness."[11]

Besides acting, Thornton delivered an address on "The American" after he was awarded a degree of Doctor of Humane Letters. His thoughts were to be reworked and expanded in his Norton lectures, but his basic theme remained unchanged: there was an essential loneliness inherent in being American. It was "the price that independence pays," and it was a loneliness that could not be assuaged by "joinings."

"We're very famous joiners," he said, "and the Europeans laugh at us. We just rush in to sign our names to belong to this and that, that they think that's a very unEuropean thing to do. Fraternities and women's clubs and men's business clubs Mondays, and alumni associations. We all sign up for these joinings. And they don't find that they are any way near as valid as they ought to be. And the very protests and the oaths with streaming eyes you take when you join them are not necessarily a sign of their validity or their depth. From our independence and our loneliness we do try to reach out to find a human community, but the American way of being a community is not the same as the European." Americans exhibit a "superficial gregariousness" because of their heritage of independence and because they live in a new world, in geometrically planned cities "exposed to sky."

And yet, he continued, there is among Americans a very deep unity based on common beliefs. ". . . We are joined really in our belief in education, our belief in democratic institutions, our belief in America's relation to the whole world." The independence of each American need not separate, but should, instead, be the basis of deep commitment, not only to America, but to humanity as a whole. One must be prepared, however, to take the risk involved, and he urged the students in the audience to take such a risk. ". . . You only learn about life from venturing yourself, by placing stakes, and taking risks. There is no contemplation of life from an armchair; you interlock, you engage; that you only know what you know by engaging yourself into the fabric and activity of life itself, by committing yourself.

"Now this is what the founders of this country very dramatically did. They made the choice, and nothing is sadder than to see people who don't make choices, for refusal of a choice is a choice. They took the risk—the perils of the unknown were preferable to the perils of being spiritually suffocated in the habitual, the known, and the accepted. That is what independence always had to do; that is what loneliness should drive the independent man to do."

He cautioned the audience that Americans placed a peculiar emphasis on attaining perfection, believing in their characteristically idealistic way that perfection might, after all, be possible to achieve. In *Our Town*, he told them, Emily urged George to be as perfect as her father, and George replied that he thought girls were perfect. Thornton maintained that only American audiences understood those lines. In translation—in France, in Germany—one might understand "impeccable manners," but no one "would even think of applying that adjective to the requirements of life." He was saddened by the prospect of "young people driven in on themselves by a too lofty, self-punishing idealism, into shyness, introspection, and, worst of all, into the inability to plan largely and to devote themselves deeply for fear of failure and humiliation in their own eyes. . . ." He urged them instead to begin "not a form of gregariousness, but a commitment. . . ."[12]

Yet he was not encouraging about their making a commitment to the theater. In more informal meetings, addressing students, Thornton urged his listeners not to consider seriously a life's work in the theater, knowing "that the irresistibly gifted will not take . . . advice and will build a career there with however much difficulty." The costs of production, he said, were so high that only rarely could a successful living be made in the theater.

It takes $60,000 before you can raise a curtain on Broadway. . . . High costs of transportation caused the decline of the road com-

pany and the centralization of the theater in New York. Seventy-
five percent of the actors in Equity are unemployed.

For every 'South Pacific' there are scores of plays that have very
short runs. The success of 'South Pacific' seems to indicate a pros-
perous theater epoch. It is not true. . . .

The forms of entertainment are themselves passing through a transition. . . . Certain parts of the larger audiences are staying away
from the theater and the movies because they have outgrown the
routine entertainment that has been successful hitherto and because
managers have not yet seen the way to furnish a type of newer entertainment which would give them satisfaction.[13]

Thornton was enthusiastic about repertory companies and small
theaters and tried to encourage such groups whenever he found
them. In the fall of 1950, when he came to Cambridge for the
Norton lectures, he spent many evenings at the Brattle Theatre or
at the Poets' Theater near Harvard Square. To Thornton the
young companies reflected the best of the spirit of American theater. He was impressed by the Brattle's productions of *Six Characters in Search of an Author* and *Henry IV, Part II*. "What struck
me most," he said in "A Playwright's View of Brattle," "was the
mixture of insight into the plays themselves, the theatre experience evident in every portion of the productions and the freshness
and vigour of their projection."

One evening, when he was at the Poets' Theater for the opening of a verse play, the audience became loudly disapproving and
even disorderly. Thornton was shocked and stood up to scold the
viewers sternly. The actors, he told them, deserved a chance and
their talent needed to be encouraged. He reproved them for their
rudeness and lack of consideration. There was a stunned silence
after he finally sat down—and the audience was well behaved
throughout the rest of the performance.

Besides delivering the prestigious Norton lectures, he conducted
a humanities course in the spring term, in which he did his "imitation Dr. Wager." The course included readings of *Don Quixote,
The Red and the Black, Great Expectations, Moby-Dick,* and
*War and Peace,* and required the grading of three short papers
from each student. Thornton was greatly lionized during his year

at Harvard, and he found it difficult to refuse the many social engagements he was offered. In addition to his Harvard commitments, he was still working on *The Emporium* and other writings.
"I start my day at 6 o'clock with my first breakfast, a cup of coffee
at an all-night restaurant in the square," he said; "I return to
Dunster and from 8:30 to 10 o'clock I answer my own telephone
calls. Then, I go to Widener Library." There, besides conducting
his own research, he was editing letters that Alexander Woollcott
had bequeathed to the university. Thornton found the task tedious. "I haven't the kind of curiosity which would make this interesting," he said. "Frankly, I don't like reading other people's
mail."[14]

He was more comfortable as a lecturer, and for him an American lecture was very different from its European counterpart. In
Europe, he thought, "a lecture tended to be a discourse in which
an Authority dispensed a fragment of the Truth."[15] Such dis-
courses appealed to the middle-class in particular, and the Swiss
especially had a penchant for lectures. "Conrad Ferdinand Meyer
said that if the citizens of Zurich were required to make a choice
between going to Heaven or going to a lecture about Heaven they
would hesitate only a moment." But the American audience was
more incredulous and less submissive. An American lecturer,
therefore, would do well to dispense with formality and offer instead a personal view on whatever topic he chose. Thornton's
series of talks dealt with "The American Characteristics of Classical American Literature," by which he meant how the English
language—in speech and in writing—was becoming transformed
into the American language.

He maintained that the chief characteristic among the British
settlers in America was their independence. Rather than allow
their environment to shape their identity, these rugged men and
women "did not need to be supported, framed, consoled, by the
known, the habitual, the loved. . . ." They did not need the sight
of the village their families had lived in for generations, the
church in which their ancestors were baptized. Even after they
had settled in the new country, a vast ocean away from their
homeland, they constantly felt the need to push on, farther and
farther away from whatever was too familiar. One adage, Thorn-

ton noted, well expressed their feelings: "If you can see the smoke from your neighbor's chimney, you're too near."

Europeans achieved their identity from their environment and immediate community. But Americans, he thought, were "disconnected." They did not feel the physical boundaries of mountains or rivers that separated them from those who spoke a different language and celebrated different festivals. They did not identify with any one particular place, nor any one particular time. "Place and environment," Thornton said, "are but *décor* to his [the American's] journey. He lives not on the treasure that lies about him but on the promises of the imagination." Americans, therefore, feel more comfortable than Europeans with the idea of a multiplicity of lives. In part, this acceptance of the hugeness of humankind comes from their vast country and their independent heritage; in part, from one book that shaped their literature: the Bible.

The Bible, Thornton said, presented the individual opposed to the vast uncounted numbers of all who have lived. "Its characters hang suspended upon the promises of the imagination. . . . Those (one and one and one . . .) to whom destiny has extended a promise and a plan have this consolation, that they feel themselves to be irreplaceable. Each one is a bundle of projects." Writers in America addressed themselves to a classless audience. Melville, Emily Dickinson, Whitman, wrote for the entire community and used earthy images that would have been considered crass by a European elite. Inherent in American writing is an essential independence and, as he told his Wooster audience, an essential loneliness.

No one embodied the American loneliness more dramatically than Thoreau. "It is difficult to be an American," Thornton knew, and the difficulty is exemplified in Thoreau's life.[16] Thoreau attempted to simplify his own life in an effort to know his inner self. He found it necessary to cut himself off from the larger community to understand his singularity. Thoreau, like every American, was an autodidact. ". . . Every American," Thornton said, "feels himself capable of being the founder of his own religion." But Thoreau was "defeated in his impassioned demands upon Love, Friendship, and Nature" because he did not fully understand the concept of the multiplicity of human lives and because he had "a parochial, a wood-lot view of nature and her mighty laws." Yet Thoreau earned Thornton's respect while Emerson received his derision. Emerson, who knew he was incapable of friendship and did not allow the defect to bother him, gave himself up to abstractions and exhorted others to attain a moral excellence by which he himself did not live. Emerson did not struggle with the contradictions faced by an American like Thoreau.

For the independent spirit, both friendship and kinship pose unresolvable problems. In the United States, Thornton said, the family nurtures "an unusually powerful ambivalence." The child wants to break his familial ties and gain his independence, but as an American he realizes the loneliness inherent in that independence: he is merely one among millions. His family actually precludes the attainment of complete independence, and yet it is the only group in which he feels necessary, celebrated, important, part of a community.

For Thoreau, every confrontation with love, family, even nature only emphasized his own physical and metaphysical loneliness. And yet his life serves as an example and, Thornton believed, Thoreau "fought some battles for us." "Is there a Thoreau," he asked, "who can tell us that once one has grasped and accepted a basic solitude, all the other gifts come pouring back—love, friendship, and nature? One reads the life story of Thoreau with anxious suspense."

The sadness we feel from knowing of Thoreau's frustrations comes because we know he suffered not only a broad philosophical loneliness, but a chilling, personal desolation. Yet another American writer, Emily Dickinson, though she appeared lonely was, Thornton said, not really as emotionally isolated as Thoreau. She was able to resolve what Thoreau could not "by loving the particular while living in the universal."

Thornton believed that Dickinson was a genius, "charged with extra-ordinary resources of the life-force which could break through dams and repair ravage." She was physically withdrawn from a larger community and she had suffered deep disillusionment from her relationships with her family and few friends; yet, Thornton said, she wrote for Everybody. Though she lived alone, unmarried, in her home in Amherst, she knew the larger world and its vast dimensions. She was an astute observer of nature: of plants and animals. ". . . She knows well that they are living their life engaging in no tender or instinctive dialogue with man, and that their life is part of a millennial chain. . . ." With her intuitive knowledge of the world, time, and space, "she is the least parochial of American poets and exceeds even Walt Whitman in imaginative sweep."

In assessing the American spirit during his year at Harvard, Thornton had occasion not only to reflect on his literary heritage, but to observe students as he worked with them and lived beside them. His faith was constantly reaffirmed, he admitted, and he felt that the generation of the fifties faced "the too long delayed task of consolidating its liberty and of impressing upon it a design, a meaning, and a focus." While others accused young people of apathy and lethargy, he saw them "fashioning the Twentieth Century Man. . . . The Silent Generation (loquacious enough among its contemporaries) holds its tongue because it cannot both explore itself and explain itself."[17]

Thornton saw great hope in the new generation. He believed that they were "the first truly international men and women." Where previous generations knew they were "one among millions," the new generation "feel themselves to be one among billions." In a sense, they were the first generation to transcend national boundaries and understand universality as Goethe implied it. ". . . We went to war against and among 'foreigners' and 'enemies,'" Thornton wrote. "That attitude was narrow; henceforward all wars are civil wars."

He also admired their determination "not to find themselves in 'false situations.'" The young people he met were not necessarily bowed by authority. They were more likely to have opinions different from those of their parents or teachers; they were more likely to rely on themselves rather than on precedents and expected behavior. They did not carry on beliefs as they were handed down, but were "interested in the nature of belief itself." Thornton believed that it was wrong to accuse them of apathy, of not actively protesting causes as did the generation of the twenties and thirties. "This generation is silent," he said, "because these changes call not for argument but for rumination. . . . These young people are setting new patterns for the relation of the individual to the society about him." Thornton advised those who would dismiss or exhort the new generation to try to understand them. ". . . They wish to live correctly by their lights and not by ours. In proportion as we are free we must accord them that."

However much inspired he might have been by again working with young people, Thornton found the Norton year exhausting. In March he entered Massachusetts General Hospital suffering from a sacroiliac dislocation that had caused him much discomfort. He felt fortunate to be attended by excellent nurses, and his hospital experience was far different from what others of his family had endured in New Haven. But even by late spring he still had not fully recovered his energies.

In June he was awarded two doctorates—one by Northeastern and another by Harvard. According to poet Wallace Stevens, who met him at the Cambridge ceremonies, Thornton "was by all odds the top speaker . . . ," and "a very good egg" besides.[18] Thornton was an admirer of Stevens' poetry and in the fall wrote to him asking if they might meet one day for some good conversation. They were neighbors in New Haven, but Thornton proposed that they might meet in Bucks County, Pennsylvania, where he was visiting and where Stevens set some of his poems. That meeting never took place.

Thornton stayed in Cambridge through the summer, though his duties at Harvard were over. By July he wrote to a friend that he was tired—very tired—and needed solitude, rest, and silence.[19]

# EIGHTEEN

H E planned to sail for France on September 14, 1951, hoping at first to stay in Europe for several months. He was exhausted, he admitted, and needed rest. The last days at Harvard were spent furiously correcting bluebooks and editing his Norton lectures for publication by Harvard University Press. The press customarily published a volume of the addresses of each Norton lecturer, but Thornton, busy with other projects, never completed his manuscript for them.

A letter from his Chicago friend Robert Stallman, proposing an edition of the letters of Stephen and William Benét, brought to mind his undergraduate days at Yale and his friendships with the two brothers. He cautioned Stallman about collecting their letters, saying that his generation was not given to writing literary analyses to each other. Though the Benét brothers were enormously kind to younger writers, Thornton doubted that their letters would reveal anything of their commitment to poetry or their thoughts about writing. Stallman would be more likely to find light-hearted, humorous interchanges.

By August, Thornton's trip was more definite. He and Isabel

would travel together, but now he thought he would return after a month to continue his writing near one or another of the libraries in which he enjoyed working. He sailed home from Genoa in October, leaving Isabel to go on to Rome.

In November and December he settled in Bucks County, driving twenty-five miles to the Princeton library a few times each week for a supply of books. He was happiest near a good library, he often said, and now he was content to rest in the countryside of Pennsylvania for the fall. Bucks County and the Pennsylvania Dutch Country were, he thought, fine backgrounds for good talk. He knew the special atmosphere of the land from the poetry of Wallace Stevens, but his proposed meeting with Stevens never took place.

By mid-January he had gone south to Daytona Beach, Florida. There he met Montgomery Clift, and their conversation centered mostly on Clift's career and choice of parts. Thornton believed Clift to be a talented actor, but thought he needed guidance in selecting and interpreting parts to allow his talent to develop. Neither man especially liked Florida: Thornton complained about the food, though he found two Spanish restaurants that pleased him; Clift thought he'd be happier somewhere in Upper Mongolia.[1] In February, Thornton was joined by his friend C. Leslie Glenn, then associated with St. John's Church in Washington, D.C.

He spent part of May in Newport, Rhode Island, a more congenial setting and one to which he often returned. There he worked on an address to be given at Oberlin College, following his receiving of an honorary doctorate. "Wrestling with Henry David Thoreau" was delivered on June 9, 1952, and contained many of the ideas he had presented in his Norton lectures at Harvard.

Thoreau, a unique spirit, was in some ways "an outrageous American." At the age of twenty-nine, he claimed that he had yet to hear a word of good advice from his elders. Thornton admitted that he had heard nothing but "good advice" during his childhood, but that, like Thoreau, he never heard any advice that touched him; like Thoreau, he was self-taught. Like Thoreau, he had asked: "Life! who knows what it is, what it does?"[2]

One peculiarity of being an American, Thornton continued, was the need to start from scratch and to travel alone. Yet all endeavors must be entered into with enthusiasm and full commitment. Thornton felt sorry when he met young people who held themselves back from complete involvement in their pursuits and who complicated their lives with extraneous activities or pastimes to avoid that real involvement. He admonished his audience to remember Thoreau's advice: "Simplify!"[3] And he told them, too, that cultivating a passion for life, realizing their goals, would not be found from books, but from involvement and activity. More than three decades after *The Cabala*, Thornton still warned against becoming a James Blair.

While at the college, Thornton told friends of a play he was writing that would be perfect for Oberlin's auditorium. *The Sandusky, Ohio, Mystery Play* was, he said, about a Christmas pageant presented by the townspeople of Sandusky, Ohio, in one of their Congregational churches. The various merchants and their families would comprise the cast, and Thornton himself offered to play St. Joseph as if he were the town policeman. But he admitted that the play still needed much work and would not be finished soon.

He was working on other ideas and spent some of the summer at the MacDowell Colony. But in recent years he had been finding the atmosphere at the colony less conducive to creativity than it had been when he first visited there in the twenties. This time there were several divorcées who, though admirable, serious artists, competed for the attentions of some of the guests—and strained the informal camaraderie that might have existed otherwise. Thornton's stay did not last into the fall. He left in September to attend the Venice Arts Conference, sponsored by UNESCO.

Thornton felt that the city was a most suitable site for the conference, "for Venice is peculiarly the work of man and of the artist —without his energy and creativity this marvel of the world would be a marsh." While most of the writers who attended the conference were assigned to one or another of the various committees, Thornton, who was to deliver the General Report at the conference's close, was able to observe each group and obtain a broad

view of the progress of the meetings. He found that the conference reaffirmed his belief that "the artist through his creating, has
been in all times a force that draws men together and reminds
them that the things which men have in common are greater than
the things that separate them: and that the work of the artist is
the clearest example of the operation of freedom in the human
spirit."

He believed that it was the purpose of the conference to set
forth certain basic principles that to others might appear to be
"vague generalizations." But it was necessary, he said, to lay
strong foundations for future action on certain important problems. One of these problems was censorship. Here the committees
were strong in their condemnation, yet they admitted that the
problem was difficult because existing laws were enacted by conservative courts, and artists must by nature "reveal new modalities
of the true and the beautiful before the majority of men are aware
of them."

Another problem was the relation of the artist to government,
especially concerning subsidies, and some participants expressed
lack of confidence in their governments' good will toward artists
and art. Freedom, Thornton concluded, was necessary for the pro-
ductivity of the artist. The artist must be free to create what he
wishes. "Freedom presents itself to an artist not as a void but as a
severe summons. Of all men, artists and men of religion have the
clearest vision of what freedom is; and we live in fear lest we
abuse it. . . . The only freedom we desire is a servitude to the
truth. For the interior struggles of the artist we can do nothing."[4]

That the interior struggles of the artist were often misinterpreted was something that Thornton knew well. For him, *Our
Town* was a victim of misunderstanding on the part of critics and
audiences, readers and directors. But in January 1953 one critic
published an article about *Our Town* that pleased and gratified
him. Winfield Townley Scott's " 'Our Town' and The Golden
Veil" appeared in *Virginia Quarterly* and was forwarded by Isabel
to Baden-Baden in March. Scott defended the play against being
called sentimental and nostalgic. He saw it in the genre of *Tom
Sawyer, Spoon River Anthology,* and *Winesburg, Ohio,* but said
that "it is a more intelligently managed work of art . . . ; it is not

lacking in the instinctiveness which makes those other books great primitives—that is to say, it is not lacking in poetry—though no doubt it is more self-conscious and literary; yet in the very skillful construction of the play is the secret of why *Our Town* does rank as one of the most moving and beautiful of American books." Thornton gently painted the patterns of everyday life in a small town, and yet the theme of the play is not one particular small town, Scott saw, nor one set of particular lives. ". . . Wilder sets in countermotion to the little wheel a big wheel; and as the little one spins the little doings, the big one begins slowly—slowly—for it is time itself, weighted with birth and marriage and death, with aging and with change. This is the great thing that *Our Town* accomplishes; simultaneously we are made aware of what is momentary and what is eternal. . . . What Wilder's art has reminded us is that beauty is recognizable because of change and life is meaningful because of death."

Scott compared Thornton's play favorably with Booth Tarkington's classic *Seventeen* and O'Neill's *Ah! Wilderness*; found sources in Robert Frost's *To Earthward*, and Joyce's *Portrait of the Artist as a Young Man*. His article was one of the few to deal with the play as if it were as deep and important as the works of some of the major playwrights of the day. To Thornton, Scott's article made the play, at last, respectable.

Though Thornton had won his first Pulitzer Prize twenty-five years before, he was not usually taken as seriously as some of his contemporaries—either as playwright or novelist. In college courses on American drama, students might study Tennessee Williams' *The Glass Menagerie* or *A Streetcar Named Desire*, O'Neill's *Mourning Becomes Electra* or *The Iceman Cometh*, Miller's *Death of a Salesman*. But rarely would *Our Town* or *The Skin of Our Teeth* be required reading. In curricula on modern novels, Thornton's name would usually be omitted in favor of Sinclair Lewis, William Faulkner, Hemingway, Fitzgerald, or Sherwood Anderson.

In gaining respectability for his works, he was undermined by his conscious aim of writing for the middle class. Some critics thought he provided too easy an evening's entertainment. His plays could be viewed superficially and only a rare critic like Scott delved beneath the surface to try to analyze Thornton's real intent.

Yet at the same time that Thornton was being ignored by departments of English and graduate students, he was celebrated by colleges and universities. Among his accumulated doctorates was one awarded by the University of New Hampshire in June 1953 for his apt portrayal of "the New England mind," especially in *Our Town*. "In that play," it was decided, "he has interpreted our state and made it known in memorable words and scenes for all times and all peoples."

In August and September 1953 he was at the MacDowell Colony working on a new play. For some time he had been a member of its board of directors, but in the fall he resigned—not because he had any conflicts with the administration of the colony, but because he felt the job was being done so well his position might be better filled by someone more interested in administration than he was.

He was pleased with his work at MacDowell, and believed that to be a successful playwright one had to be truly interested in other people—to be ardent in observing them. When T. S. Eliot told him he was going to devote more time to plays and less to poetry, Thornton was dismayed: he thought Eliot too removed from others to be a fine playwright.

Isabel was then in Europe, first in Venice and then planning to go to Florence, and their house in Hamden, which they had shared since their mother's death, was rented for the fall. Thornton stayed at MacDowell through September; until mid-November he again returned to Newport, Rhode Island, but then decided to drive south to the Florida Keys. He planned no stops along the way, though, hoping to keep the industrious pattern he had set for himself in New Hampshire and Rhode Island. But when he arrived at Key West he could find no accommodations because of the large population of Navy personnel. Instead of a warm respite there, he went on to Sanibel Island and collected shells before he returned late in the year.

While Thornton had been in Newport, the poet Dylan Thomas died in New York at the age of thirty-nine. Thornton had met Thomas when he toured the United States and one night spent hours trying to convince him that he was destroying himself and wasting his considerable talents. He and several other writers —W. H. Auden, e. e. cummings, Arthur Miller, and Wallace Stevens among them—formed the Dylan Thomas Fund Committee in December and published an open letter in the *Saturday Review* to ask for contributions for his widow, Caitlin, and his three children.

In May, Thornton stayed at a small hotel on Long Island where he secluded himself to work. Now, at fifty-six, he was in many ways unchanged from the person he was ten, twenty, or thirty years before. For all his exuberance in public, he still needed to retire from the world to devote himself to his books or plays, and he still needed to reread Goethe or listen to Mozart for solace. During his last trip to Europe, he had met Albert Schweitzer at a restaurant in Paris and asked him: ". . . At the age you have reached, how do you feel about the loves of your youth—Bach, Wagner, Goethe, Kant, Hegel? One does change in the course of a lifetime." But Schweitzer answered as Thornton himself would have: "Moi? Je suis fidèle."[5]

# NINETEEN

I N 1952 British director Tyrone Guthrie was in New York, living at the apartment of Katharine Hepburn while he worked on a production of *Carmen* at the Metropolitan Opera House. Among his neighbors were Garson Kanin and his wife, Ruth Gordon, whom Guthrie had directed in *The Country Wife* at the Old Vic. Guthrie was then interested in finding new plays to bring to England, and when Gordon suggested *The Merchant of Yonkers* it seemed an exciting possibility. She had long hoped to see a new production of the play, staged as Thornton meant it, with her own interpretation of the role of Dolly Levi. "The most serious drawback," Guthrie thought, "seemed to be that it bore the stigma of failure—something which . . . is in present-day America far more damning than a conviction for rape or arson."[1] But he was delighted by the play, and he had for many years held a high regard for Thornton.

Guthrie had met Thornton in Glasgow some thirty years before, and his first introduction to his plays was an excellent performance of *The Long Christmas Dinner* by an amateur dramatic society. "This short play fascinated me," Guthrie said, "because it discarded a lot of theatrical conventions of which I had become tired (and have since become more tired), notably the pretense of naturalistic illusion. . . . I bought the printed text, liked it as much as the performance, and bought the author's other dramatic work, a book of short plays called *The Angel That Troubled the Waters*. These seemed to me no less interesting, congenial and original than *The Long Christmas Dinner*. . . . Two at least of them still seem to me masterpieces of their kind: *The Happy Journey to Trenton and Camden* and *Pullman Car Hiawatha*. Again they discarded naturalistic illusion in favor of symbolism, a symbolism which is not at all pompous or pretentious, but is, on the contrary, extremely simple and full of a dry, rather Puritan humor."[2]

*The Merchant of Yonkers*, though, was more traditional in its style and setting. The farce employs standard techniques of mistaken identity, disguises, eavesdropping, and bumbling. But, Guthrie noted, "there is no attempt to make the audience accept illusion." Thornton, he knew, was not trying to create illusion, but give "a constant reminder that the theatre is a symbol of life. The stage is the world. The characters are not merely themselves, but representatives of humanity. The elaborate and preposterous plot derives not from life, which it only faintly resembles, but from the theatre."[3]

Guthrie admired the play almost as much as he admired the playwright. He was charmed by Thornton's exuberance and impressed by his erudition.

If you sat opposite to him in a plane or train . . . perhaps you took him, with that clipped gray moustache, to be a slightly eccentric major on leave or an excitable country doctor or, noticing those strong, incredibly restless hands, an artificer, a maker of precision instruments, or maybe, a piano tuner. You would expect him to be anything but a *savant*, a notable wit and the author of three or four works which, of all written in our time, are probably at the head of the queue for classical status—not because they are learned and funny and technically accomplished, not even because they are filled with wisdom and feeling, but because . . . they express the profound intuition with which, over and above the literal meaning, between the lines of story or play, one human soul speaks to another.

I once traveled with him in a local train in Canada. For two hours on a baking summer morning he gave me an absorbing critique and intimate biography of Henry James. Thornton left the train and I went on. An old man came along the coach and plumped down in the empty place.

"Say," he said. "Been watchin' the two of yer. Couldn't hear a word, mind ya; but that was a jolly old joker. Bet he could tell ya a few good yarns."[4]

But though Thornton was at times a nonstop talker, Guthrie noticed that he would invariably come away with "a shrewd and tolerant and comprehensive impression of the interlocutor." For all his ebullience, there was "a stillness at the center of the maelstrom." And for all his allusions to actresses, writers, and academicians, he was never a name-dropper or snob. "I treasure particularly happy memories of him at Stratford, Ontario . . . , attending rehearsals, buzzing like a bee in the actors' canteen, splashing dye onto costumes for plague-stricken Thebans, sitting up far into the night at parties, cross-legged on the floor among the youngsters of the company, listening to them with grave attention, drawing them out and pumping them full of philosophy, psychology, religion, gossip, jokes and just plain, practical horsesense."[5]

*The Merchant of Yonkers*, which had failed under Max Reinhardt's direction in 1938, was to be staged with some changes and would appear as *The Matchmaker*, with Ruth Gordon in the role that was created for her: Dolly Levi. Hugh Beaumont presented the play in London, with sets designed by Tanya Moiseiwitsch, and the play was then staged at the prestigious Edinburgh Festival during the summer of 1954. Eileen Herlie played Mrs. Molloy; Sam Levene, Horace Vandergelder; and Alec McCowen, Barnaby Tucker. Beaumont, Guthrie remembered, "as usual, was courteously, gently relentless in keeping us on our toes. Thornton was compelled to rewrite and the cast to rerehearse. The first act gave us a lot of trouble; as so often with farce, the exposition took rather long and the laughs were slow in the first twenty minutes."[6]

*The Matchmaker* then crossed the Atlantic and was given a second chance where it had first failed. The opening in Philadelphia was disappointing. The British company was not accustomed to the size of the theater or the temper of the audience. Laughs came at unexpected places, and the play's humor was not received as it had been in England. The producer, David Merrick, became worried over the play's success, and even Thornton became nervous. "He saw a matinee performance in which every line was spoken, every bit of business performed, as exactly and meticulously as it had been for more than a year by an experienced and well-disposed company," Guthrie recalled. But both men were unhappy. "He and Merrick fell upon me as if I were a fraudulent dog-breeder who had sold them a mongrel with a forged pedigree. Undignified scenes in hotel rooms kept coming to the boil and were only averted by the extreme tact and good sense of Garson Kanin who, an old friend both of Thornton and myself, could act as a sort of umpire and impose order and restraint on us two foolish, excited, elderly gentlemen."[7]

In Boston the situation improved, and the company felt the play was getting a better reception. In New York, all knew they finally had achieved success. The audience was congenial and appreciative and the critics were kind. In fact, Guthrie said, "The notices could not have been better if we had written them ourselves. . . ."[8]

From his success in Edinburgh, Thornton went to the Continent for a two-week lecture tour at German universities. On September 27 he arrived in Paris, joined by Isabel, where they visited with Alice Toklas and saw exhibitions of Cézanne and Picasso paintings. Isabel then went to Italy, Thornton to Aix-en-Provence for a working vacation. Both took an excursion to Rapallo, Italy, where they visited with Max Beerbohm, who had been living there for the past forty years.

In mid-January 1955 Thornton returned to England for discussions about producing another play at the Edinburgh Festival—*The Alcestiad*, on which he had been working for several years. When he read his newly completed third act to Tyrone Guthrie and his wife, Judith, they were much impressed by the play, and Thornton hoped that it might be first produced at the Shake-

speare Festival in Ontario, then brought to Scotland.[9] But it was
soon decided that *The Alcestiad* would open in Edinburgh for the
festival in the summer of 1955.

*The Alcestiad, or A Life in the Sun,* is Thornton's reworking of
the legend of Alcestis, the wife of King Admetus. Admetus, ill and
dying, is told by the gods that he may go on living if he can find
someone to die in his stead. His faithful wife, Alcestis, determines
that she is the only one who can perform such a sacrifice, since
she is the one who has the most to live for, and gives her life for
her husband.

Like *The Emporium, The Alcestiad* was written with Montgomery Clift in mind. But a few weeks before the opening, Clift
met with Thornton to propose some changes. When Thornton refused, Clift dropped out of the company, and the part of Admetus was taken over by Michael Goodliffe. The cast included
Irene Worth and Laurence Hardy, and the sets on the apron stage
of the Assembly Hall were again designed by Tanya Moiseiwitsch.
This play, however, did not meet the enthusiastic reception of
Thornton's previous work.

Reviews were mixed, with some critics pronouncing the play irritating and a few not knowing whether it was a comedy or a tragedy. In an interview in Edinburgh, Thornton explained that the
play was "existentialist in its philosophy . . . ," and offered the
metaphor of "two trains—one headed for negation and atheism,
and the other headed for 'the Leap of Faith.'" When asked
which train he was on, Thornton joked, "Week-end journey to
Brighton."[10]

In early spring 1955 he had gone back to America, traveling to
Berea in May and to Rhode Island. There he checked into the
Castle Hill Hotel in Newport and worked on a project different
from any he had previously done—an opera libretto. He was collaborating with composer Louise Talma on a full-scale opera of
*The Alcestiad.* Although the libretto was to be his first attempt
at the art form, he felt no worries about its restrictions. "Every
form is a restriction. . . . All the arts are conquered differently.
After all, why write a sonnet? Why limit yourself to jumping
through the hoops of complicated rhyme schemes? A restriction
can be a challenge."[11]

He had met Louise Talma at the MacDowell Colony in 1952 but had known her work before. He admired her talent, her seriousness, and her modesty. During their collaboration, he was consistently encouraging and took great pleasure when she would admit that even a phrase was beautifully wrought.

Thornton continued work on the libretto until he was scheduled to sail for Scotland on July 22. At the end of June, Isabel went to Europe for him to confer with the German producers while he remained in Newport, and in August he was back at work in New Haven.

His work was often interrupted even though he tried to keep time for writing. He was asked to help publicize the movie version of *The Matchmaker*, and to attend its premiere on August 12, 1955. He was among the guests at a birthday party for his friend Marion Preminger, and in early August met with Louise Talma in New York. His commitments kept him so busy that he was forced to stay away from a dinner honoring Robert Frost, held on November 13. Thornton had a deep respect for Frost and for some time had been corresponding with Elizabeth Sergeant, a fellow MacDowell writer and Stockbridge resident, on her book *Robert Frost: The Trial by Existence*. On March 26, 1954, he had been one of four speakers at a dinner at the Lord Jeffrey Inn in Amherst, Massachusetts, celebrating Robert Frost's eightieth birthday. Among the one hundred guests were Archibald MacLeish, Elizabeth Sergeant, and Curtis Canfield. Frost sat at a raised table between Thornton and MacLeish, but stepped down to "say" some of his poetry, including *West-Running Brook*.

One of Thornton's favorite Frost poems was *Come In*, first printed in 1941.

> As I came to the edge of the woods,
> Thrush music—hark!
> Now if it was dusk outside,
> Inside it was dark.
>
> Too dark in the woods for a bird
> By sleight of wing
> To better its perch for the night,
> Though it still could sing.

*The last of the light of the sun*
*That had died in the west*
*Still lived for one song more*
*In a thrush's breast.*

*Far in the pillared dark*
*Thrush music went—*
*Almost like a call to come in*
*To the dark and lament.*

*But no, I was out for stars:*
*I would not come in.*
*I meant not even if asked,*
*And I hadn't been.*

To Thornton, Robert Frost was a poet who only through great effort managed to communicate his secrets, his private sensibilities, to the world. His poetry was an answer to a question Thornton had asked Ruth Gordon: "What does man do with his despair?" Unlike Carl Sandburg, whom Thornton described as a public poet, Frost revealed a darkness and inner struggle.

In December 1955 Thornton sailed for Italy to meet with Louise Talma. He suffered from insomnia on shipboard, but determined that it was caused by the air conditioning rather than by any personal agitation. He spent a few days in Naples, then ten days with Talma in Rome. After a month of traveling in Europe, he returned to Rome to continue work with Talma, who was then on a Fulbright scholarship, on leave from her position as professor of music at Hunter College, New York.

In February he was still in Naples, where he unexpectedly found snow and ice, and he returned to New Haven with a bad cold.

His fame brought him requests from publishers to read the works of young writers, from applicants for Guggenheim fellowships, and even from the chairman of the Miss America Pageant. In April 1956, he was invited to serve as one of eleven judges to select Miss America 1957. This time, though he still always tried to be obliging, he refused.

# TWENTY

---

"WELCOME to the Great Decades," Justice Felix Frank-furter cabled to Thornton in 1957. At sixty, Thornton decided to take advantage of certain "new privileges" and not allow himself to become trapped in any more "false situations." For Thornton, these included speech-making and lecturing, writing critical articles, and formulating polite answers to would-be authors who wanted him to collaborate with them on books. ". . . From now on," he said, "I'm not going to be kind to strangers any more. I have a reputation for being kind to people I don't know, and that's the only explanation for the number of time-demanding, energy-depleting things I've been asked to do every week of my adult life. Maybe I haven't been kind, but I've certainly been obliging.

"Take the schoolchildren of America. How many letters have I answered that began: 'Dear Mr. Wilder, our English teacher has told each one of us to pick an American author and I've picked you . . . When did you first start writing poetry? . . . Do you believe in God? My paper must be in by the 16th so please reply at once.'

"I hereby serve notice on the schoolchildren of America that now that I have reached 60 years old I'm going to dump all their letters in the incinerator without reading them. I will refuse all responsibility if they flunk their courses."

Furthermore, he added, he would not be part of any more cultural tours, however flattering the invitations might sound. "I've done my share. I've done that. I did it very badly, but so did most of my colleagues. But the higher-ups don't seem to care much how it's done; it's felt to be sufficiently valuable and edifying to do it at all.

"Maybe the spoken word in assembly had a conviction in the nineteenth century, but it's lost it in the twentieth. Apparently I look like a dean, and a cultural chairman, and a forensic mouthpiece, but I'm not.

"From now on I shall refuse all invitations to attend world-shaking conferences, no matter how free the rides."[1]

He spent the beginning of April in Newport before leaving for a trip to Europe that included Paris, Lausanne, and the Alps. His itinerary was loose, and he thought he might stay abroad until mid-September, when he was expected in Berlin. Instead, he returned to the States during the summer and again visited Stockbridge, where Room 101 at the Red Lion Inn was waiting for him.

Thornton claimed that he did some of his best work in Stockbridge, and perhaps his preoccupation with writing was the cause of his absent-mindedness when he drew a bath for himself. His presence at the Inn could often be detected by water dripping from the bathroom floor when Thornton let the tub overflow.

A mere five months after his birthday, when he had vowed he would no longer agree to cultural tours, Thornton flew to Berlin at the request of the State Department. He was master of ceremonies at the dedication of the new Congress Hall, where some one-act plays, including *The Wreck of the 5:25* and *The Drunken Sisters*, were to be performed.

*The Wreck of the 5:25* deals with a train commuter who might be any of those who must leave their homes each morning, ride to work, and then, after a mindless day, reverse their travels. At first movies, mysteries, or television provide enough diversion, but gradually the commuter feels imprisoned by his routine and sees suicide as the only way out. His wife convinces him that life is still worth living, but the monotony of the man's existence does not change, and probably never will change. For Thornton, his solitary commuter represented the Americans "haunted by a feeling of the insignificance of the proverbial 70 years they are permitted to live. . . . This feeling undoubtedly relates to the much discussed religious revivals of our day."[2]

*The Drunken Sisters* was a short play written to follow *The Alcestiad*, in the manner of a Greek satyr play, which offered some comic relief to a longer drama. Here we see three drunken sisters, the Fates, confronted by Apollo. The insipid hags are tricked into agreeing that Admetus' life may be lengthened by the death of another. Apollo contrives that the sacrifice will be a life he considers worthless: ". . . some slave. Some gray and greasy thread on your lap. . . ." But the sisters, sly and artful, turn the trick against him. "Someone must *give* his life for Admetus. Of free choice and will. Over such deaths we have no control. Neither Chance nor Necessity rules the free offering of the will. Someone must choose to die in the place of Admetus, King of Thessaly." Apollo, then, suddenly realizes what he has done; and the audience, having just witnessed *The Alcestiad*, realizes how the tragedy came to pass.

A few weeks later, Thornton went to Frankfurt, where he was awarded the Peace Prize by the German book industry. His speech, "Culture in a Democracy," pointed to the responsibility of artists in a democracy to take full advantage of the freedom granted to them. On November 14 Thornton was awarded an honorary doctorate by the University of Frankfurt. A reception was held afterward at the Park-Hotel, where Thornton was greeted by a professor of English, Helmut Viebrock. ". . . The kind and radiant honorary doctor asked me about my field of research," Viebrock remembered; "I told him it was John Keats, which was the cue for a lively talk about his poetry and letters." Viebrock had previously met Thornton at Marburg when he spoke there after the war.[3]

Thornton's popularity in Germany was undiminished from what it had been ten years before. He knew that he appealed to

middle-class countries like Germany, while he had less success in
Britain and France, where he perceived an intellectual elite. After
World War II, his German translator noted, Thornton became
"a German *Klassiker* almost overnight. His plays, including *The
Matchmaker*, in which almost every German actress of distinction
celebrated a triumphant success as Dolly, have been performed all
over West Germany. . . . His novels, especially *The Bridge of
San Luis Rey* and *The Ides of March*, are equally considered to be
among the most important contributions to modern literature.
Many books about his books have been written, and there is
scarcely one German university whose English or drama department has not promoted at least one doctoral thesis about Wilder,
and of various aspects of his work." While other playwrights
achieved success, Wilder's works met with an "almost religious"
response. "There seemed to exist a certain affinity between Wilder
and the German postwar mind . . . because . . . *music* played a
considerable part in the development of their philosophical outlook.

"German metaphysical thought always liked to link music with
the idea of death and eternity. Mozart, to whom Wilder feels
deeply indebted . . . once wrote to his father that he never went
to bed without visualizing the possibility that he might not wake
up the next morning. But this thought did not make him feel sad
or discouraged; on the contrary, it helped him to survive and to
feel serene, even cheerful." To the Germans, Thornton conveyed
the same feeling of serenity. "It is the serenity of those who know
about the ambiguities of human endeavor without losing sight of
their ultimate goal, which is the reaffirmation of human existence,
the serenity of Mozart's late chamber music, and of Wilder's acceptance of small-town life as an ironic reflex of some supreme
order unknown to man."[4]

From Frankfurt he went to Switzerland, then returned home in
time for Christmas. But he was adamant about his vow of the previous spring: he would no longer be a public speaker. His appearance in Germany was the one exception to his promise to himself,
and he admitted to friends that he already felt better and younger
after having given up touring and lecturing. In March 1958 he
renounced all pretense of public life and drove West. By late

spring he was in happy retreat in Aspen, Colorado, which he said had the ambiance of an old western town. He enjoyed his new-found freedom, and even wondered if he might not be wise to give up speaking in private about weighty matters such as litera-ture and art and instead confine his daily dialogue to talk about the weather and other niceties.

He loved driving, though he admitted that his sister Isabel and his lawyer were nervous passengers. "I'm very good, really," he said, "but they don't think I know how. They are comforted by the thought that the excellence of the machine compensates for the deficiency of the driver. I love the open road, the gas stations, the little towns and the motels. I love the hushed elegance of the motels."[5]

Many years before, he had wistfully told Alexander Woollcott that he'd like to roam the world in old clothes and "just be a bum." "You wouldn't have far to go," Woollcott replied.[6]

He dropped in several times at Mabel Luhan's in Taos, New Mexico, where they reminisced about her salon days in New York, and he saw Witter Bynner in Santa Fe. Then he drove to Califor-nia to meet with Louise Talma, who was working at an artists' colony there, having extended her leave from Hunter College.

He was, of course, writing. His latest project was a series of plays based on the seven deadly sins. The one-acters were, he said, experimental, and he hoped they would be produced on an appro-priate stage, such as The Circle in the Square in Manhattan.

"I'm all for theater in the round," he said. "Scenery binds, con-stricts, imprisons a play in a certain time and place. The prosce-nium is deadly. I swear I will never see Shakespeare again except in the round. . . . At first, in the round is hard on the audience, requires more concentration at the start, but it soon gets a grip, and once it gets hold, you don't think about something you forgot to buy today or that appointment for tomorrow."[7]

A companion project to his work on *The Seven Deadly Sins* was a series of seven plays on the *Ages of Man*, beginning in in-fancy and ending in old age. "I am interested in the drives that operate in society and in every man. . . . Pride, avarice and envy are in every home. I am not interested in the ephemeral—such subjects as the adulteries of dentists. I am interested in those things that repeat and repeat and repeat in the lives of the millions."[8]

Of all the sins, wrath and envy were causing the most difficulty for Thornton. "I haven't got much of them in me," he said. "All the other sins I've got just great."[9] But even the other themes required a great deal of work and reworking. "I constantly rewrite, discard, and replace the cycle plays," he admitted. "Some are on the stove, some are in the oven, some are in the wastebasket. There are no first drafts in my life. An incinerator is a writer's best friend."[10]

His retreat to the West came to an end in early June, and his writing continued in New Haven. Though he had taken a course in typing long years ago at Berea, he handed in manuscripts to his agent in longhand and his study contained no typewriter. The House the Bridge Built was quiet, homey, and unpretentious—a place to bring friends. In his study he kept sets of Lope de Vega and Shakespeare, his much annotated copy of *Finnegans Wake*, and volumes by Whitman, Dickinson, Thoreau, Poe, and Melville.[11] There was—before it was given to Yale—a bronze bust by Noguchi that he thought was "a wonderful piece, really a wonderful piece."

When he wasn't traveling, he enjoyed the house near New Haven for its proximity to the Yale library. "I must live near a great library," he said, "and Yale has a great library. You might say that I am a lazy loafer without an idle minute." In describing the house, he went beyond its siding and plantings to make it sound almost like a set for *The Skin of Our Teeth:* "I live on a heap of dirt pushed down by an icecap from the North. Look at that odd red cliff there! I call it our Dolomite, and it has come all the way from the North on an icecap."[12] It was a house conducive to contemplation, and when the sky was clear he could see out to Long Island Sound.

Thornton usually rose early and ate breakfast at a diner or restaurant a mile or two away, where he would meet truck drivers or workmen. Conversations with them often inspired writing, just as his evenings in Chicago speakeasies had. Thornton had once remarked to a colleague at the University of Chicago that he had

had dinner with several members of the Capone gang and found their "singular naïveté" surprising.[13]

Thornton's long walks were still his favorite diversion, and he claimed that they aided his creativity. He was a man without hobbies, but with boundless interests. ". . . My head has always seemed to me to be like a brightly lighted room, full of the most delightful objects, or perhaps I should say, filled with tables on which are set up the most engrossing games."[14]

His home was a touchstone, but he was never tied to it for very long. His wanderings were a necessary part of his life. "Leave time and timetables to whom it may concern," he once told Ruth Gordon; "go and wander." He reminded her of Arnold's "Scholar-Gypsy," who left Oxford to learn the secrets of "the Gypsy lore / And roamed the world with that wild brotherhood. . . ." Thornton needed to wander, too, in his own way, to create the worlds of his novels and plays.

Years before, in 1936, Edward Weeks, then of *The Atlantic*, went to Chicago and asked Thornton to team up with him as an editor, even for half of each year. But Thornton knew he must refuse. "I remember his looking out over the lake, and saying quietly, as if he were speaking of someone else, 'Well, you see, Ted, there are several Wilders, and I'm not sure that any one of them should be tied down for as long as that. There's the Wilder who loves to teach, and who must do so, periodically. And there is the Wilder who wants to go off by himself and write. And then there's the Wilder who enjoys being shouted at and having his work cut to ribbons by Sam Goldwyn in Hollywood. There is the Wilder who will never know all that he wants to know about Lope de Vega. And finally there is the fellow who is beginning to feel the urge to write plays of his own. I am touched that you should want me, but I don't see how this Wilder could also become an editor.' "[15]

In November 1958 Thornton gave a reception at the Algonquin for Alma Werfel, to celebrate the publication of her autobiography. Alma Werfel, the widow of Gustav Mahler and of the novelist and playwright Franz Werfel, met Thornton on shipboard when they both were returning from Rome. She was sitting on deck reading when a man approached and said simply, "I'm Thornton Wilder." "We began to talk," she remembered, "and we seemed to go on talking until the ship docked in New York. The days passed like minutes. His every word was a joy—and so, later, was his every letter. Since Franz Werfel's passing I have treasured nothing more than Thornton Wilder's friendship."[16] She had been so impressed by *The Bridge of San Luis Rey* that she entitled her own memoir *And the Bridge Is Love*.

A letter from Mark Schorer, at work on his biography of Sinclair Lewis, prompted memories of Lewis, whom Thornton had met several times. Thornton recalled the novelist with affection, but said he had always felt uncomfortable at Lewis' strained appeal for his audience's approval. This need was at first obvious to him when he met Lewis at gatherings or parties, but he saw it, too, in his novels. Nevertheless, Thornton praised Lewis' creation of characters, many of which were true to Thornton's memories of a midwestern childhood.[17]

Thornton spent the winter in Europe, visiting Zurich and St. Moritz, still working on the deadly sins. "You can find many of the sins right here in St. Moritz," he said. "Of course one mustn't overdo it. I've made it a principle to work five days and then break out on the sixth, tearing up a few cobblestones along the way." When he emerged from his solitary work, he found that many of the other guests in the village welcomed his appearance as a new face. Life among the very rich was the same as life in any group, he observed. "The proportion is the same of hopeless self-destructive wastes as against amiable contacts and lovable, rewarding human beings. I have never believed that poverty totally destroys nor that wealth totally corrupts." He found, however, that the rich seemed always to need reassurances "that they are somebody. The rich may claim to detest the press," he said, "but without the reassurances of the society columns that they are what they think they are, they would have a completely empty feeling in their stomachs and it would be impossible for them to know if other people thought them precious."[18]

Thornton returned from his trip in late March. In New York he visited with Louise Talma, now back at her teaching position at Hunter and finding it difficult to adjust to academic life after several years of freedom. She was still at work on their opera, *The Alcestiad*. At home, Isabel was recovering from an operation and their youngest sister, Janet, had come from Amherst to help run the house and care for Isabel. By June, Isabel was well enough to manage alone, and Thornton went to Stockbridge for a few days. He was working on "Wrath" for his *Seven Deadly Sins* series and found his thoughts on the subject engrossing.

In August he performed as the Stage Manager in the Williamstown Summer Theater's production of *Our Town*, directed by Nikos Psacharopoulos. Though Thornton had been visiting the Berkshires since 1939, he first "discovered" Williamstown and its newly begun theater in 1957. With Thornton in residence, a special reading of the play was scheduled one morning in the library of Williams College's Adams Memorial Theater, and Thornton was often at the Williams Inn after performances chatting with students and the cast, who were frequently his guests for after-theater drinks.

Nikos Psacharopoulos remembered that Thornton was very pleased with the Williamstown production of *Our Town*. He wanted to remain uninvolved with the production, but once Nikos did turn to him for help. In the stepladder scene, when George asks Emily for the solution to a math problem, Nikos tried to ply the actors with "acting solutions" to the question. Think about life, he told them; think about the universe. But nothing seemed to work. Finally he asked Thornton, "What do you think George wants?" And Thornton, of course, replied, "The solution to the math problem." He wanted the facts of his play to speak for themselves. If facts are important, he told Nikos, they have their own value.

Nikos found Thornton to be a precise and articulate man, "more educated than anybody I know," he said later. He wanted his play clearly, crisply stated, as his own portrayal of the Stage Manager showed. He did not complain to Nikos, however, of his disappointment with previous *Our Town* productions, except for the musical television version in which Frank Sinatra sang the role of the Stage Manager. There was only one reason he allowed the musical to be done, Thornton admitted: it "kept him in Martinis" for a year.[19]

In the fall, Thornton again sailed for Europe, this time stopping at Hamburg, Cologne, Frankfurt, Zurich, St. Moritz, and Naples. He read Ellmann's biography of James Joyce, but found it pedestrian and wished it had revealed more about Joyce's imagination. To Elizabeth Sergeant, who had just completed a study of Frost, *The Trial by Existence*, he acknowledged the difficulty of conveying a poet's spirit rather than giving a minute dissection of his work.

Though Thornton's writing and conversation were weighted with references to past writers, he did not ignore contemporary literature. But he was dismayed that many modern novels dealt with little more than sex. Sometimes, he wrote to Elizabeth Sergeant, he would skim through books trying to find parts *not* about sex—and often failed. He would return to Trollope, he told her, rather than suffer through another writer's obsessions.

In December 1959 he left Naples, where he had had incomparable weather, and sailed West—to Caracas and the West Indies. He looked forward to writing, walking, lying undisturbed on sunny beaches, listening to calypso music. Isabel would join him, but since she was convalescing she would be allowed no liquor. Thornton was content to drink alone.

Early in 1960 he again went to Sanibel Island in Florida, where a letter from Robert Stallman caught up with him. Stallman was working on a study of Henry James, to be published as *The House That James Built* and dedicated to Thornton Wilder. Thornton warned Stallman not to be fooled by James's prefaces to Scribner's New York Edition of his works. He felt James was trying to lead his readers astray in explaining his themes. There was one abiding theme in James, Thornton told Stallman: the tragedy of love between mismatched individuals—one vastly superior to the other.

Thornton spent a leisurely summer, partly in Martha's Vineyard, where Isabel had rented a house, with a brief trip to Peterborough to accept the MacDowell Colony's First Edward MacDowell Medal on August 13. Van Wyck Brooks, Archibald MacLeish, and Robert Penn Warren chose Thornton as the recipient of the honor, and among the guests at the reception were Edward Weeks and Louise Talma. In his impromptu acceptance speech, Thornton recalled the support of Edith Isaacs and acknowledged his indebtedness to the special atmosphere the colony provided, "the friendship, the good will, the urgency that really flows from studio to studio. . . . Really, there is no better kind of both benison and good than those boards in the studios. Art is difficult; no one can help you at all. You are alone with the demands upon yourself; but other persons likewise have had to face it. And that is dramatized for us in this place."

He had written many of his best works at the colony, he went on, including a favorite, *The Happy Journey to Trenton and Camden*, and as a gesture of thanks to the audience, he began to read a new play—one from *The Seven Ages of Man*, entitled *Childhood*.

*Childhood* brings Freudian psychology to a light one-acter. Caroline, Dodie, and Billee are three youngsters who often play at wishing their parents dead. Their mother is somewhat shocked at their morbid fantasies, but their father takes the games coolly. He wishes, in fact, that ". . . just once . . . I could be an invisible witness to one of my children's dreams, to one of their games." Thornton grants his wish, and suddenly "We are in the game, which is a dream." He learned a bit from the experience of witnessing his children's celebration at their freedom in imagining themselves being orphans. "Children don't like being treated as children *all the time*," Caroline tells him. And Dodie adds that grownups spend all their time doing the same boring things— golfing and shopping. The children allow themselves to confide in the adults during their game because they are "not *really* alive. . . . We've found that it's best not to make friends with grownups," she says, "because . . . in the end . . . they don't act fair to you."

The new year, 1961, found Thornton again in the warmth of Florida, first at Palm Beach, where he had driven from New Orleans, and then at Sanibel Island. He was in his car on January 20 when Robert Frost's voice was broadcast during the presidential inauguration. Thornton praised Kennedy's noble gesture, a cultural boon, he thought, for the entire country.

The year brought pleasure in his work, too. Louise Talma's opera of *The Alcestiad* had found a theater in Frankfurt, and

Paul Hindemith's opera of *The Long Christmas Dinner* was presented in December in Mannheim, Germany. Thornton was pleased both by Hindemith's score for his short play and by the reception in Germany. Even more, he was delighted by the production plans for *The Alcestiad*, which included an excellent cast.

Three of his plays from *The Seven Ages of Man* were presented in New York, to mixed reviews. But Thornton had learned, at last, not to be hurt by critics. Gertrude Stein had cautioned him against reading reviews, and he claimed to have taken her advice. In any case, he realized that even those works which were dismissed by many critics were being read and reread years later. So many plays had been anthologized that he stopped granting permission for their use, sending prospective editors to lesser-known playwrights.

In February 1962 he and Isabel sailed to Europe for the Frankfurt production of *The Alcestiad*. The premiere, in which soprano Inge Borkh sang the role of Alcestis, received a twenty-minute ovation. And on April 20 he arrived at the State Department Auditorium in Washington to read from his works in one of Kennedy's Cabinet-sponsored programs on the arts. Thornton admired Kennedy's efforts to recognize the cultural life of the country. "It reminds us that in happier ages than this one, citizens in the arts were regarded as making contributions to the life blood of their nations."[20] He did not meet the President, however, though an aide suggested the possibility. He was told that "it is not standard procedure for the guest artist to meet with the President," an exception being Marian Anderson, who was a friend of Robert and Ethel Kennedy.

At the gathering, Abraham Ribicoff, then Secretary of Health, Education, and Welfare, introduced the author. "I knew the Kennedy administration was getting older, wiser, more successful," he said, "—but Wilder?"

Though he was honored at being invited to participate in the program, Thornton came dressed in his usual careless attire, his suit rumpled, his hat limp. "When others come they send a suit out to be pressed ahead of time," he told the black-tie audience. "I jump on it."[21]

Thornton read from *The Cabala, Our Town*, and *The Drunken*

*Sisters.* "I am filled with great pleasure," he told his audience, "that Washington is becoming the lighthouse on the hill for things which we have spent our lives."

But within a month, Thornton would be far from the lighthouse on the hill, from the House the Bridge Built, from his favorite libraries and his friends. All he would admit was that he would be "somewhere in Arizona," and that, for the next two years, he would "be a bum." ". . . It's going to be two years without neckties, without shoelaces and without cultivated conversation," he said. His desire for retreat, which he had been nurturing for thirty years, was now to become his reality. "It's like suicide with some people who always talk about it yet never do it," he said, "but now I'm going to realize my ambitions. . . . I'm going to choose some place halfway between Nogales and Tucson —a place where I can hit the bars with equal ease in both towns. . . . No matter where it is, it's going to be my ideal of getaway quarters—a little white frame house with a rickety front porch where I can laze away in the shade in a straight-backed wooden rocking chair."[22] He was quick to add that he had not given up loving humanity, and he was not getting irritable because of all his obligations. He just wanted to enjoy quiet and solitude. At dawn on May 20, 1962, he began his drive West.

# TWENTY-ONE

---

HIS first two weeks were spent rambling happily, looking for a place to settle and "put out saucers of milk for the snakes." He wanted to find a special town, "a place where I'll pat little Mexican children on the head and greet my neighbors every day, a place where they wouldn't point at you if you didn't keep up with the niceties of life and say, 'he's teched in the haid.' "[1]

He planned to mingle with the townspeople, to go to the post office and the supermarket, arrange to borrow books from the University of Arizona library, and drive to Tucson a few evenings a week. He expected to emerge refreshed, with some new ideas for books and plays. One subject that interested him at the time was the study of animal behavior. "I want to see how I look through a snake's eyes," he said, "what makes them afraid, what makes them angry, whether they can learn to trust and how."[2]

The town he finally chose for his hermitage was Douglas, Arizona, with a population of some 12,500, where he lived for four months at the Gadsden Hotel. Then he found an apartment of his own a few blocks away, at 757 Twelfth Street. There he cooked for himself and enjoyed only passing acquaintanceships with his neighbors. Many evenings were spent at the Roundup, a bar in Douglas, where he had long conversations—in Spanish—with bartender Albert Morales.

He always wore his seersucker suit and a white shirt and tie, unusual in the desert heat. Some evenings he drove the 115 miles to the University of Arizona at Tucson; sometimes he dined in Tombstone or crossed the border to Agua Prieta. And sometimes he drove in the mountains, alone.

His stay in Douglas was somewhat short of two years. In July 1963 he learned he was to be the recipient of the Medal of Freedom, to be awarded by then President Kennedy in September. He had planned to attend the award ceremony, then return to Douglas until early winter. But the presentation was postponed twice —first when the Kennedys' infant son died, and then in November 1963 when Kennedy was assassinated.

The award ceremony was finally set for early December, and Thornton ended his year and a half in Douglas in late November to drive east both for the ceremony and for a celebration to mark his brother's retirement from the Harvard Divinity School.

A luncheon in the Benjamin Franklin Room at the Department of State followed President Lyndon Johnson's presentation of the award on Friday, December 6, the day Jacqueline Kennedy officially moved out of the White House. Among those present were Chief Justice and Mrs. Earl Warren, Secretary of State Dean Rusk and his wife, Arthur Goldberg, George Ball, Walt Rostow, Daniel Moynihan, Ralph Bunche, James Conant, Mies van der Rohe, Rudolf Serkin, Edward Steichen, and, accompanying Thornton, his sister Isabel.

Thornton was acclaimed nationally for his work, and in New York his name was associated with the opening of yet another successful play. *The Matchmaker* was reworked and revived, this time as the musical *Hello, Dolly!*, and the role that Thornton wrote for the diminutive Ruth Gordon was reinterpreted by tall, svelte Carol Channing. The play was revised by Michael Stewart, with Jerry Herman providing such songs as "It Takes a Woman," and the title song, "Hello, Dolly!" Carol Channing played until August 1965, followed by Dollies who included Ginger Rogers, Martha Raye, and Pearl Bailey. *Hello, Dolly!* companies gave

Thornton's *The Matchmaker* enormous exposure, taking the musical throughout the United States, and to Europe and Asia.
Eventually, Barbra Streisand was Dolly in the film version.

Thornton was sixty-seven in 1964, and his health was beginning
to fail. In June he had a malignant wart removed from his cheek,
and through the summer he had to undergo radium treatments.
By fall he felt he again needed a rest, and planned another retreat
—this time, he thought, to Europe.

He was coming to the end of a long work—longer than he had
anticipated, and one that had occupied his days and nights in Arizona. In working on such a lengthy novel, Thornton wrote to his
editor, Cass Canfield, he had felt a few moments of doubt and only
the briefest period when he could not persevere in his writing.

The novel, which would be his first to appear since *The Ides of
March*, was, like *Heaven's My Destination*, American in setting
and mood. It drew upon the emotional pain he had suffered during
the time he was writing, he explained to Canfield, and described
the ways in which one deals with personal tragedy. But there was
humor too, he added, and he hoped his editor would enjoy it.

He needed to leave "civilization" once again, and after Christmas
in Florida planned to take a leisurely trip to Europe, sailing from
Curaçao to Genoa and back. He planned to work on the book in
the solitude of his cabin.[3]

But the voyage did not speed the completion of the book, and
when Thornton returned in the spring he still did not have his
manuscript ready for Harpers. His health was worrying him again,
and in June he expected to be hospitalized for treatment of a her-
nia. Still, he was able to appear at the White House on May 4 for
the presentation of the first National Medal for Literature.

The ceremony was held in the East Room of the White House
before 150 guests seated in gilded chairs. Thornton received a me-
dallion and a check for five thousand dollars. "You have never
confused being modern in language with a dreary reliance on four-
letter words," Lady Bird Johnson told Thornton as she presented
the award. "You have never assumed that realism in writing
means a cloying self-pity or a snappish disdain for others. You
have written with that understanding, affectionate rapport with

your subjects which to me is the hallmark of genuine literature."

"Well, I'm still working . . ." Thornton replied.

The novel he saw ending in 1964 was yet to be completed in the spring of 1965. He turned sixty-eight, and was asked for the secret of a long life. Drink, good posture, and listening to Mozart, he said—though Haydn symphonies would do as well. He was jubilant now over the results of a recent medical examination and would not need to see a doctor again for a year. In early October, he left for Europe, again for solitude and seclusion. He knew he was close to the end of the novel, and it was important to him to devote all his energies to its completion.

He had once joked that he would have to live to at least one hundred to complete all the projects he had in mind. His self-description as a lazy idler meant he sometimes went for many years without a publication. But more likely his time was spent in one or another of scholarly pursuits that sometimes exasperated his friends. He should be writing more plays, more novels, they told him, not immersing himself in Lope de Vega, Joyce, or Stein.

At sixty-nine, he suddenly realized that his time was limited and still there was much he wanted to say. He was true to the vow he made years before—lectures, public appearances, tours were given up. His health again was a problem, and in late spring 1966 he underwent an operation that had been postponed from the year before. He now limited his writing, too. He would work only on novels, plays, and scholarly articles, refusing requests for essays, short stories, or other pieces. He completed his latest work in progress, a long, detailed novel he titled *The Eighth Day*.

*The Eighth Day*, which Thornton dedicated to his sister Isabel, differed from his previous novels in structure and plot, but not in theme. Like *Heaven's My Destination*, *The Eighth Day* was set in America, but without George Brush to lighten the story with his wide-eyed self-righteousness. Thornton's latest novel was a mystery, the unfolding of a tale that begins with a murder trial in 1902, the Ashley Case. John Barrington Ashley is tried for the murder of Breckenridge Lansing, found guilty, and sentenced to death. Five days later, he escapes and is never found. Five years

later, evidence is turned up which proves that Ashley was innocent of the crime. For Thornton, John Ashley became a modern
version of a Greek hero whose life was manipulated by malevolent
or benevolent fates; Coaltown, Illinois, was Athens, or Palestine,
where some yet-to-be-understood intelligence reigned. And the
people of the Kangaheela Valley were, of course, archetypal.

Coaltown was Our Town enlarged, sprawled out, untidy at the
edges. As he did in *Our Town*, Thornton took up his archaeologist's pickax to unearth the physical strata of the place, to give
it a particular unique identity while at the same time linking it—
geographically and philosophically—to the universe. The four
themes that are dominant in virtually all of Thornton's works are
seen again in *The Eighth Day*: the disaffected personality, twin-
ship, righteousness and self-righteousness, and gods as men. Lines
from his previous novels are paraphrased and the sentiments
recur.

The novel is divided into six parts, several of which cover the
same time period from different points of view. We come to know
the history of the Ashleys and the Lansings and receive intimations of their futures. Thornton is not concerned, though, with
analyzing a particular personality, with developing a particular
character. He does not ask, "What happened to John Ashley?"
but rather, "What will happen to mankind?" He does not ask,
"Who was Breckenridge Lansing?" but rather, "Who is the man
of the Eighth Day?"

His character Dr. Gillies, a country doctor who is one of Thornton's mouthpieces, muses about the state of humanity on New
Year's Eve 1899. "Nature never sleeps," he observes. "The process
of life never stands still. The creation has not come to an end.
The Bible says that God created man on the sixth day and rested,
but each of those days was many millions of years long. That day
of rest must have been a short one. Man is not an end but a beginning. We are at the beginning of the second week. We are
children of the eighth day." While his listeners thought they
heard a note of optimism in Dr. Gillies' talk, the wise physician
meant no such thing. "He had no doubt that the coming century
would be too direful to contemplate—that is to say, like all the
other centuries. . . . There are no Golden Ages and no Dark

Ages. There is the oceanlike monotony of the generations of men under the alternations of fair and foul weather."

The book opens with a look at The Elms, the Ashley homestead, where Beata Ashley and her three daughters have taken refuge from the real and imagined rebuffs of the townspeople after their husband and father was arrested and condemned. Beata Ashley, like Thornton's mother, is in love with culture. A proud and somewhat aloof woman, she is sensitive and devoted to her husband. Yet she is not the source of action in the family, however much she may be its strength. The middle daughter, Sophia, is the real backbone. It is she who sells lemonade to help the family's finances; it is she who decides to turn the rambling Elms into a boardinghouse—and who succeeds, with the good will and kindnesses of her neighbors. The other daughters are Lily, endowed with a beautiful voice and an artistic nature; and Constance, exuberant, loving, gregarious.

Thornton's portrayal of a family's plight is hardly believable. Poor though they have become, the Ashleys never lack an aristocratic elegance, and their morale never drops too low to end their nightly reading of Shakespeare. Beata, though she does not dare to leave her house for months, seems to walk in a special radiance, unimpaired by poverty. Evidently Thornton meant to create a family whose strength does not buckle under hardship, but we have instead four transparent women—and one son, Roger, whose story is told separately—always cool, clean, and everlastingly polite.

While his family grows close and strong in Coaltown, John Ashley flees south to the copper mines of Chile. In Part Two, Thornton follows Ashley's escape (Ashley does not know who freed him from prison) until he arrives in Rocas Verdes, a mining town high in the Andes, where he becomes a character much like Samuele in *The Cabala*. Here, with Dr. Gillies left in Coaltown, Thornton creates two women to speak for the author—María Icaza, "midwife, abortionist, *maga*, teller of fortunes, interpreter of dreams, go-between, exorcisor of devils"; and Mrs. Wickersham, the worldly-wise proprietress of a hotel near the mining camp.

Ashley is Thornton's "disaffected personality," an agent who intervenes in the lives of others without emotional involvement, who lives by his own lights, who can witness happiness and tragedy with equanimity and remain intact, self-contained, self-sufficient. In *The Cabala* we had Samuele; in *The Bridge*, the Abbess and Uncle Pio; in *The Woman of Andros*, Chrysis; in *Heaven's My Destination*, George Brush.

Ashley is Thornton's self-righteous personality, too. He is told by María Icaza that God chooses some to know the highest happiness and the greatest tragedy in order to truly understand the miracle of being alive. He who is chosen must be someone with the morality and strength to use his knowledge well—and Ashley is just such a man. As Mrs. Wickersham observes, Ashley is one of the few people on earth who really works, instead of scurrying aimlessly or being occupied with busy-ness. "We work," she tells him. "And we forget ourselves in our work." Others are deluded into thinking they are making changes for progress. But progress, Mrs. Wickersham decides, is illusory. "From time to time," she says, "everyone goes into an ecstasy about the glorious advance of civilization—the miracle of vaccination, the wonders of the railroad. But the excitement dies down and there we are again—wolves and hyenas, wolves and peacocks." Yet anyone who knows John Ashley would be tempted to admit that he is involved in "progress." He is a tireless putterer and tinkerer, making innovative changes for the workers' comforts as effortlessly as he fixes a pipe or mends a roof.

If John Ashley is a man of the Eighth Day, then this new man's chief characteristic is his faith: faith in some providence that protects him, some spirit that guides him, and most of all, faith in humanity. For the John Ashleys—and the Thornton Wilders—of the world, time is not marked as it is for everyone else. "Time does not present itself to them as an infinite succession of endings." Each moment might be an eternity; and surely, they know, a man's eternity is no more than a moment.

*The Eighth Day* uses many devices that appear in Thornton's earlier books. Paired characters show a superior consciousness contrasted with one that is flawed: John Ashley and Breckenridge Lansing; John's wife, Beata, and Eustacia Lansing; John's son, Roger, and Lansing's son, George. The Ashleys, after all, are literary descendants of the Greek gods, prudent children of Saturn, the characters of the Cabala loosed in turn-of-the-century America. History repeats itself in their spirits, and their innate nobility enables them to rise above the unfortunate and sometimes tawdry circumstances in which they find themselves. They conduct their lives with a dignity and purpose that transcend time and place.

Roger travels to Chicago where, using a *nom de plume*, he quickly becomes a well-respected newspaper reporter. Lily, also using a pseudonym, fulfills her destiny as an opera singer. Sophia, of course, upholds the Elms, and Constance, the youngest, eventually devotes her life to good works among the Japanese.

Thornton's philosophy is clearly expounded in *The Eighth Day*, so clearly that the reader often winces at the familiarity of some sentiments that seem to be lifted unchanged from earlier works. As in *The Woman of Andros*, each glimpse into a family's life reveals puzzled hearts and puzzled minds. A glimpse at the stars evokes the same feelings about the multiplicity of lives that Thornton expressed in *Our Town*. As in *The Bridge of San Luis Rey*, Thornton is ambiguous about the meaning of life, the possibility of a "design in the arras" or a pattern to history. Like all of Thornton's works, *The Eighth Day* is an expression of guarded optimism.

The book, despite a nod to Joyce in its unfinished ending, is essentially a traditional tale told in a straightforward, traditional way. It is an old-fashioned story, with a plot, a dollop of suspense, a roster of identifiable characters, and a moral that resounds again and again. Writing in a time of crisis, Thornton responds with his unflagging hope for the future. Nineteen hundred sixty-seven is just another beginning, another chance for humanity to shape its destiny, another chance to aspire to perfection, to goodness, to moral righteousness, to justice. The Ashleys' strength, he tells us, lies in their ability to "invent the explanation for existence." Their knowledge of the world comes, not from books, not from "fruitless introspection," not from sterile philosophical discussions that begin and end in theories, but in sensitive, astute observations. The Ashleys, like Thornton, listen passionately and absorb whatever they see. They construct reality from their experience, their sensibilities. Nearly forty years after *The Cabala*, Thornton again warns against becoming James Blair. Thirty years after *Heaven's My Destination*, he still believes in George Brush.

But 1967 was not the right time for Thornton's message. However sincere his intentions, he was read as an old-fashioned moralist. While other novelists bared body and soul to convey their themes, Thornton insisted on his polite, restrained prose, his archetypal characters, and failed to offer an honest exploration into a personality—the author's or one of his creations. Even Edward Weeks, kindly disposed toward Thornton, found the ending contrived. "The flaw in the book," he wrote in *The Atlantic*, "is in the last third, where the denouement, and especially within the Lansing family, is too obviously stage-managed by Mr. Wilder."[4] Thornton, who in 1948 tried to modernize his style by using fictional "documents" to tell *The Ides of March*, now reverted to traditional nineteenth-century narrative. Stanley Kauffmann, in *The New Republic*, found the novel "shockingly and unredeemedly bad. . . . The writing . . . is without grace, though he strains for it constantly; the characters are stagy, hollow, unrealized, though they are laden with characteristics; the plot, full of arthritic twists, is attenuated and undramatic although the author himself seems generally breathless with excitement; the theme, as apprehended here, is sophomoric, although Wilder has dealt with it before with at least some immediate effect. What the book conveys basically is the wrong kind of urgency: that Wilder was conscious of the nearly twenty years since his last novel and that he wanted to publish at least one more."[5]

Yet, despite some negative reviews, *The Eighth Day* was hardly dismissed by the literary world. In March, John Updike, Granville Hicks, and Josephine Herbst chose the novel as the winner of the National Book Award for fiction published in 1967 over Norman Mailer's *Why are We in Vietnam?*, Joyce Carol Oates's *A Garden of Earthly Delights*, Chaim Potok's *The Chosen*, and William Styron's *The Confessions of Nat Turner*. John Updike wrote the citation: "Through the lens of a turn-of-the-century murder mystery, Mr. Wilder surveys a world that is both vanished and coming to birth; in a clean gay prose sharp with aphoristic wit and the sense and scent of Midwestern America and Andean Chile, he takes us on a chase of Providence and delivers us, exhilarated and edified, into the care of an ambiguous conclusion."

The thousand-dollar prize was presented in Lincoln Center's Philharmonic Hall on March 6, but, with Thornton vacationing in Italy, it was accepted by his editor and friend Cass Canfield.

Thornton's links to the Europe of his youth were slowly dissolving. In 1967 Alice Toklas died, nearly ninety, feeble and ill. Her admiration of Thornton had never diminished, and she was always cheered by his visits. She had converted to Catholicism in her eighties and Thornton, who saw her reading more and more devotional literature, said nothing to dissuade her. He knew she was being influenced by some of her Catholic friends, especially writer Bernard Faÿ, whom Thornton did not particularly like, but even so he remained silent, allowing her to do whatever was necessary to mitigate the loneliness she felt for Gertrude Stein. He knew his visits with her brought to life happier days, and he enjoyed reminiscing.

Alice, who could be unforgiving over any real or imagined slight, did overlook an unintended insult. Once, on the terrace at Bilignin, she disclosed to Thornton that she intended to write a cookbook filled with anecdotes as well as recipes. Thornton was surprised. "But, Alice," he asked, "have you ever tried to write?" Alice, who well knew the trials of creativity from having lived with a self-proclaimed genius, did not reply. "As if a cookbook had anything to do with writing," was all she thought.[6]

Still, even with fewer friends to visit, Thornton, at seventy-one, enjoyed "gadding about" Europe, letting no museum or historical sight go unvisited. Once, in Baden-Baden, he stayed at a hotel where Dostoevsky and Balzac were supposed to have stopped, and enjoyed reflecting on its illustrious guests. He delighted in tidbits of knowledge, especially anything concerning theater. He had seen a play by Gotthold Lessing in Germany and learned from the program notes that many eighteenth-century Jews, having to choose surnames when they left the ghetto, called themselves Lessing after the dramatist in gratitude for his work. The idea so excited him that he shared his discovery with Brooks Atkinson in a letter written days later.[7]

Often he returned to Switzerland—St. Moritz or Zurich—and

often to Germany. Since his early trip there with his bored young companion, Thornton felt very much at home in Germany. He could always work there, he once told Ernest Hemingway, where he couldn't settle down in Paris.

In the States, he often returned to the Inn at Castle Hill in Newport, Rhode Island, where Room 9, with its turreted windows overlooking Narragansett Bay, awaited him. The small, secluded hotel offered solace and silence. His privacy was respected, and he had only to listen to the sea, the cry of the gulls, the ringing of the buoys. From the windows of his room he could gaze out at the bay and the cliffs of Newport and watch the shallow waves break against the rocks. It was a setting conducive to a writer's contemplation. Or he might relax at Martha's Vineyard, or in Stockbridge, where the Stockbridge Inn extended its hospitality to him long after its bar should have been closed.

Once Thornton stayed there until the early hours of the morning, talking openly about life and literature with owner-bartender Dick Carlotta. Carlotta had mentioned to Thornton his own idea for a book about his inn and the assorted characters who passed through at one time or another. Thornton—"Cousin Thornie" to Carlotta—thought the idea splendid and immediately wrote a preface and introduction for the yet-to-be-written book on the only blank sheets he could find—cocktail napkins.[8]

Thornton's thoughts reflect his own strivings more than Carlotta's. He admitted that in any man's life only a few facts will be truly important and afford the lights by which he lives. For Thornton, the individuals he knew, each personality in all its intricacies, provided endless fascination. It was upon these individuals that he drew for his inspiration and creativity. Each human being embodied the hopes and suffering of countless generations. Life, in its deepest philosophical meaning, was embodied in each human being.

No matter how privileged or deprived one individual might be, his life is no more or less significant, no more or less deserving of celebration. Each individual is the nexus of dreams fulfilled and unfulfilled, and each lives with a varying intensity according to his desires.

It was Thornton's hope to find some key to understanding the human spirit and, in doing so, to understanding himself. And yet he discovered that just as he began to touch the real spirit of any individual, that being might become fragmented into a kaleidoscope of beings and elude him, just as his own psychic identity in some ways eluded him.

Thornton believed himself destined to bestow a gift: the gift of literature, of art, to his fellow human beings. At times he felt that his destiny was beyond his control—that the crucial moments of his life occurred with no exertion of his own will—yet he knew he, too, was guided by dreams and desires as much as any other individual, and knew he had suffered for his failures, just as he had been buoyed by his successes. And yet he was not sure—he would never be sure—whether or not his gift had any meaning, whether or not he was able to communicate his feelings in beauty and sensitivity, whether or not his contribution to art and to the ages would endure with any meaning.

Unlike the sharp, precise, exuberant face he showed the world, Thornton revealed a fragility to his friend that few were privileged to see. He feared, he told Carlotta, that in the end he might have failed.

# TWENTY-TWO

———————◆◆———————

THORNTON was on Martha's Vineyard in 1969 when Edward Kennedy's car accident at Chappaquiddick caused the streets to become crowded with camera-toting tourists. Thornton was dismayed and disgusted, and took off for Europe, where he relaxed for several months.[1] His health was becoming a problem again, and he tried to devote as much time as he could to his newest writing venture, another novel.

Though he claimed not to be bothered by criticism, Thornton's books usually show evidence of reviews of earlier works. He heard a call for a book which could be seen as autobiographical, one which revealed more of Thornton Wilder and less of archetypal, one-dimensional characters. He began just such a book, hoping that readers would see him in a character he called Theophilus North.

Theophilus is a young man who, after teaching for some years at a boys' preparatory school in New Jersey and spending summers at a tutoring camp in New England, suddenly decides to quit his job and explore the possibilities of life. He does not want to be a writer—not yet—though he can see himself writing later on, maybe twenty years into the future. He knows only that he no longer

wants to teach. He needs to live—to live fully and passionately—
and he sets himself upon the course of life.

He has no real plan for his time, but on impulse decides to visit
Newport, Rhode Island, where he had served in the Coast Artillery some years before. It was a city he liked, a city of quality,
with multilevels of humanity to be uncovered. This young man, it
must be noted, has the penchant of an archaeologist about him.
He loves people; he delights in involving himself in their lives
without becoming changed by the involvement. He has high
moral standards, faith in the good of humankind, compassion for
his fellows. He is religious in the broadest sense, without espous-
ing any particular doctrine or creed. One is never sure, in fact, if
his extraordinary inner peace comes from belief in a unique deity
(which he denies) or from belief in the permanence of the universe
and in the unalterable Good to which he thinks all must aspire.

He is a gentle young man, with a ready sense of humor and a
sound base of knowledge. He is well read; well educated; above
all, well mannered. One might call him genteel. Certainly he is everlastingly polite.

His father was born in Maine; was a newspaper editor in
Madison, Wisconsin, before he was sent to China as a consul; attended Yale and received his doctorate there; was a Protestant
and an officer of the Temperance League in Madison. He was a
moralistic, self-righteous man; one might go so far as to call him
preachy and dogmatic. Nevertheless, his influence on his son could
not be denied.

Theophilus had attended schools in China; in one, a German
school, he learned German well enough to offer himself as a tutor
later. The experience in China opened up to him a world he never
knew: he was suddenly aware of the multitudes of people who
existed, of the vastness of the land, of a history more ancient than
anything he had conceived until then. He had also spent some
time in Rome, where his archaeological perspective was honed.

He had attended Yale, where he published a play called *The
Trumpet Shall Sound* in the Yale Literary Magazine. He had
roomed at Berkeley Hall, a coincidence since he had spent some
of his boyhood in Berkeley, California. He had been a member of
the Elizabethan Club. He had once met Sigmund Freud. He had

lived "a sheltered academic life" until he came to Newport. Similarities between Theophilus North and Thornton Wilder abound.

For the plot, Thornton reverts to the technique he used in *The Cabala*. Theophilus North comes to Newport and becomes involved in "adventures" with one or another of the town's inhabitants. He is sometimes asked to intervene; sometimes he becomes entangled by a quirk of circumstance. But always he is looked upon as "a Yale man and a Christian," and his upright character is unquestioned.

Theophilus has had many ambitions in life. At various times he has wanted to be a missionary, an anthropologist, an archaeologist, a detective, an actor, a magician, a *picaro*. Understandably, for he is young, energetic, literate, and intelligent, he wants to be free. He does not want to be someone's subordinate. He does not want to be involved with business or politics. He wants to spend his time with people. One "ambition" stands out: he wants to be a lover. Certainly, coming from Thornton Wilder, that needs an explanation, and one is given. He is not seeking a goddess, he says, nor is he a would-be Casanova. But he can't help being attracted to perky, vivacious females—young women whose spirit matches his own.

Theophilus is adventurous and playful. There is nothing jaded about him. He is ready, he decides, to light into other people's lives, to court danger, to have fun. He goes to Newport.

Though Theophilus is at loose ends, Thornton's character shows no anxiety over his state. He is trying, one might say, to find himself, but he expects the process to be leisurely and entertaining. He suffers no identity crisis. Wherever his ambitions might lead, he will remain solidly Theophilus North. He may not know *what* he is; he is sure about *who* he is.

Newport offers as much interest for him as ancient Rome. He finds no less than nine cities, each with a certain fascination. The first is the oldest, the remnants of a seventeenth-century village. The second is the town that stood in the eighteenth century, a graceful and tidy place. The third is the seaport; the fourth, the naval base; the fifth, the home of the nineteenth-century intellectuals who came from other New England cities—Henry James, Julia Ward Howe, Louis Agassiz. The sixth is the city of the

wealthy: the summer villas modestly called "cottages." Their servants formed the seventh city. Those who prey on wealth formed
the eighth. And the merchants and their families formed the
ninth.

Theophilus decides to advertise himself both as a tennis coach
and a tutor of English, French, German, Latin, and algebra. He
also offers to read aloud to anyone who might require such a service. Of course, he finds employment almost immediately. Of
course, he is well liked.

His first adventure concerns a wealthy young socialite, Diana
Bell, who has run off to elope with a retiring schoolteacher. Theophilus is called in—for no other reason than that he is a Yale man
and has common sense—to stop the elopement and bring Diana
home. Though he makes clear his distaste for interfering in the
lives of other adults, he consents to perform his task. He contrives
a scene in which Diana's true colors clash with her fiancé's. The
match dissolves. The two lovers part as friends. And of course,
Theophilus has succeeded in his mission. His reputation begins to
be spread around Newport.

Next he is called in by one Miss Wyckoff—again, because of his
Yale connection—to read family letters to her in an effort to discover why her house has a reputation of being haunted. Theophilus finds a letter which reveals that the house suffered the same
fate as the one he described in *The Trumpet Shall Sound*. When
the Wyckoffs were away, the servants took over, and their raucous
doings were misinterpreted. But he is not content merely to dis-
close the cause to Miss Wyckoff. Instead, he contrives to rescue
the house's reputation. He meets a journalist, the lovely Flora
Deland, and feeds her wondrous tales about the mansion. She
publishes them, and suddenly Miss Wyckoff finds she is living in
an enviable home. This adventure, more demanding than the previous one, does have its compensation: Theophilus manages to
seduce Flora.

At "Nine Gables" he meets Dr. Bosworth, an elderly, scholarly
Harvard man who delights in Theophilus even though he knows
he comes from Yale. Dr. Bosworth is being manipulated by his
children, especially his oldest daughter, into believing he is frail
and ill. His spirit is drained, and he often feels dejected. He even

wonders if he might be going crazy. Theophilus takes it upon himself to liberate the old gentleman from his children's domination. He manages to convince him that he is in perfect health, strong, able, and intellectually stimulating. He restores Dr. Bosworth to his rightful position in his own house and makes him a free man.

Liberation is the theme of the next adventure, too, when Theophilus meets an old classmate of his, Nicholas "Rip" Vanwinkle, who is dominated by a shrewish wealthy wife. Here Theophilus arranges a scene that shames her into repentance, and she reconsiders her treatment of her husband.

Next Theophilus meets Elbert Hughes, who unwittingly is entangled with forgers of antique documents—autographs and letters—and desperately wants to be freed. Theophilus makes plans to have him kidnapped and spirited off to a mental hospital (since he often thinks he is Edgar Allan Poe, there is some logic here) for his own safety, and even arranges to have the forgers undone.

Charles Fenwick, the unhappy adolescent of the next adventure, is lonely, haughty, and distant until Theophilus allows him to regress into an earlier stage where he can laugh at "forbidden" words and think "forbidden" thoughts. Theophilus' friendship with Charles culminates happily: the young man is able to relax somewhat and is freed of the pent-up anxieties that made him so aloof. Theophilus has drawn upon his experience as a teacher to play amateur psychiatrist, but, as always, he succeeds.

Theophilus, liberator of men, is able also to mend strained marriages and inspire downhearted women. Myra and George are expecting a child, but, with Myra's history of miscarriages, she must rest and take all precautions. George, dismayed at having to abstain from sex for six months, takes up with a lovely Frenchwoman; besides, he finally confesses to Thornton, Myra's all-consuming love for him is smothering. Though Theophilus is hired to read to Myra during lonely afternoons, he performs the more important task of inspiring in her a love for great literature and inspiring in George repentance for his sins and acceptance of the love that is offered. Theophilus purports not to give advice. Of course, he always does; and of course, his wise words are heeded.

The episode of "Mino" is a hard test of Theophilus' "disaffected" personality. Mino is a brilliant young Italian who lost both feet when, as a child, he was run over by a train. He is an autodidact, a genius, but he is haunted by his handicap and secretly fears he will be unable to attract and keep a woman. Theophilus arranges to convince him otherwise, and the episode ends with the beautiful Agnese (whose name alludes to purity and chastity) throwing her arms around Mino.

The involvement with Mino is one of the most sensitive of the book. The next adventure, with Alice, is the most preposterous. Theophilus meets Alice, a Navy wife, at a restaurant-bar called Mama Carlotta's, suspiciously like Dick Carlotta's Stockbridge Inn. Alice is married to George, who is sterile, and desperately wants a baby. George is away on a ship. Alice is sincere, unaffected, simple, and good. Of course, Theophilus obliges her, and we are left with no doubt about the result.

"The Deer Park" is the site of the next entanglement, the home of Elspeth Skeel, a lovely girl suffering from migraine headaches. Theophilus is called in because he has acquired a reputation—unfounded and embarrassing to him—of being a "healer." Elspeth hopes he can rid her of her headaches and free her from proposed brain surgery. He does heal her by discovering her father's domination over her and her brother and revealing the psychological cause of her problem to the child's eminent physician. Elspeth is sent to a school in Switzerland, where she will be very happy.

Theophilus' reputation continues to spread throughout the city. He is again called in, this time to help an aged woman racked by rheumatism. He cannot help her to live without pain, but he manages to help her die peacefully. Theophilus reflects, then, on the unique "constellation" of friends each individual should have. Each person should have eighteen friends: three men and three women older than he, three each of equal age, and three each younger. As one leaves, another should come as a replacement. The "constellation" will support and nourish him or her.

Theophilus is a loyal and devoted friend to those he respects. He brings together the Baron Stamm, "Bodo," and Dr. Bosworth's daughter Persis Tennyson, a widow, two young people eminently suited to each other and yet at first forced to forsake their possible happiness. Persis' husband had killed himself, and rumor spreads that he had committed suicide in a state of deep depression. Such a state is unthinkable to an optimist, a good Protestant, a Yale man, and a lover of life, and Theophilus learns the truth from Persis: Tennyson killed himself on a dare, playing Russian roulette. This fact will save Persis' reputation, he is sure, and he has it publicized, thus enabling her to consider Bodo as a suitor; previously she wanted to protect him from her shame.

Throughout the book we are treated to mention of a certain Edweena, who is the fiancée of one of Theophilus' friends, Henry Simmons. Only at the end do we meet the elusive lady, and she turns out to be a woman Theophilus once slept with and never forgot. His reunion with her—of course, they let no one know they had met before—brings the book full circle, and we leave Theophilus on his way to another city, where he will find new faces and more puzzled hearts.

Despite superficial coincidences, Theophilus North is not Thornton Niven Wilder. Though he claims to have been changed by his experiences in Newport, Theophilus at the end is still the same "disaffected" young man he was at the start of the tale. He is essentially another Wilder archetype, a saintly man, for all his sexual encounters. He is Samuele. He is John Ashley. He is a man of faith, of good will, and he proves, again and again, that Goodness can overcome Evil. He becomes neither sadder nor wiser from his entanglements, though one must admit it would be difficult to become wiser. Though Thornton frequently has Theophilus' eyes fill with tears, the reader somehow cannot believe that he cares fully, deeply, and passionately about those with whom he becomes involved. His life touches that of many, but he himself remains untouched. What he does care about is injustice, enslavement of the spirit, and the inability of any human being to exercise his own will.

"Memory and imagination," Thornton wrote in his final sentence, had combined in *Theophilus North*. But the character of Theophilus was more imagination than Thornton's memory of himself in 1926.

When the book was published in 1973 reviewers rightly saw it as Thornton's last, and many had praise for the work. His friends Glenway Wescott, Malcolm Cowley, and Archibald MacLeish all came forward with kind words. Thornton had earned a position as the kindly granddad of American letters, and his newest novel was warmly greeted.

By late in the year, Thornton's health became so poor that he spent the winter at the Hotel El Convento in San Juan and Bluebeard's Castle on St. Thomas. He had had a slipped disk and was recovering slowly. He had hypertension. He was nearly blind in his left eye and was gradually becoming deaf. He thought spring might relieve some symptoms, but he felt as ill in April as he had in December.

Early in 1975 he was in Sanibel Island, Florida, trying to work. He was no better, and now was forced to give up smoking and drinking. To Robert Stallman in France he admitted that he was an old man, and did not think he would ever see Europe again.[2] His gait was halting, but still his spirit could soar. His imagination never suffered the ravages of age.

Thornton Wilder died in his sleep on December 7, 1975. His face was calm, accepting, quiet.[3] He was brought by ambulance to the Hospital of St. Raphael in New Haven and was pronounced dead on arrival at 7:25 P.M. The funeral was private, and a memorial service was held on January 18, 1976, in the Battel Chapel at Yale.

"It was once suggested that my tombstone read, 'Here lies one who tried to be obliging,'" Thornton had said. "The Germans heard of this and got it all mixed up, made it grandiose, and, to my horror, translated it, 'Here lies one who tried to help mankind.'"[4]

"How does one live?" he had asked in *The Woman of Andros*. His faith was in people, in humankind, in the slow, sure perfection of the species with each new birth. He tried to impart a bit of truth in his novels and plays, yet did not fully believe that he had succeeded. His own life, he admitted, may have been special, privileged, enviable. But like any other human being, he had known despondency and despair; like few others, he was able to turn those feelings into optimism and hope. He believed in something eternal, he wrote in *Our Town*, "and that something has to be with human beings."

He was the writer of plays and novels, and the lover of humanity. Like his character Chrysis, he asked to be remembered for his gift, however tenuous or frail it may prove to be. "Remember some day, remember me as one who loved all things and accepted from the gods all things, the bright and the dark. And you do likewise. Farewell."[5]

# NOTES

All references below are fully annotated in the bibliography. For simplification, annotations were not made where the source of a quote is obvious from the text. In compliance with the wishes of the Estate of Thornton Wilder, no quotations from unpublished writings of Thornton Wilder appear in the biography.

CHAPTER ONE

1. Thornton Wilder (TW) to Alexander Woollcott.
2. Unless otherwise noted, information about Amos's childhood and youth comes from the Yale Class History, 1884.
3. Amos Parker Wilder (APW) to Louis Bridgman, January 19, 1912.
4. "Thornton Wilder: A Biography in Sound," April 30, 1956, recorded for NBC (NBC tape).
5. Barnes, 177.
6. Information about Amos's career in the foreign service comes from the files of the Department of State and was kindly provided by the National Archives and Records Service, Washington, D.C.
7. NBC tape.
8. Wooster *Daily Record*, May 10, 1950.
9. APW speech, Central China Famine Relief Committee, October 31, 1911.

CHAPTER TWO

1. *Theophilus North*, 12.
2. "The Old Days."
3. *Theophilus North*, 104.
4. Ibid., 274.
5. Thacher School Bulletin.
6. *The Angel That Troubled the Waters*, vi.
7. NBC tape.
8. *The Angel That Troubled the Waters*, v.
9. Ibid., 23.
10. Ibid., 26.
11. Hutchins, *No Friendly Voice*, 90.
12. Ibid., 93.
13. Daniels, 16.
14. Artz.
15. Hutchins, op. cit., 89.
16. Artz to LS, November, 1976.
17. Francis Hutchins to LS, July 11, 1977.
18. Parmenter, 11.
19. *Theophilus North*, 67.
20. Ibid., 12.
21. New York *Times*, April 15, 1962.


CHAPTER THREE

1. Phelps, "As I Like It," 224.
2. Boston *Traveler*, December 14, 1955.
3. Farrar, Hartford *Courant*, July 15, 1928.
4. *The Angel That Troubled the Waters*.
5. *Theophilus North*, 61.
6. Ibid., 328.
7. New York *Times*, May 16, 1977.
8. *The Cabala*, 1.
9. *Theophilus North*, 349.
10. Goldstone, *Writers at Work*, 113 (Goldstone interview).
11. *Time*, January 12, 1953.
12. Glenn, 195–96.
13. Mulford, 251.
14. *Time*, loc. cit.
15. Garson Kanin, speech at Wellesley College, May 9, 1977.
16. Isaacs, 21–22.
17. Ibid.

## CHAPTER FOUR

1. Daniels, 15.
2. Smith, 15.
3. Smith, 40.
4. Stallman, *The Houses That James Built*, viii.
5. TW to Mr. Jelliffe, April 21, 1939.
6. Smith, 25.
7. TW to Mary Seccombe, October 12, 1924.
8. NBC tape.
9. New York *Times*, May 9, 1926.
10. *Saturday Review*, May 8, 1926, 771.
11. Wilson, *The Wound and the Bow*, 221.

## CHAPTER FIVE

1. TW to Lewis Baer, November, 1926.
2. TW to Seccombe, February, 1927.
3. New York *Times*, December 11, 1926.
4. TW to Frederic Prokosch, December 25, 1936.
5. Boston *Traveler*, December 14, 1955.
6. Luke 13:4 (King James Version).
7. Goldstone interview, 108.
8. December 3, 1927, 371.
9. December 28, 1927, 173.
10. February 28, 1928.
11. TW to Henry Blake Fuller, May 12, 1928.
12. Phelps, *Autobiography*, 798.
13. Wilson, *Shores of Light*, 381.
14. Ibid., 376.
15. Ibid., 379.
16. *Time*, January 12, 1953, 44.
17. Hermine Popper, interview with Isabel Wilder (unpublished).

## CHAPTER SIX

1. Farrar, Hartford *Courant*, July 15, 1928.
2. Ibid.
3. TW to Fuller, May 18, 1928.
4. New York *Times*, June 13, 1928.
5. New York *Times*, June 29, 1928.
6. Andrews, "To Us He Was Always 'T.W.'"
7. Maurois, 38–39.

8. Maurois, 39.
9. Steward to LS, October 14, 1978.
10. Maurois, 41.
11. Beach, 111.
12. NBC tape.
13. TW to Rankin, November 12, 1928.
14. Wescott, 243–44.
15. Ibid., 248.
16. Ibid., 247.
17. TW to Edith Isaacs, January 16, 1928.
18. *New Republic*, November 26, 1928, 49.

CHAPTER SEVEN

1. Phelps, *Autobiography*, 811.
2. Kansas City *Star*, April 18, 1929.
3. TW to Alexander Woollcott, March 12, 1929.
4. William Hutchins to TW, April 16, 1929.
5. TW to Phelps, April 11, 1929.
6. Hutchins, *Center Magazine*, 19.
7. Robert Hutchins Memorial Program, WAMC radio, October 3, 1977.
8. Hutchins, *No Friendly Voice*, 191.
9. Loring Holmes Dodd, 280.
10. Minnesota *Daily*, February 7, 1930.
11. Wilson, *Shores of Light*, 445.
12. *The Nation*, February 26, 1930.
13. March 1, 1930, 771.

CHAPTER EIGHT

1. William Hutchins to TW.
2. New York *Times*, May 16, 1977.
3. Glenn, 30–31.
4. Louis Engel taped reminiscences, September 1977 (Engel tape).
5. Stallman, "To Thornton Wilder," 28.
6. Dexter Masters to LS, September 6, 1977.
7. Ulrich, "TW: Professor and Playwright," 7, 8.
8. Glenn, 195–96.
9. Ardrey, 10.
10. Ibid., 13.
11. *Time*, January 12, 1953.

12. Honolulu *Star-Bulletin*, November 4, 1933.
13. Ibid.
14. Goldstone interview, 105.
15. Ibid., 110–11.
16. Behrman, 134.
17. Engel tape.
18. Ibid.
19. Ibid.


CHAPTER NINE

1. Hatcher, 271.
2. Wilson, *Shores of Light*, 501.
3. Ibid., 503.
4. Honolulu *Advertiser*, November 5, 1933.
5. Kaufman and Hennessey, xviii.
6. TW conversation with LS, April 1975.
7. Adams, 212.
8. TW to Alexander Woollcott, 1933.
9. Preminger, 147.
10. TW to Katharine Cornell, May 19, 1932.
11. Buffalo *Evening News*, December 13, 1932.
12. *New Republic*, January 18, 1933.
13. Cleveland *Plain Dealer*, January 18, 1933.
14. Ibid.
15. Boston *Globe*, March 15, 1959.
16. Goldstone interview, 104.
17. Cleveland *Plain Dealer*, December 7, 1932.
18. Honolulu *Star-Bulletin*, November 4, 1933.
19. Honolulu *Advertiser*, November 5, 1933.
20. Honolulu *Star-Bulletin*, November 2, 1933.
21. Honolulu *Advertiser*, November 5, 1933.
22. Honolulu *Star-Bulletin*, November 10, 1933.
23. Honolulu *Star-Bulletin*, November 17, 1933.
24. TW to Alexander Woollcott, August 31, 1934.
25. Hahn, 191.
26. Witter Bynner, *Guestbook*, New York: Knopf, 1935, 75.


CHAPTER TEN

1. Stein, *Everybody's Autobiography*, 201.
2. Stein, *Geographical History*, 38.
3. Stein, *Writings and Lectures*, 150.

4. Stein, *Geographical History*, 54.
5. Stein, *Everybody's Autobiography*, 203–4.
6. Glenn, 31.
7. Stein, *Everybody's Autobiography*, 207.
8. Stallman, "To Thornton Wilder," 29.
9. Stein, *Everybody's Autobiography*, 220.
10. Ibid., 263.
11. Ibid., 267.
12. Goldstone interview, 104.
13. Wilson, *Letters*, 256.
14. Goldstone interview, 111.
15. Harry Levin conversation with LS, October 11, 1977.
16. Hermine Popper interview with Isabel Wilder.
17. *New Republic*, January 16, 1935.
18. January 5, 1935.
19. *Nation*, January 30, 1935.
20. TW to Witter Bynner, June 16, 1935.
21. TW to Alexander Woollcott, May 4, 1935.
22. TW to Mr. Davis, May 5, 1935.
23. TW to Alexander Woollcott, May 4, 1935.
24. TW to Alexander Woollcott, June 23, 1935.
25. Stein, *Geographical History*, 14.
26. Ibid., 180–81.
27. Stein, *Everybody's Autobiography*, 301.
28. Stein, *Geographical History*, 9–10.
29. TW conversation with LS, April 1975.
30. Stein, *Geographical History*, 35.
31. Ibid., 35–37.
32. Ibid., 61.
33. TW conversation with LS, April 1975.
34. Stein, *Geographical History*, 64.
35. Ibid., 204.
36. Stein, *Everybody's Autobiography*, 301.
37. TW to Robert Stallman, August 8, 1935.
38. Gallup, 306–7.
39. "Joyce and the Modern Novel," 16.
40. Gallup, 306–7.
41. Ibid., 303–5.
42. Ibid., 305–6.
43. Stein, *Everybody's Autobiography*, 302.


CHAPTER ELEVEN

1. Stein, *Everybody's Autobiography*, 132–33.

2. *Theophilus North*, 299.
3. TW to Witter Bynner, June 16, 1935.
4. *Time*, January 12, 1953.
5. NBC tape.
6. TW to Alexander Woollcott, September 27, 1936.
7. TW to Alexander Woollcott, September 17, 1936.
8. TW to Alexander Woollcott, October 2, 1936.
9. Wescott, 148–49.
10. Gordon, *My Side*, 287.
11. Barnes, 264.
12. TW to Alexander Woollcott, May 31, 1937.
13. Stein, *The Making of Americans*, 3.
14. Ibid., 3.
15. Stein, *How Writing Is Written*, 43–47.
16. Steward, 62.
17. Ibid., 37.
18. Ibid., 32.
19. New York *Times*, December 28, 1937.
20. Ibid.
21. Harris, 79.
22. New York *Herald Tribune*, February 15, 1938.

CHAPTER TWELVE

1. Honolulu *Advertiser*, November 17, 1933.
2. New York *Times*, November 6, 1961.
3. Honolulu *Star-Bulletin*, November 4, 1933.
4. New York *Herald Tribune*, February 15, 1938.
5. Goldstone interview, 110.
6. Ibid., 110–11.
7. "Some Thoughts on Playwriting," 85–86.
8. Ibid., 90–91.
9. "A Platform and a Passion or Two."
10. McCarthy, 27–29.
11. Ibid., x.
12. Kaufman and Hennessey, 201.
13. Harris, 82.
14. Connelly, 232.
15. Harris, 79.
16. Ibid., 79–80.
17. Ibid., 112–13.
18. Connelly, 234.
19. February 5, 1938.
20. March 1938, 172–73.

21. *New Republic,* February 23, 1938, 74.
22. Brown, *Two on the Aisle,* 189, 193.
23. New York *Herald Tribune,* March 13, 1938.
24. Wisconsin *State Journal,* October 6, 1940.


CHAPTER THIRTEEN

1. Kaufman and Hennessey, 215.
2. Gallup, 333–34.
3. March 1939, 173–74.
4. *Newsweek,* January 9, 1939.
5. Wilder, "A Platform and a Passion or Two," 51.
6. Gallup, 338–39.
7. Behrman, "Thornton Wilder—America's Universal Man," 133.
8. Parmenter, 11.
9. "Our Town—from Stage to Screen," 815.
10. Ibid., 816.
11. Ibid., 816.
12. Ibid., 817.
13. Ibid., 818.
14. Ibid., 821.
15. TW to Mary Seccombe, February 2 and February 6, 1940.
16. "Our Town—from Stage to Screen," 822.
17. Ibid., 824.
18. Parmenter, 10.
19. Ibid., 11.
20. Ibid., 11.
21. Montreal *Gazette,* November 8, 1940.
22. Wisconsin *State Journal,* October 6, 1940.


CHAPTER FOURTEEN

1. Wisconsin *State Journal,* October 6, 1940.
2. Ibid.
3. Wilson, *Letters,* 184.
4. "James Joyce," 373–74.
5. "Joyce and the Modern Novel," 12.
6. Ibid., 14–15.
7. Ibid., 14.
8. Ibid., 18.
9. TW to Esther Bates, January 12, 1941.
10. TW to Mrs. Anderson, n.d.
11. Barnes, 221.

12. Kaufman, 346.
13. Truffaut, 109.
14. TW to Alexander Woollcott, June 10, 1942.
15. TW to Alexander Woollcott, July 1942.
16. TW to Alexander Woollcott, September 28, 1942.
17. Kaufman and Hennessey, 345.
18. Bankhead, 250.
19. Ibid., 259.
20. Ibid., 254–55.
21. Ibid., 249.
22. Ibid., 251–52.
23. November 28, 1942, 35.
24. *Time*, November 30, 1942, 57.
25. *New Republic*, November 30, 1942, 714–15.
26. Gilder, 9.
27. *Newsweek*, November 30, 1942.
28. Kaufman and Hennessey, 374.
29. Ibid., 368.
30. Ibid., 385.
31. Harry Levin conversation with LS, October 11, 1977.
32. Adams, 311.
33. Woollcott, 245.
34. Ibid., 393.

CHAPTER FIFTEEN

1. Newlove, 135.
2. Eckermann, 107.
3. Ibid., 154.
4. Ibid., 187.
5. Miriam Lens to TW, October 7, 1957.
6. TW conversation with LS, April 6, 1975.
7. Introduction to *Four in America*, x.
8. Ibid., xiv.
9. TW conversation with LS, April 6, 1975.
10. Introduction to *Four in America*, xxvii.
11. Ibid., xxvii.

CHAPTER SIXTEEN

1. TW to Chauncey Brewster Tinker, April 18, 1947.
2. July 31, 1948.
3. February 21, 1948.

4. February 21, 1948.
5. Montreal *Gazette*, March 13, 1948.
6. Berkshire *Eagle*, June 19, 1948.
7. Franklin Heller to LS, October 17, 1977.
8. Bosworth, 99.
9. Kay Boyle to LS, November 11, 1977.
10. Kay Boyle, introduction to *The Bridge of San Luis Rey*, New York: Time-Life Books, 1967, xiii, xiv.
11. Fussell, *The Nation*, May 3, 1958, 394.
12. TW to Esther Bates, March 16, 1953.
13. Cleveland *Plain Dealer*, August 10, 1975.

CHAPTER SEVENTEEN

1. Bergstraesser, vii.
2. TW to George Odell, June 27, 1949.
3. "The American Loneliness," 68.
4. New York *Times*, April 15, 1962.
5. *Rocky Mountain News*, June 28, 1949.
6. *Rocky Mountain News*, June 27, 1949.
7. *Rocky Mountain News*, June 29, 1949.
8. Elizabeth Paepcke to LS, October 29, 1977.
9. William Miles conversation with LS, May 24, 1977.
10. Wooster *Voice*, May 11, 1950.
11. Wooster *Daily Record*, May 11, 1950.
12. TW speech upon receipt of Doctor of Humane Letters, Wooster College typescript.
13. Cleveland *Plain Dealer*, May 10, 1950.
14. Boston *Herald*, March 12, 1951.
15. "Toward an American Language"; all quotations in this section are from the article as noted in the bibliography.
16. "The American Loneliness"; all quotations in this section are from the article as noted in the bibliography.
17. "The Silent Generation"; all quotations in this section are from the article as noted in the bibliography.
18. Wallace Stevens to Norman Holmes Pearson, June 25, 1951.
19. TW to Francis Hutchins, July 24, 1951.

CHAPTER EIGHTEEN

1. TW to Libby Holman, January 20, 1952; TW and Montgomery Clift to Frank Sullivan, n.d.
2. Wilder, "The American Loneliness," 69.

3. Ibid.
4. UNESCO, *The Artist in Modern Society*, 124.
5. Anderson, 158.

CHAPTER NINETEEN

1. Guthrie, A *Life in the Theatre*, 233.
2. Guthrie, "The World of Thornton Wilder," 110–11.
3. Ibid., 116.
4. Guthrie, A *Life in the Theatre*, 231.
5. Guthrie, "The World of Thornton Wilder," 118.
6. Guthrie, A *Life in the Theatre*, 234.
7. Ibid., 235.
8. Ibid., 235.
9. TW to Elizabeth Sergeant, January 16, 1955.
10. "Mr. Wilder's Confession," *The Scotsman*, August 24, 1955.
11. Boston *Traveler*, December 14, 1955.

CHAPTER TWENTY

1. Boston *Herald*, June 18, 1957.
2. Boston *Daily Globe*, September 18, 1957.
3. Helmut Viebrock to LS, April 25, 1977.
4. Sahl, 9.
5. "Afternoon," *New Yorker*, May 23, 1959, 35.
6. Gordon, *Myself Among Others*, 14.
7. "Afternoon," 34.
8. New York *Times*, November 6, 1961.
9. Berkshire *Eagle*, June 16, 1961.
10. New York *Times*, November 6, 1961.
11. Haberman, *The Plays of Thornton Wilder*, 8.
12. "Afternoon," 35.
13. NBC tape.
14. Goldstone interview, 106–7.
15. Edward Weeks, Address at MacDowell Colony, MacDowell Colony *News*, August 13, 1960.
16. Werfel, 306–7.
17. TW to Mark Schorer, February 29, 1959.
18. Boston *Globe*, March 15, 1959.
19. Nikos Psacharopoulos conversation with LS, July 27, 1978.
20. Unidentified newspaper, May 1, 1962.
21. Arizona *Daily Star*, May 1, 1962.
22. Arizona *Daily Star*, March 9, 1962.

CHAPTER TWENTY-ONE

1. Arizona *Daily Star*, March 9, 1962.
2. New York *Times*, April 15, 1962.
3. Canfield, 102–3.
4. June 1967, 124, 126.
5. January 8, 1967, 26, 45–46.
6. Toklas, *The Alice B. Toklas Cookbook*, 298.
7. TW to Brooks Atkinson, December 4, 1969.
8. The manuscripts are in the possession of Mr. Carlotta and were read with his kind permission.


CHAPTER TWENTY-TWO

1. TW to Dick Carlotta, December 5, 1969.
2. TW to Robert Stallman, February 14, 1975.
3. Isabel Wilder to Dick Carlotta, December 18, 1975.
4. "Afternoon," *The New Yorker*, May 23, 1959.
5. *The Woman of Andros*, 107.

# BIBLIOGRAPHY

## BY THORNTON WILDER

I. NOVELS AND PLAYS:

*The Alcestiad, or A Life in the Sun*. New York: Harper & Row, 1978.
*The Angel That Troubled the Waters and Other Plays*. New York: Coward-McCann, 1928.
*The Bridge of San Luis Rey*. New York: A. & C. Boni, 1927.
*The Cabala*. New York: A. & C. Boni, 1926.
*The Eighth Day*. New York: Harper & Row, 1967.
*Heaven's My Destination*. New York: Harper & Bros., 1935.
*The Ides of March*. New York: Harper & Bros., 1948.
*The Long Christmas Dinner and Other Plays in One Act*. New Haven: Yale University Press, 1931.
*Lucrèce*, by André Obey. Translator. Boston: Houghton Mifflin, 1933.
*The Matchmaker* (see *Three Plays*).
*The Merchant of Yonkers*. New York: Harper & Bros., 1939.
*Our Century*. New York: The Century Association, 1947.
*Our Town* (see *Three Plays*).
*The Skin of Our Teeth* (see *Three Plays*).
*Theophilus North*. New York: Harper & Row, 1973.

*Three Plays: Our Town, The Skin of Our Teeth, The Matchmaker.* New York: Harper & Bros., 1957.

*The Woman of Andros.* New York: A. & C. Boni, 1930.


II. ARTICLES AND SHORT PIECES

"After a Visit to England," *Yale Review.* December 1941, pp. 217–24.

"The American Loneliness," *The Atlantic.* August 1952, pp. 65–69.

"And the Sea Shall Give Up Its Dead," *S4N.* January–February 1923, pp. 9–13.

*Childhood,* in *The Atlantic.* November 1960, pp. 78–84.

"A Diary: First and Last Entry," *S4N.* February 1924, pp. 7–11.

"The Drunken Sisters," *The Atlantic.* November 1957, pp. 92–95.

"Emily Dickinson," *The Atlantic.* November 1952, pp. 43–48.

"For Henry Blake Fuller," *Tributes to Henry B.,* edited by Anna Morgan. Chicago: Ralph Fletcher Seymour, December 20, 1929, p. 106.

"Giordano Bruno's Last Meal in Finnegans Wake," *Hudson Review.* Spring 1963, pp. 74–79.

"James Joyce (1882–1941)," *Poetry: A Magazine of Verse.* March 1941, pp. 370–74.

"Joyce and the Modern Novel," *A James Joyce Miscellany,* edited by Marvin Magalaner. James Joyce Society, 1957, pp. 11–19.

"Kultur in einer Demokratie," Frankfurt am Main: Borsenverein des Deutschen Buch-handels E.V., 1957.

"Lope Pinedo, Some Child-Actors, and a Lion," *Romance Philology.* August 1953, pp. 19–25.

"Noting the Nature of Farce," New York *Times.* January 8, 1939, IX, p. 1.

"The Old Days," *Saturday Evening Post Number of the Thacher School Semicentennial Publications.* September 1919–June 1929.

"on translators," *Translation.* Winter 1974, p. 5.

(with Sol Lesser) "Our Town—from Stage to Screen," *Theatre Arts.* November 1940, pp. 815–24.

"A Platform and a Passion or Two," *Harper's Magazine.* October 1957, pp. 48–51.

(with Isabel Wilder) "Playgoing Nights: From a Travel Diary," *Theatre Arts Monthly.* June 1929, pp. 411–19.

"A Playwright's View of Brattle," *The Prompter.* Spring 1951, pp. 3–4.

"Pride of Intellect," *Yale Review.* October 1927, pp. 178–80.

"Queens of France," *Yale Review.* September 1931, pp. 72–85.

"Sentences," *Double Dealer.* September 1922, p. 110.

"The Silent Generation," *Harper's Magazine.* April 1953, pp. 34–36.

"Some Thoughts on Playwriting," *The Intent of the Artist,* edited by Augusto Centeno. Princeton: Princeton University Press, 1941, pp. 83–98.

"Toward an American Language," *The Atlantic.* July 1952, pp. 29–37.

"The Turn of the Year," *Theatre Arts Monthly.* March 1925, pp. 143–53.

"The Unerring Instinct," NCCJ Scripts for Brotherhood, 1948.

"The Victim, Not the Murderer, Is Guilty," *The Lit* (The Student Magazine of the Lawrenceville School), October 1978, p. 6.


III. INTRODUCTIONS

Abbott, Elsie. *Days from a Year in School.* Cornwall, New York: Cornwall Press, April 12, 1930.

Beer-Hofman, Richard. *Jacob's Dream.* New York: Johannes-Presse, 1946.

Sassoon, Sir Philip. *The Third Route.* New York: Doubleday, 1929.

Stein, Gertrude. *Four in America.* New Haven: Yale University Press, 1947.

——. *The Geographical History of America.* New York: Random House, 1936.

——. *Narration.* Chicago: University of Chicago Press, 1935.


IV. OBERLIN LITERARY MAGAZINE (*arranged chronologically*)

*St. Francis Lake: A Comedy in Cages,* December 1915, pp. 44–46.

*Flamingo Red: A Comedy in Danger,* January 1916, pp. 93–96.

"The Language of Emotion in Shakespeare," March 1916, pp. 140–44.

"Sealing Wax," April 1916, pp. 190–92.

*Brother Fire: A Comedy for Saints,* May 1916, pp. 200–2.

"Two Miracles of Doma y Venuzias," November 1916, pp. 6–7.

*A Christmas Interlude,* December 1916, pp. 47–49.

*Proserpina and the Devil: A Play for Marionettes,* December 1916, pp. 50–51.

"The Marriage of Zabett," June 1917, pp. 166–68.

*To a Teacher,* September 1917, p. 269.


V. YALE LITERARY MAGAZINE (*arranged chronologically*)

*The Angel on the Ship,* October 1917, pp. 15–17.

*The Message and Jehanne,* November 1917, pp. 94–96.

*The Last Measure of the Graal, To a friend enlisting,* December 1917, pp. 151–53.

*Three-Minute Plays For Three Persons. No. 12, The Penny That Beauty Spent. No. 13, The Walled City,* March 1918, pp. 303–8.

"Review of *Per Amica Silentia Lunae* by Yeats," March 1918, p. 314.

"Review of Rupert Brooke's *Death and Burial,*" March 1918, p. 315.

*That Other Fanny Otcott,* April 1918, pp. 328–31.

*Improving the Time,* May 1918, pp. 363–64.

*In Praise of Guynemer,* December 1918, pp. 27–29.

"An Imaginary Preface [to] Four Comedies of Menander, paraphrased by Cosmo Davies: *Captain Braggart, The Statue in the Market Place; The Two Shady Ladies; Sailor, How Long Are You in Town?,*" April 1919, pp. 166–68.

*Not For Leviathan,* April 1919, pp. 160–63.

*Childe Roland to the Dark Tower Came,* June 1919, pp. 208–40.

*The Trumpet Shall Sound,* Act One, October 1919, pp. 9–26; Act Two, November 1919, pp. 78–92; Act Three, December 1919, pp. 128–46; Act Four, January 1920, pp. 192–207.

"Eddy Greater," June 1920, pp. 373–82.

## GENERAL BIBLIOGRAPHY

"The Abiding Truths of 'Our Town,'" *Life,* September 7, 1962, pp. 52–67.

Adams, Samuel Hopkins. *A. Woollcott, His Life and His World.* New York: Reynal & Hitchcock, 1945.

Adcock, St. John. "Thornton Wilder," *The Bookman,* March 1929, pp. 316–19.

Adler, Henry. "Thornton Wilder's Theatre," *Horizon,* 1945, XII, pp. 89–99.

Adler, Mortimer J. *Philosopher at Large.* New York: Macmillan, 1977.

"Afternoon," *The New Yorker,* May 23, 1959, pp. 34–35.

"American Playwrights Self-Appraised," *Saturday Review,* September 3, 1955, pp. 18–19.

Anderson, Erica. *The Schweitzer Album.* New York: Harper, 1965.

Andrews, Clark. "To Us He Was Always 'T.W.'" *Yankee,* September 1978, pp. 120–25, 152–68.

Ardrey, Robert. *Plays of Three Decades.* New York: Atheneum, 1968.

Arnavon, Cyrille. "La Vogue de Thornton Wilder," *Etudes Anglaises* (Paris), 1957, X, pp. 421–30.

Artz, Frederick B. "Thornton Wilder in Oberlin—A Few Memories," *The Oberlin Alumni Magazine*, January 1957, p. 14.

"As We Remember Him: In Memory of Stephen Vincent Benét," *Saturday Review of Literature*, March 27, 1943, p. 9.

Atkinson, Brooks, and Hirschfeld, Albert. *The Lively Years*. New York: Association Press, 1973.

Ballet, Arthur H. " 'In Our Living and in Our Dying,' " *English Journal*, 1956, XLV, pp. 243–49.

Bankhead, Tallulah. *Tallulah*. New York: Harper, 1952.

Barnes, Eric Wollencott. *The Man Who Lived Twice*. New York: Scribner's, 1956.

Beach, Sylvia. *Shakespeare and Company*. New York: Harcourt, Brace, 1956, 1959.

Beckerman, Bernard, and Seegman, Howard. *On Stage*. New York: Quadrangle, 1973.

Behrman, Samuel Nathaniel. *Portrait of Max*. New York: Random House, 1960.

——. "Thornton Wilder—America's Universal Man." *Reader's Digest*. May 19, 1974, pp. 132–36.

Bennett, Arnold. *The Journal of Arnold Bennett (1921–1928)*. New York: Viking, 1933.

Bentley, Eric. *In Search of Theater*. New York: Knopf, 1953.

——. *The Playwright as Thinker*. New York: Reynal & Hitchcock, 1946.

Bergstraesser, Arnold, ed. *Goethe and the Modern Age*. Chicago: Regnery, 1950.

Bessy, Maurice. *Orson Welles*. Trans. Ciba Vaughan. New York: Crown, 1971.

Blackmur, R. P. "Thornton Wilder," *Hound and Horn*, 1930, III, pp. 586–89.

Blakeslee, George, ed. *Recent Developments in China*. New York: Stechert, 1913.

Boleslavsky, Richard. *Acting, The First Six Lessons*. New York, Theatre Arts, 1933.

Bosis, Lauro de. *Icaro*. Trans. Ruth Draper. New York: Oxford University Press, 1933.

——. *The Story of My Death*. New York: Oxford University Press, 1933.

Bosworth, Patricia. *Montgomery Clift*. New York: Harcourt Brace Jovanovich, 1978.

Brown, E. K. "A Christian Humanist," *University of Toronto Quarterly*, April 1935, pp. 365–70.

Brown, John Mason. *Two on the Aisle*. New York: Viking, 1938.

Bryer, Jackson R. "Thornton Wilder and the Reviewers," *Papers of the Bibliographical Society of America*, 1964, LVIII, pp. 34–49.

Buchwald, Art. "Life Begins at Sixty," New York *Herald Tribune*, May 21, 1957, II, p. 1.

Burbank, Rex. *Thornton Wilder*. New York: Twayne, 1961.

Burnett, Whit, ed. *The World's Best*. New York: Dial, 1942, 1950.

Cahn, Sammy. *I Should Care: The Sammy Cahn Story*. New York: Arbor House, 1974.

Campbell, Joseph, and Robinson, H. M. "The Skin of Whose Teeth?" *Saturday Review of Literature*, December 19, 1942, pp. 3–4, and February 13, 1943, pp. 16, 18–19.

Canby, Henry Seidel. *American Memoir*. Boston: Houghton Mifflin, 1947.

Canfield, Cass. *Up & Down & Around*. New York: Harpers Magazine Press, 1971.

Clurman, Harold. *All People Are Famous*. New York: Harcourt Brace Jovanovich, 1974.

——. "Theater," *Nation*, September 3, 1955, p. 210.

Cole, Toby, ed. *Playwrights on Playwriting*. New York: Hill & Wang, 1960.

Connelly, Marc. *Voices Offstage*. New York: Holt, Rinehart & Winston, 1968.

Cornell, Katharine. *I Wanted to be An Actress*. New York: Random House, 1939.

Corrigan, Robert W. "Thornton Wilder and the Tragic Sense of Life," *The Theatre in Search of a Fix*. New York: Delacorte, 1973, pp. 239–46.

Cowley, Malcolm. *Exile's Return*. New York: Viking, 1951.

——. *The Literary Situation*. New York: Viking, 1954.

——. "The Man Who Abolished Time," *Saturday Review*, October 6, 1956, pp. 13–14, 50–52.

——. *A Second Flowering*. New York: Viking, 1973.

——. *A Thornton Wilder Trio* (introduction). New York: Criterion, 1956.

Daniels, Mabel. "Thornton Wilder: A Musical Memoir," *Radcliffe Quarterly*. May 1964, pp. 15–22.

Deckle, Bernard. *Profiles of Modern American Writers*. New York: Tuttle, 1969.

Delpach, Jeanine. "Thornton Wilder auteur de 'Notre petite ville' et 'Ides de mars' à Paris," *Les Nouvelles Littéraires*. October 4, 1951, pp. 1, 6.

Dodd, Lee Wilson. "The Ways of Man to Man," *Saturday Review of Literature*. December 3, 1927, p. 371.

Dodd, Loring Holmes. *Celebrities at our hearthside*. New York: Dresser, 1959.

Dreiser, Theodore. *Plays of the Natural and the Supernatural*. New York: John Lane, 1916.

Eckermann, Johann Peter. *Conversations of Goethe*. Trans. John Oxenford. London: Bell, 1875.

Edelstein, J. M. *A Bibliographical Checklist of the Writings of Thornton Wilder*. New Haven: Yale University Press, 1959.

Eliot, T. S. "Eliot contra Thornton Wilder," *Die Zeit*, Hamburg, November 14, 1957, pp. 11–12.

Esslin, Martin. *The Theatre of the Absurd*. New York: Anchor, 1961.

Farrar, John. "Wilder Crosses the Bridge to Success," Hartford *Courant*, July 15, 1928, p. E8.

Fergusson, Francis. "Three Allegorists: Brecht, Wilder and Eliot," *The Human Image in Dramatic Literature*. New York: Anchor, 1957, pp. 41–71.

Firebaugh, Joseph J. "Farce and the Heavenly Destination," *Four Quarters*, May 1967, pp. 10–17.

——. "The Humanism of Thornton Wilder," *Pacific Spectator*, Autumn 1950, p. 438.

Fischer, Walther. "The Bridge of San Luis Rey und Prosper Mérimée's La Carosse Du Saint-Sacrement," *Anglia*, January 1936, pp. 234–40.

Flexner, Eleanor. *American Playwrights, 1918–1938*. New York: Simon & Schuster, 1938.

Franchey, John. "Mr. Wilder Has An Idea," New York *Times*, August 13, 1939, IX, p. 2.

Frenz, Horst. "American Playwrights and the German Psyche," *Die Neuren Sprachen*, 1961, X, pp. 170–78.

——. *American Playwrights on Drama*. New York: Hill & Wang, 1965.

——. "The Reception of Thornton Wilder's Plays in Germany," *Modern Drama*, 1960, III, pp. 123–37.

——. "Thornton Wilder's Visits to Postwar Germany," *American-German Review*, 1957, No. 1, pp. 8–10.

Frey, John R. "Postwar German Reactions to American Literature," *Journal of English and Germanic Philology*," 1955, LIV, pp. 173–94.

Friedman, Paul. "The Bridge: A Study in Symbolism," *Psychoanalytic Quarterly*, January 1952, p. 72.

Fuller, Edmund. "Thornton Wilder: 'The Notation of the Heart,'" *Books with Men Behind Them*. New York: Random House, 1962, pp. 36–62.

Fussell, Paul, Jr. "Thornton Wilder and the German Psyche," *Nation*, May 3, 1958, pp. 394–95.

Gaither, Mary, and Frenz, Horst. "German Criticism of American Drama," *American Quarterly*, 1955, VII, pp. 111–22.

Gallup, Donald, ed. *The Flowers of Friendship*. New York: Knopf, 1953.

Gardner, Marvin. "Thornton Wilder and the Problem of Providence," *University of Kansas City Review*, 1940, VII, pp. 83–91.

Gassner, John. *Dramatic Soundings*. New York: Crown, 1968.

------. *Theatre at the Crossroads*. New York: Holt, Rinehart & Winston, 1960.

------. *The Theatre in Our Times*. New York: Crown, 1954.

Gelb, Arthur. "Thornton Wilder, 63, Sums Up Life and Art in New Play Cycle," New York *Times*, November 6, 1961, pp. 1, 74.

Gilder, Rosamond. "Broadway in Review," *Theatre Arts*, January 1943, pp. 9–11.

Glenn, C. Leslie. *A Scornful Wonder*. New York: McKay, 1977.

Goethe, Johann Wolfgang. *Autobiography*. Trans. John Oxenford. Philadelphia & Chicago: Moore, 1901.

------. *Literary Essays*. Arranged by J. E. Spingarn. New York: Ungar, 1921, 1964.

Gohdes, Clarence Louise Frank. *Essays on American Literature in honor of Jay B. Hubbell*. Durham, N.C.: Duke University Press, 1967.

Gold, Michael. "Wilder: Prophet of the Genteel Christ," *New Republic*, October 22, 1930, pp. 266–67. See letters November 5, 1930, pp. 325, 326; November 12, 1930, pp. 352–53; November 26, 1930, p. 49; December 3, 1930, pp. 75–76; December 10, 1930, pp. 104–5; December 17, 1930, p. 141.

Goldstein, Malcolm. *The Art of Thornton Wilder*. Lincoln: University of Nebraska Press, 1965.

Goldstone, Richard. "Thornton Wilder," *Writers at Work*, ed. by Malcolm Cowley. New York: Viking, 1959, pp. 99–118.

------. *Thornton Wilder*. New York: Saturday Review Press/E. P. Dutton, 1975.

------. "The Wilder Image," *Four Quarters*, May 1967, pp. 1–7.

Gordon, Ruth. *Myself Among Others*. New York: Atheneum, 1971.

------. *My Side*. New York: Harper & Row, 1976.

Grebanier, Bernard. *Thornton Wilder*. Minneapolis: University of Minnesota Press, 1964.

Guthrie, Tyrone. *A Life in the Theatre*. New York: McGraw-Hill, 1959.

------. "The World of Thornton Wilder," *In Various Directions*. New York: Macmillan, 1965.

Haberman, Donald. "The Americanization of Thornton Wilder," *Four Quarters*, May 1967, pp. 18–27.

------. *The Plays of Thornton Wilder: A Critical Study*. Middleton: Wesleyan University Press, 1967.

Hahn, Emily. *Mabel*. Boston: Houghton Mifflin, 1977.

Hamburger, Käte. *From Sophocles to Sartre*. New York: Ungar, 1969.

Harris, Jed. *Watchman, What of the Night?* New York: Doubleday, 1963.

Hart-Davis, Rupert. *Hugh Walpole*. New York: Macmillan, 1952.

Hatcher, Harlan. *Creating the Modern American Novel.* New York: Farrar & Rinehart, 1935.

Hayes, Helen. *On Reflection.* New York: Evans/Lippincott, 1968.

Hazlitt, Henry. "Communist Criticism," *Nation,* November 26, 1930, pp. 583–84.

Hewitt, Barnard. "Thornton Wilder Says 'Yes,'" *Tulane Drama Review,* December 1959, pp. 110–20.

Hicks, Granville. *The Great Tradition.* New York: Macmillan, 1933.

Hoffman, Frederick J. *Freudianism and the Literary Mind.* Baton Rouge: Louisiana State University Press, 1945.

Hopper, Stanley R., ed. *Spiritual Problems in Contemporary Literature.* New York: Institute for Religious and Social Studies, 1952.

Hutchins, Francis S. *The Telescope and the Spade: Berea College.* New York: The Newcomen Society, 1963.

Hutchins, Robert M. *The Learning Society.* New York: Praeger, 1968.

———. *No Friendly Voice.* Chicago: University of Chicago Press, 1936.

———. "Remarks at a memorial service for Thornton Wilder January 18, 1976," *The Center Magazine,* September/October 1977, p. 19.

"In Charge," *The New Yorker,* March 30, 1963, p. 37.

Isaacs, Edith J. R. "Thornton Wilder in Person," *Theatre Arts,* January 1943, pp. 21–30.

Israel, Jerry. *Progressivism and the Open Door.* Pittsburgh: University of Pittsburgh Press, 1971.

Kanin, Garson. *It Takes a Long Time to Become Young.* New York: Doubleday, 1978.

Kaufman, Beatrice, and Hennessey, Joseph, eds. *Alexander Woollcott Letters,* New York: Viking, 1944.

Kohler, Dayton. "Thornton Wilder," *English Journal,* January 1939, pp. 1–11.

Kosok, Heinz. "Thornton Wilder: A Bibliography of Criticism," *Twentieth Century Literature.* IX, 1963, pp. 93–100.

Krutch, Joseph Wood. *The American Drama since 1918.* New York: Braziller, 1957.

Kuner, Mildred Christophe. *Thornton Wilder; the bright and the dark.* New York: Crowell, 1972.

LaGuardia, Robert. *Monty: A Biography of Montgomery Clift.* New York: Arbor House, 1977.

Lewis, Allan. *American Plays and Playwrights of the Contemporary Theatre.* New York: Crown, 1965.

Lewis, Flora. "Thornton Wilder at 65 Looks Ahead—and Back," *New York Times Magazine,* April 15, 1962, p. 28.

Li, Chien-Nung. *The Political History of China, 1840–1928.* New York: Van Nostrand, 1956.

Loggins, Vernon. *I Hear America.* New York: Crowell, 1937.

Lumley, Frederick. *New Trends in Twentieth Century Drama.* New York: Oxford University Press, 1967.

MacKaye, Percy. *Playhouse and the Play.* New York: Greenwood, 1969.

MacLeish, Archibald. "The Isolation of the American Artist," *The Atlantic Monthly,* January 1958, pp. 55–59.

Marx, Arthur. *Goldwyn: a biography of the man behind the myth.* New York: Norton, 1976.

Maurois, André. *A Private Universe.* Trans. Hamish Hiles. New York: Appleton, 1932.

Mayer, H. *Steppenwolf and Everyman.* New York: Crowell, 1971.

McCarthy, Mary. "Class Angles and a Wilder Classic," pp. 21–29, and "The Skin of Our Teeth," pp. 53–56, *Sights and Spectacles.* New York: Farrar, Straus and Cudahy, 1956.

McNamara, Robert. "Phases of American Religion in Thornton Wilder and Willa Cather," *The Catholic World.* September 1932, pp. 641–49.

Miller, Arthur. "The Family in Modern Drama," *The Atlantic Monthly.* April, 1956, pp. 35–41.

Modic, John. "The Eclectic Mr. Wilder," *Ball State Teachers College Forum,* 1961, I, pp. 55–61.

Morgan, H. Wayne. "The Early Thornton Wilder," *Southwest Review,* 1958, XLIII, pp. 245–53.

Morley, Sylvanus G. *Chronology of Lope de Vega's Comedies.* New York: Oxford University Press, 1940.

Morse, Samuel French. *Wallace Stevens: Poetry as Life.* New York: Pegasus, 1970.

Mulford, Roland J. *History of the Lawrenceville School, 1810–1935.* Princeton: Princeton University Press, 1935.

Nathan, George Jean. *Theatre Book of the Year,* 1942–1943, pp. 132–36; 1943–1944, pp. 205–6. New York: Knopf, 1943, 1944.

Newberry, W. *The Pirandellian mode in Spanish literature from Cervantes to Sartre.* Albany, N.Y.: State University of New York Press, 1973.

Newlove, Donald. "The Professor with a Thousand Faces," *Esquire,* September 1977, pp. 99–103, 132, 134–36.

Noble, Peter. *The Fabulous Orson Welles.* London: Hutchinson, 1956.

Obey, André. *Noah.* London: Heinemann, 1953.

"An Obliging Man," *Time.* January 12, 1953, pp. 44–49.

Odell, George Clinton Densmore. *Annals of the New York Stage.* New York: Columbia University Press, 1927–1949.

*One in Spirit: A Retrospective View of the University of Chicago.* Chicago: University of Chicago Library, 1973.

Oppel, Horst. "American Literature in Post-War Germany: Impact or Alienation?," *Studies in Comparative Literature,* ed. Waldo F. McNeir. Baton Rouge: Louisiana State University Press, 1962, pp. 259–72.

Oppenheimer, George. *The Passionate Playgoer: A Personal Scrapbook*. New York: Viking, 1958.

Papajewski, Helmut. *Thornton Wilder*. Trans. John Conway. New York: Ungar, 1968.

Parmenter, Ross. "Novelist into Playwright," *Saturday Review of Literature*, June 11, 1938, pp. 10–11.

Perez, L. C. "Wilder and Cervantes: in the spirit of the tapestry," *Symposium*, Fall 1971, pp. 249–59.

Phelps, William L. "As I Like It," *Scribner's*, 1928, LXXXIII, pp. 224–25.

———. *Autobiography with Letters*. New York: Oxford University Press, 1939.

Popper, Hermine I. "The Universe of Thornton Wilder," *Harper's*, June 1965, pp. 72–78, 81.

Porter, T. E. *Myth and Modern American Drama*. Detroit: Wayne State University Press, 1969.

Preminger, Marion Mill. *All I Want Is Everything*. New York: Funk and Wagnalls, 1957.

Quintero, Jose. *If You Don't Dance, They Beat You*. Boston: Little, Brown, 1974.

Rabkin, Gerald. "The Skin of Our Teeth and the Theatre of Thornton Wilder," *The Forties: Fiction, Poetry, Drama*, ed. Warren French. Deland, Florida, 1969.

Robinson, Henry M. "The Curious Case of Thornton Wilder," *Esquire*, March 1957, pp. 70–71, 124–26.

Sahl, Hans. "Wilder and the Germans," *Four Quarters*, May 1967, p. 8.

Sayler, Oliver M. *Max Reinhardt and his theatre*. New York: Brentanos, 1924.

Scott, Winfield Townley. "'Our Town' and the Golden Veil," *Virginia Quarterly Review*. January, 1953, pp. 103–17. (Also appears in *Exiles and Fabrications*, New York: Doubleday, 1961.)

Sergeant, Elizabeth Shepley. *Robert Frost: The Trial by Existence*. New York: Holt, 1960.

Sievers, W. David. *Freud on Broadway*. New York: Heritage, 1955.

Smith, Chard Powers. *Where the Light Falls*. New York: Macmillan, 1965.

Sprague, Marshall. "Remembering Mr. Wilder," New York *Times Book Review*, January 27, 1974, p. 31.

Squires, Radcliffe. *Frederic Prokosch*. New York: Twayne, 1964.

Stallman, Robert W. *The Houses That James Built and other Literary Studies*. East Lansing, Mich.: Michigan State University Press, 1961.

———. "To Thornton Wilder: A Note in Gratitude," *Four Quarters*, May 1967, pp. 28–29.

Stein, Gertrude. *Everybody's Autobiography*. New York: Random House, 1937.
——. *The Geographical History of America*. New York: Random House, 1936.
——. *How Writing Is Written*, ed. Robert B. Haas. Los Angeles: Black Sparrow Press, 1974.
——. *The Making of Americans*. New York: Something Else Press, 1966, 1972.
——. *Reflection on the Atomic Bomb*, ed. Robert B. Haas. Los Angeles: Black Sparrow Press, 1974.
——. *Writings and Lectures, 1909–1945*, ed. Patricia Meyrowitz. Baltimore: Penguin, 1967.
Stephens, George D. "Our Town—Great American Tragedy?," *Modern Drama*, 1959, I, pp. 258–64.
Steward, Samuel. *Letters to Sammy*. Boston: Houghton Mifflin, 1977.
Stresau, Herman. *Thornton Wilder*. New York: Ungar, 1963.
"Talk with the author," *Newsweek*, January 22, 1962, p. 51.
Teichmann, Howard. *Smart Aleck*. New York: Morrow, 1976.
Toklas, Alice B. *The Alice B. Toklas Cookbook*. New York: Doubleday/Anchor, 1960.
Tritsch, Walther. "Thornton Wilder in Berlin," *The Living Age*, September 1931, pp. 44–47.
Truffaut, François. *Hitchcock*. New York: Simon & Schuster, 1967.
Tunney, Gene. *A Man Must Fight*. Boston: Houghton Mifflin, 1932.
Ulrich, Dorothy Livingston. "Thornton Wilder, a Classic of Tomorrow," *Associations*, December 1936, pp. 249–55.
——. "Thornton Wilder: Professor and Playwright," *University of Chicago Magazine*, April 1938, pp. 7–9.
UNESCO. *The Artist in Modern Society*. International Conference of Artists, Venice, 22–28 September 1952. Published July 1, 1954.
Valentine, Lucia and Alan. *The American Academy in Rome 1894–1969*. Charlottesville: University of Virginia Press, 1973.
Van Dyke, Henry. *The Man behind the Book*. New York: Scribners, 1929.
Varg, Paul. *The Making of a Myth, The U.S. and China, 1897–1912*. East Lansing: Michigan State University Press, 1968.
Weales, Gerald. "Unfashionable Optimist," *Commonweal*, 1958, LXVII, pp. 486–88.
Weeks, Edward. *In Friendly Candor*. Boston: Little, Brown, 1959.
Werfel, Alma Mahler. *And the Bridge Is Love*. New York: Harcourt, 1958.
Wescott, Glenway. *Images of Truth*. New York: Harper & Row, 1962.
"What shall we play? Repertories for a National Theatre," *Theatre Arts*, February, 1941, pp. 148–49.

Wilder, Amos Niven. *Arachne: Poems*. New Haven: Yale University Press, 1928.

———. *Modern poetry and the Christian tradition*. New York: Scribners, 1952.

———. *Spiritual Aspects of the New Poetry*. New York: Harper & Row, 1940.

———. *Theology and Modern Literature*. Cambridge, Mass.: Harvard University Press, 1958.

Wilder, Amos Parker. *The municipal problem; a discussion of the conditions which make difficult the government of American cities, of defects in charters which provoke evils, and of remedies for these evils already under trial or proposed*. New Haven: 1891.

Wilder, Charlotte. *Mortal Sequence*. New York: Coward-McCann, 1939.

———. *Phases of the Moon*. New York: Coward-McCann, 1936.

Wilder, Isabel. *Heart, Be Still*. New York: Coward-McCann, 1934.

———. *Let Winter Go*. New York: Coward-McCann, 1937.

———. *Mother and Four*. New York: Coward-McCann, 1933.

Williams, Tennessee. *Memoirs*. New York: Doubleday, 1975.

Wilson, Edmund. "The Antrobuses and the Earwickers," *The Nation*, January 30, 1943, pp. 167–68.

———. *Letters on Literature and Politics, 1912–1973*, ed. Elena Wilson. New York: Farrar, Straus & Giroux, 1977.

———. *The Twenties*, ed. Leon Edel. New York: Farrar, Straus & Giroux, 1975.

———. *The Shores of Light*. New York: Farrar, Straus & Young, 1952. Includes "The Economic Interpretation of Wilder" (1930) and "Thornton Wilder: The Influence of Proust" (1928).

———. *The Wound and the Bow*. New York: Oxford University Press, 1947.

Wixon, C. "Dramatic techniques of Thornton Wilder and Bertolt Brecht: a study in comparison," *Modern Drama*, Summer 1972, pp. 112–24.

Woollcott, Alexander. *Long, Long Ago*. New York: Viking, 1943.

Young, Stark. "Sorrow's Sharp Sustaining," *New Republic*, January 18, 1933, p. 268.

# INDEX